IMPACT!

A SELF-ESTEEM BASED
Skill Development Program for
Secondary Students

Gerry Dunne

Dianne Schilling

David Cowan

Cover design: Doug Armstrong Graphic Design

Copyright © 1990, Innerchoice Publishing • All rights reserved
Revised February, 1993.

ISBN: 0-9625486-1-8

INNERCHOICE PUBLISHING
P.O. BOX 1185
TORRANCE, CA 90505
(800) 662-9662 • Email: jalmarpress@att.net • www.jalmarpress.com

Acknowledgments

All over the nation, innovative changes have been initiated to improve the quality of education. ***IMPACT!*** supports these initiatives by providing the social-emotional and skill development necessary for young people to enjoy a successful school experience. It is the product of the creative input of educators throughout the country; it reflects the things that have worked best to bring about higher levels of student academic and behavioral performance; and it has been developed to address a broad range of educational concerns and has wide potential for application and implementation.

IMPACT! is used in a great many settings including advisor/advisee programs, career development, and as a practical approach to promoting personal and social responsibility, developing personal and interpersonal skills, and fostering inter-group harmony.

We deeply appreciate the many educators who have contributed their successes to this project, but especially Priscilla Chavez-Reilly, Director of Guidance Services for New York City Public Schools, her associate Christina Casanova, and the teachers and counselors of New York City. As a result of their valuable input, ***IMPACT!*** reaches across and deals effectively with cultural diversity and a wide range of socio-economic conditions.

The Authors

ABOUT IMPACT!

IMPACT! has been created to deal with major issues facing public education in general and every classroom teacher and counselor in particular. Research indicates the need to attend educationally to the social-emotional as well as intellectual development of students. For the latter, educators utilize a wide range of academic curricula and programs that teach cognitive skills. For the former, we have created *IMPACT!*.

IMPACT! is a self-esteem based program that facilitates growth in the social and emotional domains. It develops specific non-academic attributes and skills in individual students and refines them within the social context of structured peer interaction. *IMPACT!* encourages students to acknowledge their own progress and that of others, and in so doing expands personal self-esteem, helping each student more effectively manage the ever-changing landscape of his or her environment.

IMPACT! increases the ability of students to function effectively in a multicultural environment. Cultural diversity is transformed from a source of racial and ethnic tension to a wellspring of understanding from which students derive an appreciation of their commonalties and differences. Just as they learn to draw esteem from individual uniqueness, they learn to draw strength from cultural diversity.

Finally, *IMPACT!* encourages students to recognize their broader role as members of society. The program culminates by reaching beyond the classroom, offering students opportunities to interface in productive ways with individuals and organizations in the community.

IMPACT!

CONTENTS

IMPACT!

INFORMATION FOR TEACHERS AND COUNSELORS

. . . over time, a continuing and steadfast focus on the positive in life, on our strengths, and on the strengths of others can help to restore in our students their personal energy, their feelings of power, their sense of worth so that they can see themselves as positive forces who can contribute to the task of building a better world.

Robert C. Hawley

- ***IMPACT!*** Theory
- The ***IMPACT!*** circle session
- How to set up ***IMPACT!*** circle sessions
- Leading the ***IMPACT!*** circle session
- Training student leaders
- Strategies for using ***IMPACT!*** activities
- Creating your own ***IMPACT!*** circle session topics
- Questions and answers
- Cross Curriculum Reference Guide

IMPACT! Theory

An Eclectic Foundation

In an age when many people and systems have become alienated and confused, the educational system is in a unique position to alter this trend. In order for students to be ready for a fulfilling, productive adult life, they need to experience the fullness of themselves first. They need to know who they are, how they function, and how they relate to others. They also need to believe in themselves.

A product of synergistic thinking, the *IMPACT!!* program addresses these ideals. *IMPACT!* combines carefully selected features from many theories, schools, and systems. For example:

- Alfred Adler's concern for positive self-regard
- Harry Stack Sullivan's recognition that the principle of universality (the realization that everyone experiences the broad range of human emotions) is crucial to mature behavior.
- As students participate in circle sessions, some of their behaviors are positively reinforced, while others are not. Thus the program also utilizes some behavior modification strategies.
- Processes, and content areas throughout the program reveal the influence of other theorists in psychology and education, such as Carl Rogers, Abraham Maslow, Fritz Perls, Sam Keen, Harvey Jackins, Thomas Gordon, Haim Ginott, Albert Ellis, and George Brown.

Psychotherapists generally assume that people grow if their feelings are dealt with first, allowing behavioral change to follow. Rational-emotive therapists seek to influence and reeducate thoughts to facilitate effective and appropriate expression of feelings. Behavior modifiers focus on the behavior of individuals and try to change that. The aim of the *IMPACT!* program is to allow all three of these approaches to occur.

We view human beings as whole people—not a collection of parts. We see feelings, thoughts, and behavior as interactive, relating to one another in a multitude of ways. All must be included when we strive for self-understanding and growth. Throughout the program, a wide variety of experiences is offered in order to approach our goals by many roads and with many different tools.

A Definition of Self-Esteem

Because *IMPACT!* is a self-esteem based program, further discussion of its theory ought to be preceded by a definition and description of self-esteem. We offer the following:

Self-esteem is the sum of all that we have come to believe about ourselves in a *qualitative* sense. It is our unique perception of our worth and worthiness.

Self-esteem is fluid; that is, it is constantly subject to change. Changes in self-esteem occur in response to specific experiences—both deliberate and natural—and, in a narrower sense, simply because our perceptions of ourselves vary from environment to environment. For example, a student may esteem him/herself more at home than at school; an adult may esteem him/herself more at work than at home—or vice versa. In summary, our self-esteem is the reflection of our belief about self colored by an ever changing environmental landscape.

We have charge over our self-esteem and possess the capacity to change it. However, the *current* state of our self-esteem determines the quality of our experience in every situation. If we have done nothing to enhance our self-esteem, we are its servant, for better or worse. On the other hand, if we know how to control our self-esteem—and choose to do so—it serves as an invaluable resource *to us*.

Our self-esteem is like clay in a potter's hand. We can mold of it what we will.

Basic Assumptions of Worth and Worthiness

In order to create an environment that enhances self-esteem, the content and process of *IMPACT!* are designed to reflect these basic assumptions about human worth and worthiness:

- **There is no ceiling on self-esteem.**
- **Every individual is inherently worthwhile.**
- **Each person has the right to be self-determinlng.**
- **Everyone needs and deserves attention, acceptance and affection.**
- **Successes in life nourish the growth of self-esteem.**
- **Self-esteem is enhanced by the development and acknowledgement of identifiable skills and attributes.**

Our society has long been concerned with such matters as pathology, dysfunction, treatments, cures, and crisis intervention. Health has been viewed as the state people are in when they are not visibly sick. Yet health, like illness, exists in degrees.

The basic purpose of *IMPACT!* is to facilitate health by enhancing self-esteem. It does not focus on illness. It is neither therapy nor sensitivity training. Rather, the aim of the program is to create an environment in which people can become instrumental in their own growth and development.

If we believe there is **no ceiling on self-esteem**, we will be prepared to see students (and ourselves) learn, grow, and enjoy life—perhaps more than we had previously thought possible. If we believe that **every human being is worthwhile**, our interactions with students will reflect this attitude. We will not see any student as being

inherently unimportant, worthless, or bad. *IMPACT!* reflects the belief that all human beings are valuable, and that each individual is responsible—and must answer—for his/her own behavior.

If every person has the right to **self-determination**, we have a responsibility to make opportunities for expression and actualization known to students and then facilitate their progress as they move toward the goals they choose. *IMPACT!* helps students become aware of their own abilities and strengths and how those have been effective in overcoming obstacles they have faced in the past. In addition, it helps students develop essential skills for achieving present and future goals.

If every person has the right to receive **attention, acceptance, and affection**, we need to listen to students when they express their feelings and ideas, and help them learn to do this for each other. When genuine attention and acceptance are given and received, affection between people is free to grow. *IMPACT!* consistently provides a framework for realizing these ideals.

IMPACT! assumes that a key avenue to maintaining and enhancing self-esteem and well-being is through the process of **verbal interaction**. Our emotional and intellectual lives are so complex that we would be devastated if we could not discuss our experiences with one another. When we share our experiences and feelings at a level beyond superficiality, we see the basic commonalties among human beings and the individual differences, too.

IMPACT! also assumes that internalizing the foregoing principles leads to self-respect. On this foundation we then grow to understand and respect others, and in the process we develop the concern for humanity. It may be that we are now entering an age in which the great principles of morality—of caring and sharing—will be acted upon out of necessity, because this is the only way humanity can survive on a crowded planet. As Maurice Strong put it:

For the first time we have a situation in which the moral, philosophical, spiritual insights of the great religious leaders of the world, which used to be thought of as fuzzy-minded idealism — concepts of brotherhood, caring, and sharing—now are preconditions of survival. I think this is a profound thing that people have not yet caught onto—that the moral and physical systems of men are now converging, that one is a precondition of the other.

If we believe that **successes in life nourish the growth of self-esteem**, we will give students many opportunities to experience success. Not success in a general sense, but specific successes associated with competencies.

We will help students recognize that success reflects more than just an outcome; it also applauds the process by which it was realized. Therefore, *how* we do something is as important as *what* we do.

Consider the excitement you feel when you solve a particularly difficult puzzle. Then ponder the frustration that accompanies the realization that you *don't know how you did it!* In an effort to recreate the result, you focus on the process. As each new effort fails, it is cataloged so as not to be repeated. Then it happens. You solve the puzzle again. You experience the same thrill as before, but now it is magnified by the knowledge that you possess the process for repeating it again. This is the kind of success experienced by Edison with the light bulb, by Bell with the telephone, and by every person who has recognized a need or problem, and created or discovered a solution for it. *This is the success that we must acknowledge in ourselves and others.*

If we believe that **self-esteem is enhanced by the development and acknowledgement of identifiable skills and attributes**, we will show students what those skills and attributes are, and we will give students many opportunities to practice them. In addition, we will encourage students to acknowledge themselves and one another for every increment of progress.

We frequently overlook these critical skills and attributes because they are *non-academic.* Yet all people, young and old, require them. Research demonstrates that when deficiencies in their development exist, individuals are "at risk." On the other hand, as they are developed, performance goes up and self-esteem is enhanced. This holds true for all socioeconomic levels, all cultures, and for every other environmental condition or circumstance. *IMPACT!* addresses these skills and attributes repeatedly through activities and discussion topics. They are:

- listening
- oral communication
- trusting
- reliability/dependability/responsibility
- understanding of others (empathy)
- adaptability
- assertiveness
- initiative/work ethic
- decision making
- time management
- goal setting
- stress management
- leadership
- problem solving

As we develop necessary skills and attributes, they are reflected in accumulated successes. These refine and sharpen the accuracy of our perception of self and the value we assign to that perception.

On the next page is a visual model that reflects the mechanics of this relationship:

DEVELOPING SELF ESTEEM

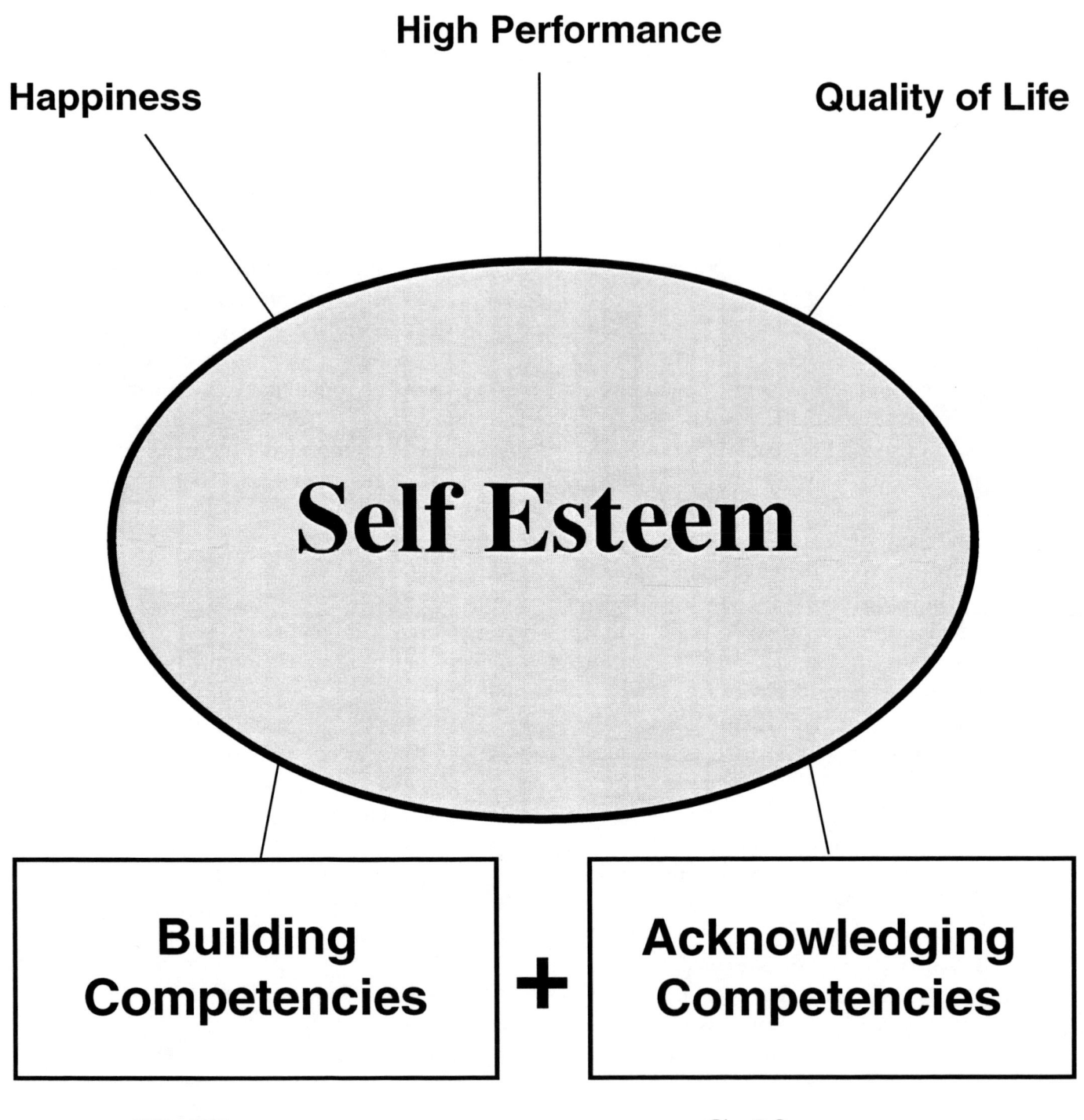

High Performance

Happiness

Quality of Life

Self Esteem

Building Competencies **+** **Acknowledging Competencies**

- **Skills**
- **Attributes**

- **Self**
- **Others**

Fundamental Life Questions

Secondary students constantly ask themselves some very basic questions about life and living. One of these questions is, **"Who am I?"** The ability to answer this question at all reflects awareness of self. Many students answer the question negatively or evasively, which may reflect what they have learned about themselves from a hostile or non-supportive environment, or from a simple lack of self-awareness.

Students also ask themselves, **"What can I do?"** Their constant testing of their physical, mental, emotional, and verbal powers often drives us to fits of distraction. Positive responses to this question reflect a degree of success in accomplishing goals. Negative responses, on the other hand, are often a result of an environment that does not recognize their constructive efforts or help them to discharge their energies in positive directions.

Students, in a variety of verbal and non-verbal ways, are also trying to find out **"Can I get along with people?"** Students who answer positively tend to feel comfortable and accepted by their peers and significant others. Negative responses originate out of fears regarding their social relations and skepticism regarding their social roles.

Students who consistently answer these questions in the negative usually grow up with great difficulty. If they have the time and money, they may visit a therapist, whose diagnosis is likely to state that the client has psychological problems in one or more of the following categories: (1) a lack of awareness or avoidance of his/her own emotions, impulses, motivations, and behavior; (2) a feeling of incompetence or; (3) an inability to function adequately in a social milieu. When we consider the debilitating problems that face many human beings, *we* may well ask, "Are these kinds of difficulties inevitable in the lives of individuals? Can something be done to prevent these kinds of problems?"

A Dynamic Response

There is reason to believe it is possible to effect a positive change in the emotional and social development of human beings when they are young by intervening in their lives in such a way as to ensure awareness, social facility, and self-esteem. This kind of intervention is the purpose of the *IMPACT!* program, which relates to three critical areas of human functioning: (1) awareness (of the feelings, thoughts, and behavior of self and others); (2) social relations (how individuals get along with other people); and (3) self-esteem (how individuals perceive their worth and worthiness). For purposes of brevity these areas are called **Awareness**, **Social Interaction**, and **Mastery**. They comprise the underlying theoretical components of the entire program. The activities and discussion topics in *IMPACT!* are built on a developmental progression from Awareness through Social Interaction to Mastery.

Students relate to others verbally in the circle sessions as each topic is discussed. They also learn to listen. The program provides practice in basic communication skills, while subject matter relating to relevant life issues is being discussed. This provides positive experiences which offer students the opportunity to grow in awareness, to learn more about effective modes of social interaction, and to feel more masterful (self-confident).

IMPACT! serves as a way of developing, maintaining, and enhancing life skills. The experiences gained from participating in circle sessions can contribute to the reservoir of strength from which we may draw when difficult life circumstances occur.

The following are descriptions of the three growth areas of the program. These may be reproduced to orient faculty, parents, or other interested persons to the fundamental purposes of the *IMPACT!* program.

Awareness

Awareness is a critical element of self-esteem. Aware people do not hide things from themselves. They are in touch with the inner world of their feelings and thoughts, and they are in control of their actions—and they understand that other people feel, think, and behave too. They are also in touch with the reality of the past, the possibilities of the future, and the certainty of the present. Awareness allows individuals to order their lives flexibly and effectively on a moment-to-moment basis.

By contrast, unawareness of what is going on in one's inner and/or outer worlds sets the stage for lack of congruence between what one believes or feels and how one behaves. Feelings of isolation ("I'm the only one who's ever felt like this before.") occur when people are unaware that everyone experiences the same triad of human functioning (feeling, thinking, and behaving) that they do. Unaware people are not in charge of their own lives. By default, their courses are plotted by others or by parts of themselves they have not recognized.

We hope to demonstrate experientially to students, through their involvement with the *IMPACT!* program, that everyone experiences all the emotions. Circle session topics, supporting activities, and experience sheets provide opportunities for students to experience and discuss their emotions in an accepting and nonthreatening atmosphere. Students discover that emotions cannot be judged right or wrong, good or bad, in a moral sense. They simply are. To try to negate one's feelings or attempt to take away a feeling in someone else only compounds the situation—as neuroses, insomnia, ulcers, and miscommunication between persons testifies. For this reason the feelings of each student are focused on and accepted in every circle session. As Carl Rogers states in *On*

Becoming a Person:
> *...when I can accept another person, which means specifically accepting the feelings and attitudes and beliefs that he has as a real and vital part of him, then I am assisting him to become a person, and there seems to me great value in this.*

Similar to a feeling, a thought, in and of itself, can hurt no one. The cognition phase of *IMPACT!* activities enables students to share their thoughts in a constructive manner. They become aware that even divergent thoughts may be discussed without fear. Students realize that their ability to think is a great power, and may be used constructively or destructively in a multitude of ways. Through their participation in the program, students become more aware of how often they personally use their thought processes to make life meaningful and productive.

Social Interaction

People effective in their social interactions are capable of understanding other people. They know how to interact with others flexibly, skillfully, and responsibly, without sacrificing their own needs and integrity. They have a good sense of timing and are effective at being heard and making needed changes in their environment. These people can process nonverbal as well as verbal messages of others, and they realize that people have the power to affect one another. They are aware, not only of how others affect them, but also of the effect of their behavior on others, and they take accompanying responsibility for their actions.

Without skills in social interaction, individuals confuse situations and give inappropriate responses. They lack positive communication skills and are unaware of how their actions affect others.

According to Harvey Jackins, author of The *Human Side of Human Beings,* every person is inherently intelligent, zestful, and capable of loving, cooperative relationships with others. What goes wrong is that we get hurt, and repeated hurts significantly affect those same inherent gifts. We then have great difficulty liking, trusting, and sometimes even respecting others, and they have the same difficulties with us. Our social interactions suffer, and we do not enjoy each other as we potentially could.

Logically, the next question is, "What can we do about this situation?" Students deal with other people every day—their peers and significant adults. They need positive interpersonal experiences and information in the social realm in order to offset prior difficulties and build healthy relationships. Yet, as Carl Rogers points out, the educational system has largely failed to in any systematic way meet the need of students to learn how to understand and get along with other people.

If they are fortunate, students are surrounded by people who give them attention. In the case of people older than they, it is highly desirable that healthy, responsible behavior be modeled. If students are listened to, if their feelings are accepted, and if they learn how to do this with others, they are indeed fortunate.

IMPACT! attempts to actualize the positive qualities that are inherent in all of us. By its format and process, it allows students to practice positive modes of communication and transfer them to other situations.

IMPACT! gives students the opportunity to discuss what goes into a relationship that makes it friendly, caring, and trusting. Further, students explore problem areas in varied human settings. Society has an ideal view of how people should ultimately behave, but no formal structure that defines or describes the intermediate steps. *IMPACT!* develops and nurtures an understanding of those intermediate steps.

Mastery

Self-confident people believe in themselves; they perceive themselves as being "OK." They are not debilitated by knowledge of their weaknesses, but have a healthy degree of self-esteem and a feeling of mastery or self-confidence. They try new challenges and do not strongly fear failure. It is likely that they have experienced success more than failure, and probably when they were successful, a significant person noted it and commented on it to them.

It has been widely observed that individuals are likely to achieve mastery in their endeavors when they have a feeling of mastery about themselves. Generally, it seems as though people who believe in themselves are the ones who continue to succeed, and the more they succeed, the more they believe in themselves. Thus, a beneficial cycle is created.

The ways in which significant others respond to what we do plays a critical role in whether or not we see ourselves as masterful. If they let us know they recognize our efforts and comment positively when we try or succeed, our awareness that we do have capabilities increases. Conversely, without favorable comment we are less aware of our capabilities, even if we experience success. This explains why so many brilliant people do not regard themselves as such. Rather, they are painfully aware of their limitations and shortcomings and miss many opportunities to actualize their potential. Our culture has numerous ways of causing us to focus on our weaknesses rather than our assets and abilities.

In the *IMPACT!* program, we call belief in oneself a feeling of "I can-ness." Through the circle sessions, supporting activities, and experience sheets, students are routinely encouraged to explore their own successes and hear positive comments about their efforts. All the activities are designed to heighten students' awareness of their own and others' successes. Failure is a reality that is also examined. The objective, however, is not to remind students that they have failed; instead these activities enable them to see that falling short is a common, universal experience.

History speaks to us of many effective and capable individuals who found great success in their endeavors. Some, however, achieved success for themselves at the expense of others. They exercised their abilities and powers irresponsibly. By focusing on their positive behaviors and accomplishments, students recognize the rewards that can be gained when one behaves responsibly. Cooperation vs. competition is another issue addressed by the mastery portion of the program. As equitably as possible, the program's structure attempts to meet the needs of all students in the group. Everyone's feelings are accepted.

Comparisons and judgments are not made. The circle is not another competitive arena, but is guided by a spirit of cooperation. When students practice fair, respectful, noncompetitive interaction with each other, they benefit from the experience and are likely to employ these responsible behaviors in other life situations. The lesson then becomes:

There need be no losers in order to have winners in a group.

IMPACT! has been developed to help students deal with such matters as improving their learning habits, taking pride in their accomplishments, dealing rationally with disappointments and problems, and making workable decisions. It is not the aim of **IMPACT!** to participate in producing a masterful but limited young adult. Rather, we hope to help students become responsibly competent.

The IMPACT! circle session

The circle session is a small-group discussion in which participants (students and circle leader) listen carefully to one another as they take turns verbally responding to a specific topic, and then freely discuss any individual and collective insights they have gained from sharing. The circle session always follows the same process even though the topic for discussion changes. In its broadest sense, the circle session is designed to facilitate communications between participating students and between the leader (usually a teacher or counselor) and students. The circle session allows participants the opportunity to explore aspects of human life

with one another, to appreciate themselves and others as developing persons, to practice effective communication skills, and to develop empathy for others.

The circle session's overall objectives are to increase students' self-understanding, self-esteem, and sense of social responsibility. Several approaches are used to achieve these objectives. They include: The use of a circular, small-group seating arrangement; ground rules that set the tone for personal privacy and safety; and a procedural structure that invites each student to share, to give and receive reflective feedback, and to cognitively summarize the learnings that he or she has gained.

Does all of this mean that leading circles is difficult? No. Circle leadership skills are quite simple. As a circle leader, you will: follow an outline; state and enforce simple rules of considerate conduct; model your own respect for those rules; lead a discus-sion; verbally communicate with students in clear, non-patronizing language; and listen carefully (and respond appropriately) to what the students say. When you lead a circle session, you are a teacher, model, coach, and co-participant all at the same time.

How to set up *IMPACT!* circle sessions

Group Size and Composition

Circle sessions are a time for focusing on individuals' contributions in an unhurried fashion. For this reason, each circle session group needs to be kept relatively small— eight to twelve usually works best. At this age, students are capable of extensive ver-balization. You will want to encourage this, and not stifle them because of time con-straints.

Each group should be as **heterogeneous** as possible with respect to sex, ability, and racial/ethnic background. Sometimes there will be a group in which all the students are particularly reticent to speak. At these times, bring in an expressive student or two who will get things going. Sometimes it is necessary for practical reasons to change the membership of a group. Once established, however, it is advisable to keep a group as stable as possible.

Length and location of circle sessions

Most circle sessions last approximately 20 to 30 minutes, sometimes a little longer. At first students tend to be reluctant to express themselves fully because they do not yet know that the circle is a safe place. Conse-quently your first sessions may not last more than 10 to 15 minutes. Generally speaking, students become comfortable and motivated to speak with continued experience.

Circle sessions may be conducted at any time during the class period. Starting circle sessions at the beginning of the period allows additional time in case students become deeply involved in the topic. If you start circles late in the period, make sure the students are aware of their responsibility to be concise.

Circle sessions may be carried out wher-ever there is room for students to sit in a circle and experience few or no distractions. Most leaders prefer to have students sit in chairs rather than on the floor. Students seem to be less apt to invade one another's space while seated in chairs. Some leaders conduct sessions outdoors, with students seated in a secluded, grassy area.

How to get started

Circle topics are provided in all units. However, on page 69 of the unit, "Communi-cating Effectively," you will find an activity especially designed to help you introduce the circle process to students. We suggest that you complete this activity with the entire class prior to holding your first circles.

Teachers and counselors have used nu-merous methods to involve students in the circle process. What works well for one leader or class does not always work for another. Here are two basic strategies lead-ers have successfully used to set up groups. Whichever you use, we recommend that you display the **Circle Session Rules poster** (included in your *IMPACT!* kit) in a location that permits easy viewing by all participants.

1. Start one group at a time, and cycle through all groups. If possible, provide an opportunity for every student to experience a circle session in a setting where there are no disturbances. This may mean arranging for another staff member or aide to take charge of the students not participating in the circle. Non-participants may work on course work or experience sheets, or, if you have a cooperative librarian, they may be sent to the library to work independently or in small groups on a class assignment. Repeat this procedure until all of the students have been involved in at least one circle session.

Next, initiate a class discussion about the circle sessions. Explain that from now on you will be meeting with each circle group in the classroom, with the remainder of the class present. Ask the students to help you plan established procedures for the remainder of the class to follow.

Meet with each circle session group on a different day, systematically cycling through the groups. In your second or third cycle, begin student leadership training. In each group, allow a student the opportunity to lead the session as you sit beside him/her, acting as leader-trainer. In time, student-led groups may meet independently at staggered times during the period, or they may meet simultaneously in different parts of the room while you circulate. Eventually you should be able to be a participant in the student-led groups. For more information on student leadership, refer to the heading, "Training Student Leaders" later in this section.

2. Combine inner and outer circles. Meet with one circle session group while another group listens and observes as an outer circle. Then have the two groups change places, with the students on the outside becoming the inner circle, and responding verbally to the topic. If you run out of time, use two class periods for this. Later, a third group may be added to this alternating cycle. The end product of this arrangement is two or more groups (comprising everyone in the class) meeting together simultaneously. While one group is involved in discussion, the other groups listen and observe as members of an outer circle. *If you wish, you may invite the members of the outer circle to participate in the review and discussion phases of the circle.*

What to do with the rest of the class

A number of arrangements can be made for students who are not participating in circle sessions. Here are some ideas:

• **Arrange the room to ensure privacy.** This may involve placing a circle of chairs or carpeting in a corner, away from other work areas. You might construct dividers from existing furniture, such as bookshelves or screens, or simply arrange chairs and tables in such a way that the circle area is protected from distractions.

• **Involve aides, counselors, parents, or fellow teachers.** Have an aide conduct a lesson with the rest of the class while you meet with a circle group. If you do not have an aide assigned to you, use auxiliary staff or volunteer parents.

• **Have students work quietly on subject-area assignments in pairs or small, task-oriented groups.**

• **Utilize student aides or leaders.** If the seat-work activity is in a content area, appoint students who show ability in that area as "consultants," and have them assist other students.

• **Give the students plenty to do.** List academic activities on the board. Make materials for quiet individual activities available so that students cannot run out of things to do and be tempted to consult you or disturb others.

• **Make the activity of students outside the circle enjoyable.** When you can involve the rest of the class in something meaningful to them, they will probably be less likely to interrupt the circle.

• **Have the students work on an ongoing project.** When they have a task in progress, students can simply resume where they left off, with little or no introduction from you. In these cases, appointing a "person in charge," "group leader", or "consultant" is wise.

• **Allow individual journal-writing.** While a circle is in progress, have the other students make entries in a private (or share-with-teacher-only) journal. Do not correct the journals, but if you read them, be sure to respond to the entries with your own written thoughts, where appropriate.

Leading the *IMPACT!* circle session

This section is a thorough guide for conducting **IMPACT!** circle sessions. It covers major points to keep in mind and answers questions which will arise as you begin using the program. Please remember that these guidelines are presented to assist you, not to restrict you. Follow them and trust your own leadership style at the same time.

IMPACT! Circle Session Procedures

1. **Setting up the circle** (1-2 minutes)

2. **Reviewing the rules** (1-2 minutes) *

3. **Introducing the topic** (1-2 minutes)

4. **Sharing by circle members** (12-18 minutes)

5. **Reviewing what is shared** (3-5 minutes) *

6. **Summary discussion** (2-8 minutes)

7. **Closing the circle** (less than 1 minute)
   *optional

Setting up the circle (1-2 minutes)
As you sit down with the students in the circle, remember that you are not teaching a lesson. You are facilitating a group of people. Establish a positive atmosphere. In a relaxed manner, address each student by name, using eye contact and conveying warmth. An attitude of seriousness blended with enthusiasm will let the students know that the circle session is an important learning experience—an activity that can be interesting and meaningful.

Reviewing the rules (1-2 minutes).

At the beginning of the first session, and at appropriate intervals thereafter, go over the rules for the circle session. They are:

IMPACT! Circle Session Rules

1. **Bring yourself to the circle and nothing else.**

2. **Everyone gets a turn to share, including the leader.**

3. **You can skip your turn if you wish.**

4. **Listen to the person who is sharing.**

5. **There are no interruptions, probing, put-downs, or gossip.**

6. **Share the time equally.**

7. **Stay in your own space.**

From this point on, demonstrate to the students that you expect them to remember and abide by the rules. Convey that you think well of them and know they are fully capable of responsible behavior. Let them know that by coming to the session they are making a commitment to listen and show acceptance and respect for the other students and you.

Introducing the topic (1-2 minutes)

State the topic in your own words. Elaborate and provide examples as each activity suggests. Add clarifying statements of your own that will help the students understand the topic. Answer questions about the topic, and emphasize that there are no "right" responses. Finally, restate the topic, opening the session to responses (theirs and yours). Sometimes taking your turn first helps the students understand the aim of the topic. At various points throughout the session, state the topic again.

Just prior to leading a circle session, contemplate the topic and think of at least one possible response that *you* can make to it.

Sharing by circle members (12-18 minutes)

The most important point to remember is this: The purpose of the circle session is to give students an opportunity to express themselves and be accepted for the experiences, thoughts, and feelings they share. Avoid taking the action away from the circle members. They are the stars!

Reviewing what is shared (optional 3-5 minutes)

Besides modeling effective listening (the very best way to teach it) and positively reinforcing students for attentive listening, a review can be used to deliberately improve listening skills in circle members.

Reviewing is a time for reflective listening, when circle members feed back what they heard each other say during the sharing phase of the circle. Besides encouraging effective listening, reviewing provides circle members with additional recognition. It validates their experience and conveys the idea, "you are important," a message we can all profit from hearing often.

To review, a circle member simply addresses someone who shared, and briefly paraphrases what the person said ("John, I heard you say....").

The first few times you conduct reviews, stress the importance of checking with the speaker to see if the review accurately summarized the main things that were shared. If the speaker says, "No," allow him/her to make corrections. Stress too, the importance of speaking *directly* to the speaker, using the person's name and the pronoun "you," not "he" or "she." If someone says, "S/he said that...," intervene as promptly and respectfully as possible and say to the reviewer, "Talk to Betty...Say you." This is very important. The person whose turn is being reviewed will have a totally different feeling when talked *to*, instead of *about*.

Note: Remember that the review is optional and is most effective when used *occasionally*, not as a part of every circle.

Summary discussion (2-8 minutes)

The summary discussion is the cognitive portion of the circle session. During this phase, the leader asks thought-provoking questions to stimulate free discussion and higher-level thinking. Each circle session in the program includes three or more summary questions; however, at times you may want to formulate questions that are more appropriate to the level of understanding in your group—or to what was actually shared in the circle. If you wish to make connections between the circle session topic and your content area, ask questions that will accomplish that objective and allow the summary discussion to extend longer.

It is important that you not confuse the summary with the review. The review is optional; the summary is not. The summary meets the need of people of all ages to find meaning in what they do. Thus, the summary serves as a necessary culmination to each circle session by allowing the students to clarify the key concepts they gained from the session.

Closing the circle (less than 1 minute).

The ideal time to end a circle session is when the summary discussion reaches natural closure. Sincerely thank everyone for being part of the circle. Don't thank specific students for speaking, as doing so might convey the impression that speaking is more appreciated than mere listening. Then close the circle by saying, "The circle session is over," or "OK, that ends our session."

More about Circle Session Procedures and Rules

The next few paragraphs offer further clarification concerning circle session leadership.

Why should students bring themselves to the circle and nothing else? Individual teachers differ on this point, but most prefer that students not bring objects (such as pencils, books, etc.) to the circle that may be distracting.

Who gets to talk? Everyone. The importance of acceptance in ***IMPACT!*** cannot be overly stressed. In one way or another practically every rule says one thing: *accept*

one another. When you model acceptance of students, they will learn how to be accepting. Each individual in the circle is important and deserves a turn to speak if
he or she wishes to take it. Equal opportunity to become involved should be given to everyone in the circle.

Circle members should be reinforced equally for their contributions. There are many reasons why a leader may become more enthused over what one student shares than another. The response may be more on target, reflect more depth, be more entertaining, be philosophically more in keeping with one's own point of view, and so on. However, students need to be given equal recognition for their contributions, even if the contribution is to listen silently throughout the session.

In most of the circle sessions, plan to take a turn and address the topic, too. Students usually appreciate it very much and learn a great deal when their teachers and counselors are willing to tell about their own experiences, thoughts, and feelings. In this way you let your students know that you acknowledge your own humanness.

Does everyone have to take a turn? No. Students may choose to skip their turns. If the circle becomes a pressure situation in which the members are coerced in any way to speak, it will become an unsafe place where participants are not comfortable. Meaningful discussion is unlikely in such an atmosphere. By allowing students to make this choice, you are showing them that you accept their right to remain silent if that is what they choose to do.

As you begin circles, it will be to your advantage if one or more students decline to speak. If you are unperturbed and accepting when this happens, you let them know you are offering them an opportunity to experience something you think is valuable, or at least worth a try, and not attempting to force-feed them. You as a leader should not feel

compelled to share a personal experience in every session, either. However, if you decline to speak in most of the sessions, this may have an inhibiting effect on the students' willingness to share.

A word should also be said about how this ground rule has sometimes been carried to extremes. Sometimes leaders have bent over backwards to let students know they don't have to take a turn. This seeming lack of enthusiasm on the part of the leader has caused reticence in the students. In order to avoid this outcome, don't project any personal insecurity as you lead the session. Be confident in your proven ability to work with students. Expect something to happen and it will.

Some circle leaders ask the participants to raise their hands when they wish to speak, while others simply allow free verbal sharing without soliciting the leader's permission first. Choose the procedure that works best for you, but do not call on anyone unless you can see signs of readiness.

Some leaders have reported that their first circles fell flat—that no one, or just one or two students, had anything to say. But they continued to have circles, and at a certain point everything changed. Thereafter, the students had a great deal to say that these leaders considered worth waiting for. It appears that in these cases the leaders' acceptance of the right to skip turns was a key factor. In time most students will contribute verbally when they have something they want to say, and when they are assured there is no pressure to do so.

Sometimes a silence occurs during a circle session. Don't feel you have to jump in every time someone stops talking. During silences students have an opportunity to think about what they would like to share or to contemplate an important idea they've heard. A general rule of thumb is to allow silence to the point that you observe group discomfort. At that point move on. *Do not switch to another topic.* To do so implies you will not be satisfied until the students speak. If you change to another topic, you are telling them you didn't really mean it when you said they didn't have to take a turn if they didn't want to.

If you are bothered about students who attend a number of circles and still do not share verbally, reevaluate what you consider to be involvement. Participation does not necessarily mean talking. Students who do not speak *are* listening and learning.

How can I encourage effective listening? The circle session is a time (and place) for students and leaders to strengthen the habit of listening by doing it over and over again. No one was born knowing how to listen effectively to others. It is a skill like any other that gets better as it is practiced. In the immediacy of the circle session, the members become keenly aware of the necessity to listen, and most students respond by expecting it of one another.

In the ***IMPACT!*** program, listening is defined as the respectful focusing of attention on individual speakers. It includes eye contact with the speaker and open body posture. It eschews interruptions of any kind. When you conduct a circle session, listen and encourage listening in the students by (1) focusing your attention on the person who is speaking, (2) being receptive to what the speaker is saying (not mentally planning your next remark), and (3) recognizing the speaker when he or she finishes speaking, either verbally ("Thanks, Shirley") or non-verbally (a nod and a smile).

To encourage effective listening in the students, reinforce them by letting them know you have noticed they were listening to each other and you appreciate it. Occasionally conducting a review after the sharing phase also has the effect of sharpening listening skills.

How can I ensure the students get equal time? When circle members share the time equally, they demonstrate their acceptance of the notion that everyone's contribution is of equal importance. It is not uncommon to have at least one dominator in a group. This person is usually totally unaware that by continuing to talk s/he is taking time from others who are less assertive.

Be very clear with the students about the purpose of this ground rule. Tell them at the outset how much time there is and whether or not you plan to conduct a review. When it is your turn, always limit your own contribution. If someone goes on and on, do intervene (dominators need to know what they are doing), but do so as gently and respectfully as you can.

What are some examples of put-downs? Put-downs convey the message, "You are not OK as you are." Some put-downs are deliberate, but many are made unknowingly. Both kinds are undesirable in a circle session because they destroy the atmosphere of acceptance and disrupt the flow of discussion. Typical put-downs include:

- overquestioning.
- statements that have the effect of teaching or preaching
- advice giving
- one-upsmanship
- criticism, disapproval, or objections
- sarcasm
- statements or questions of disbelief

How can I deal with put-downs? There are two major ways for dealing with put-downs in circle sessions: preventing them from occurring and intervening when they do.

Going over the rules with the students at the beginning of each session, particularly in the earliest sessions, is a helpful preventive technique. Another is to reinforce the students when they adhere to the rule. Be sure to use nonpatronizing, nonevaluative language.

Unacceptable behavior should be stopped the moment it is recognized by the leader.

When you become aware that a put-down is occurring, do whatever you ordinarily do to stop destructive behavior in the classroom. If one student gives another an unasked-for bit of advice, say for example, "Jane, please give Alicia a chance to tell her story." To a student who interrupts say, "Ed, it's Sally's turn." In most cases the fewer words, the better—students automatically tune out messages delivered as lectures.

Sometimes students disrupt the group by starting a private conversation with the person next to them. Touch the offender on the arm or shoulder while continuing to give eye contact to the student who is speaking. If you can't reach the offender, simply remind him/her of the rule about listening. If students persist in putting others down during circle sessions, ask to see them at another time and hold a brief one-to-one conference, urging them to follow the rules.

Suggest that they reconsider their membership in the circle. Make it clear that if they don't intend to honor the rules, they are not to come to the circle.

How can I keep students from gossiping? Periodically remind students that using names and sharing embarrassing information is not acceptable. Urge the students to relate personally to one another, but not to tell intimate details of their lives.

What should the leader do during the summary discussion? Conduct the summary as an open forum, giving students the opportunity to discuss a variety of ideas and accept those that make sense to them. Don't impose your opinions on the students, or allow the students to impose theirs on one another. Ask open-ended questions, encourage higher-level thinking, contribute your own ideas when appropriate, and act as a facilitator.

Training student leaders

A basic assumption of the ***IMPACT!*** program is that every human being (barring those having considerable subnormal intelligence) has leadership potential. Further, the best time for energizing this ability is in childhood, and the optimum time for maintaining the skills is during adolescence. Students in countless classrooms effectively lead their own circle sessions.

Leadership training can be provided in several stages. In the first stage of training, the student observes you, and begins to acquire the skills of leadership through observation and later by simple imitation. In addition, the student acquires leadership capability by taking the risk of serving in the role of leader when you ask for a volunteer.

In the next stage of leadership training, ask the student to sit next to you and perform

all of the activities for which he or she has observed you being responsible. You are now the leader-trainer. Lend support, encourage, and minimally guide the student as necessary. If a great deal of coaching is required at any given session, the student may be experiencing more failure than success. When this happens, leadership training should be tactfully stopped and postponed until another day when the student has acquired more experience in observing, more courage, or more readiness to try again. Provide only enough coaching to keep the ball rolling in the early stage of leader-training.

As students progress in their acquisition of leadership skills, phase out of the leader-trainer role as rapidly as possible until, in the final stages, student leaders are effectively serving the needs of their groups in a totally responsible way. At this point, discontinue coaching and become a participant in the group. Serve as a reinforcing agent for all of the constructive elements of a circle session—move the students forward in the direction of becoming more aware, more self-confident, and more socially effective.

Be sure to emphasize that *every* student has leadership potential, and that *everybody* can lead. All that is required is a little bit of courage and a lot of practice. Be as personal as possible when you make these remarks to the group. Try to convey to the students the feeling that you strongly believe in them.

You can begin training student leaders after two or three successful circle sessions. Invite the students to consider volunteering to lead a circle. Suggest that they watch you closely to see what steps the leader follows. At the end of the session, ask the students to describe what you did. They should be able to delineate the following steps:

The leader:
1. announces the topic and clarifies what it is about.
2. may lead a review of the circle session rules.
3. gives each person a turn who wants one.
4. may conduct a review of what each person said.
5. conducts a summary discussion by focusing on the meaning of the session and the major observations of the participants.
6. terminates the circle.

Ask the students if anyone would like to volunteer to lead the next session. If no one volunteers, accept this outcome and wait for a session or two before trying again. If several volunteer, choose a student who you think is very likely to succeed. Then tell the group the topic you have in mind for the next session.

Before the next session, give the student leader a copy of the topic, and discuss it with him/her. Also provide a copy of the **Steps in Leading a Circle Session** as an aid to following the circle process, and make sure that the **Circle Session Rules poster** is located so that the student leader can see it while conducting the circle.

As the session begins, tell the group that you will be the trainer and speak about the process when necessary, but that otherwise, the student is the leader and you are a participant. Before turning the session over to the student leader add one more thing—a new ground rule stating that the students are expected to respect fully the leadership position of the student. **If they disagree with the student leader's procedure or are aware of what he or she should do next when the student leader may have forgotten, they are not to say anything at that time unless they are asked to by the student leader.** When people are learning a new skill, it can be very upsetting to have other people constantly reminding them of what they are supposed to do next. For this reason the student leader should not be heckled in any way. (Time can be taken at the end of the session for the group to give feedback to the student leader about his/her performance).

Now, allow the student leader to proceed, interjecting statements yourself about the procedure only when absolutely necessary. Be sure to take your turn and model respectful listening. As necessary, deal with students who interrupt or distract the group.

Before ending the session, thank the student leader, and conduct a brief feedback session by asking the students, "Who would like to tell (the student leader) what you liked about the way he or she conducted the session?" Let the student leader call on each person who has a comment.

Tell the students the topic you have in mind for the next session, and ask for a volunteer to lead it. Remember that students should not lead the group until you are sure they will be successful. Be careful to appoint leaders of both sexes and all racial/ethnic groups. Continue this process until all who wish to conduct circles are competent enough to lead them independently.

Combining Teacher and Student Leadership

This procedure allows several groups to meet simultaneously during the same class period.

Begin by announcing to the class that circles will be held during the period. If necessary, review the rules with the whole class. Then announce the topic, describe it and restate it. Finally, take your turn to relate to it personally. Answer any questions the students have, and then ask them to get into their groups.

When the circles are formed, the student leaders take over. They restate the topic and facilitate the sharing phase and, if desired, a review. The students return to their regular seating for the summary discussion, which is led by the teacher.

Note: This is a particularly fruitful procedure if you are using *IMPACT!* as a supplement to your regular subject. The summary discussion can then include questions concerning the relevancy of the topic to subject matter currently being studied.

Strategies for using *IMPACT!* activities

The *IMPACT!* program utilizes a wide variety of techniques. The circle session is the central strategy, but there are others. This section describes several major strategies and presents basic points to keep in mind as you implement them.

Dyads

When first initiated, dyads are probably most effective if the students are allowed to select their own partners. After the class is well into the semester and the students know each other better, ask the students to pair up with someone they've never worked with before. If the students tend to shun the opposite sex, announce that you would like to see boys and girls pair up.

Ask the students to sit close to and facing their partner, and position themselves as far away from other students as possible so they will be able to hear each other. If the number of students is uneven, be the partner of the remaining student. In fact, it is helpful for the leader to be in as many dyads as possible.

In most dyad activities, partners take turns speaking and listening in response to one or more topics. Two advantages of dyads are that they allow maximum self-expression in a relatively short time period. And they are the most effective way for students to discuss some topics.

Triads

Some triad activities are simply very small discussion groups. Others are like dyads in that the students take turns speaking and listening in response to specific topics. The difference is that the third person in the triad acts as an observer while the other two interact. The observer role is played by each member in the triad on a rotating basis. The function of the observer is to note, as objectively as possible, the behavior of the interacting pair and give them feedback.

Small Group Discussions

When students meet in small groups to discuss a topic or engage in some phase of an

IMPACT! activity, they are usually directed to select a leader or recorder. They are also urged to observe *IMPACT!* ground rules. The intent is not to transform every small-group task into a circle session, merely to provide structure and safety. One of the main advantages of small groups is that they give the students an opportunity to collaborate—which facilitates problem-solving, stimulates creativity, and takes some of the load off you.

Class Discussions

Almost all *IMPACT!* activities include a culminating discussion, and some activities are almost entirely discussion. When leading a discussion, act as a facilitator, keeping these guidelines in mind:
- Questions should be relevant, timely, and open-ended.
- It should be understood that there are no right or wrong answers.
- Keep the discussion focused.

Without being rigid, ask students who introduce peripheral issues to bring them up again when the main discussion is over or at some other time. Digressions can ruin the effectiveness of a discussion, but very often the other thoughts that students introduce are worth discussing, too.

Brainstorming

Brainstorming is a very valuable way to promote individual creativity and group cohesiveness simultaneously. Perhaps the most important thing to remember about brainstorming is that the generation of ideas and the evaluation of ideas are two separate processes. Thanks to this distinction, individuals may contribute their ideas spontaneously without fear of criticism. Brainstorming includes the following basic steps:
- The task or problem is defined.
- The students describe all the ideas they can think of, without evaluating any of them.

- The ideas are recorded.
- The brainstorming is ended.
- Then and only then, the ideas are evaluated.
- A choice or decision is made.

Dramatizations and Role-Playing

Besides being very dynamic, acting experiences in the classroom promote direct, experiential learning. Dramatizations usually involve planning, rehearsing, and performing, and typically call for a student director. Role-playing is more spontaneous, and unfolds in a situation that simulates reality. Although the participants are playing the parts of other people, they usually end up playing themselves, as their own values surface.

Role-playing is frequently used as a problem-solving technique in which alternative actions are tested and evaluated. Opportunities for role-playing (other then those described in the activities) may evolve from unfinished stories, films, pictures, and real or imaginary situations suggested by you and the students.

Creative Writing

Sometimes students are asked to write a story, poem, play, lyrics for a song, or even create a cartoon. Frequently the class brainstorms ideas before the writing period begins in order to motivate students and give them ideas. One way teachers have successfully encouraged students to write is by following this (or a variation of this) procedure:

The students imagine how they would *say* what they want to write, and then write down those words without regard for neatness, grammar, punctuation, spelling, etc. After they record some thoughts, they go back and read what they have written. Then they proceed with the next collection of thoughts in the same way. They continue doing this (often each collection of thoughts becomes a separate paragraph) until they have finished. At this point they go back over what they have written, reading it carefully and editing their work for grammar, syntax, spelling, and punctuation. (You may prefer to have students meet in dyads or small groups and edit each other's writing, as well as make suggestions pertaining to content and style.) As a final step, the entire product is rewritten to include all editorial changes.

If you have computers, encourage the students to use word processing, spell checkers, and any other available technology.

Research

Some *IMPACT!* activities entail various kinds of research. Students may use the school or public library or other resources. Here are some suggestions to consider when research is called for:

- Select a topic area of general interest to your students.
- Allow them to select specific topics.
- Describe where the needed information may be found.
- Be specific about your expectations with respect to their written report.

Voluminous written work should not be the object of research activities. Students are far more likely to find this kind of activity meaningful when writing is included as a means to an end, rather than an end in itself.

Art and Music

The major objective of art activities is to allow students to express their feelings and ideas creatively. You don't have to be an art teacher to involve students in activities that encourage artistic expression. For example, cartooning may be an acceptable substitute for story-writing if you teach English language arts. Other examples include encouraging students to make posters, displays, timelines, charts, and other illustrations to aid them in presenting individual and group reports to the class.

Make music appreciation activities meaningful by giving the students background information on each musical selection before playing it. If the recording has been contributed by a student, ask him/her to introduce it. Before selections are played, urge the students to get into a relaxed position in their chairs. Suggest that they close their eyes. Be sure to use the best sound equipment available.

Creating your own *IMPACT!* circle session topics

How *IMPACT!* Topics Are Developed

Topics in the *IMPACT!* program are presented according to a principle of learning that has been validated in a wide variety of applications. This principle is called *successive approximation*, and simply means, *begin where learners are or where they are likely to be and proceed to steps that are in keeping with the learners' progress*. The program is designed to help students develop useful insights into themselves and others while they practice positive communication skills. Circle session topics are experiential approximations of those insights.

Generally speaking, it is relatively easy to talk about things past and less easy to talk about right now. Second, it is typically easier to talk about other people and less easy to talk about oneself. Third, it seems to be easier for most people to talk about behavior than to talk about feelings. Finally, pleasant emotions are easier for most people to describe than negative ones. The examples that follow indicate topics at each end of the continuum for each of the four dimensions.

1. **Past** .... **Present**
   "A Pleasant Memory"   "Something I Feel Good About Today"

2. **Other People** .... **Self**
   "Someone Did Something for   "A Way I Take Care of Myself"
   Someone Else"

3. **Behavior** .... **Feelings**
   "I Helped Someone Who Needed   "A Time I Felt Shy"
   and Wanted My Help"

4. **Positive Feelings** .... **Negative Feelings**
   "Something That Makes   "Something That Makes Me Feel Sad"
   Me Feel Good"

Thoughts on Developing Your Own Topics

Many teachers and students generate topics tailor-made to fit their needs. If these topics are generated so that the less complex are presented first, moving sequentially toward the more complex, the principle of learning underlying the program will be maintained. Insights may come anywhere along the continuum, but they are more likely to occur when students are on familiar ground. The test of ease for a topic will be the sharing in the circle. Here are three other points to keep in mind:

1. If you create a topic that relates to an issue of some kind, remember that in issue-oriented circle sessions there need be no agreement. The circle is not a rap session. Each person merely voices his/her own thoughts and feelings about the issue. The emphasis is on listening to one another's remarks and becoming aware of one's own thoughts and feelings. During the summary discussion, elicit comments from the students on the similarities and differences in their feelings and thoughts and ask open-ended, thought-provoking questions.

2. Do not initiate a topic that might be a lead-in for ax-grinding on the part of you or anyone else in the circle. If you need to express strong feelings to the students, find another method. The same principle applies to a situation in which one or more students have some strong feelings to express to each other. *The circle is not a setting for confrontation, not even subtle confrontation!*

3. Make sure that the topic, when it is discussed, will lead to an exploration of feelings. If you hold circle sessions and feelings are not discussed, they are not *IMPACT!* circle sessions.

Guidelines for Developing Circle Sessions Topics.

Formulate topics in light of the considerations already mentioned. To avoid the repetitious "A Time...," other starters for topics are:

"When..."
"One of..."
"Something I..."
"What..."
"One Way..."
"An Idea I..."
"The Way..."
"How..."
"Things I..."
"The Thing That..."

Consider what you are trying to achieve with the topic. Does it relate to one of the three growth areas, Awareness, Social Interaction, or Mastery? Is it in harmony with other aspects of your curriculum?

Be sure to present the topic to the students in an open-ended manner. Elaborate on it. Mention suggestions and possibilities to help them start thinking about it. State the topic at the beginning of your introduction and again at the end.

As you listen to students respond, do not feel compelled to question them. If you do ask a question, be sure it's open-ended and asked with the intention of helping them express themselves more fully. In general, questions asked to students when they are sharing should help students develop an awareness of **feelings**, their own and others. For example:

— *Do you remember how you felt at the time?*
— *How do you feel about that now?*

Questions may enable students to become more aware of their **behavior**.
— *Do you remember what you said/did when it happened?*
— *How did other people act/react in that situation?*

Questions may help students focus on their own **thoughts**, including attitudes, beliefs, preferences, etc., to learn more about how their thoughts influence their feelings and behavior.
— *Did any thought or image cross your mind when that happened?*
— *Do you remember how that idea caused you to feel or act?*

Summary discussion. The purpose of the summary is to involve students intellectually, to encourage them to examine the implications of what they have shared, and to stimulate higher-order thinking skills. The summary starters listed below relate to Awareness, Social Interaction, and Mastery.

Awareness
— *What kinds of things do people do...?*
— *If you feel...does that mean...?*
— *What is it that...?*
— *What kinds of things do...?*
— *When people...?*
— *If you want..., then...?*

Social Interaction:
— *If you want people to..., then...?*
— *Would all of us...?*
— *Are there ways we...?*
— *Are there times when...?*
— *What can you say to...?*

Mastery
— *How can a person...?*
— *Do you think...should have to...?*
— *What can you do when...?*
— *Is it too early/late to...?*

Questions and answers

Questions About the Leader's Role While Conducting Circle Sessions

1. What if I feel strange and awkward when first using the process of the circle?

For some the circle session may demand behaviors that feel unnatural at first. It is important to remember that these procedures were developed because of their proven effectiveness in promoting positive communication skills in students. You are urged to follow the format, to keep interaction positive, and to serve as a effective communication model. Use your own personal style. So long as the basic circle session procedures are followed, your style should reflect what is most comfortable and closest to the real you.

2. Do I have to share verbally in the circle session?

The rules apply to everyone equally: all the participants get a turn to speak, but they don't have to take it. Hence, there may be times when you will choose not to share. On the other hand, if you rarely share, the students will probably not see you as a real member of the group. They may begin to respond with what they think you want to hear, not their real thoughts and feelings.

3. How long should I wait for a student to share verbally the first time?

Until he or she shares. Re-evaluate what you consider to be involvement. Participation may be something other than talking. Attentiveness to others is positive participation. Verbal sharing is likely to occur when students feel comfortable, secure, and included and when they have something to say. Most teachers and counselors indicate this is generally not a serious problem in their circles after the students have experienced two or more sessions.

4. What should I do if I forget who said what during a circle session?

Be honest and ask for help. Your honesty sends the message: "It's okay to forget; everybody does. Even teachers are human."

5. There are times when I can make a very important moral or value point from the sharing that occurs in the circle. What should I do?

The basic atmosphere of the circle is one of acceptance. Moralizing has a judgmental quality. If you feel you should make a value statement, use an "I" message. That is, own the statement as a reflection of your own position or society's position, as you see it. (For example: "I think its not right for people to take things that don't belong to them." "It seems to me that most people don't like to be interrupted.") In addition, ask the students what they think about the issue during the summary discussion, and accept their responses.

6. What should I do about a parent who asks to observe a circle?

Invite all parents and community members openly and warmly to participate in the circle. Explain the rules for the session (or ask the students to explain them) with the understanding that the parents have a right to share if they desire to—the same right the students have in the circle every day. Carry out the circle as you normally do, and take the time to answer the parents' questions afterward. The experience of participating in a circle is generally a positive one and usually answers most questions parents have.

Questions About Classroom Management

7. When is the best time to begin the IMPACT! program with a particular group or class?

The best time to introduce **IMPACT!** activities is when the class or group first forms. This usually occurs at the beginning of the semester. The program helps students get to know you and each other. Teachers who wait for a few weeks before introducing **IMPACT!** activities are more likely to experience reticence in students than those who introduce the activities at the outset.

8. I like the idea, but I don't have the time. How can I fit IMPACT! into my overloaded curriculum?

If you don't have the time, you can't! Your choice is "Shall I do **IMPACT!**?" If you respond yes, you will find time. While you are leading circle sessions, other students are doing independent seat work on your subject matter.

9. How should I decide who will be in which group?

There are numerous ways. Choose the one you feel will work best for you. The important don'ts are: (1) don't ability-group; and (2) don't separate students according to sex, or ethnicity. The maximum number should be 12, and eventually everyone in the entire class should participate in a circle.

10. Do students have to attend the circle?

No. If a student is involved with a task that for him/her takes precedence over attending the circle, then you may wish to allow that student to follow his/her own interests. On the other hand, if nonattendance is avoidance, you have a different situation. By avoiding, the student may be saying that he or she feels threatened, or uncomfortable, or that sharing is required. A solution may be to reassure the student that attendance does not have to mean verbal sharing. Everyone has the right to participate silently.

11. How should I introduce a new student to the circle?

Many ways are open to you. You may have another student in the circle tell the new participant what's happening, what the ground rules are, and so on. Our experience indicates that introducing a new student to a small group facilitates acceptance in the larger group. New students have reported that the circles were especially helpful in allowing them to make friends in a new situation.

12. What should I do with the rest of the class while circles are being carried out?

The same thing you do when you use other small-group activities in the classroom. You may assign a wide variety of seat work, including free reading, catch-up time, individualized contracts, etc. This question is specifically dealt with earlier in the section.

13. How should I deal with resistant students?

Students are easily misinterpreted. Quite often their seeming hostility or impudence is a mask covering shyness and fear. You don't have to solve their problems, and your attentive listening to them shows you care. Should a student say, "But we're not learning anything!" your response may be along the following lines:
Teacher: "How do you communicate with people outside the classroom?"
Student: "Talk."
Teacher: "What for?"
Student: "To find out what's happening."
Teacher: "Is talking taught in school?"
Student: "Yeah, sort of."
Teacher: "Then maybe you are learning something."

Questions About Student Responses in Circle Sessions:

14. What can I do if students look blank, or there are long silences?

This behavior is not unusual, particularly when you first start circle sessions or if the topic is one students seldom think about. Suppose you sense the students are having difficulty grasping or relating to the topic. You can legitimize the silence by saying something like, "This topic requires some thought. Let's all take a minute to think about it."

Allow a minute or so to pass, restate the topic, and wait for someone to share. You may also decide to take your turn first if you sense the students would appreciate further clarification.

Another strategy is to announce the topic ahead of time, either the day before or at the beginning of the class period. You might also list topics on the chalkboard.

15. How should I respond when another member of the circle laughs at or puts down the student who is sharing?

Respond by letting the student know that what he or she is doing is unacceptable. Your first responsibility is to protect the speaker, even if your response to the offender appears to be a put-down. When it is his/her turn to speak, you will protect him/her just as vigorously.

At appropriate intervals remind the students of the rules, and if the unacceptable behavior persists, *excuse* the student from the circle session.

16. How do I deal with a response that indicates a student enjoys hurting others?

First of all, be sure the response is an honest one and not designed to get attention. If it is the latter kind, do not reward it with attention. If it is an honest statement, you have several options. You may accept the response without comment (probably the

most difficult for many teachers), you may send an "I" message ("Hurting others gives me a bad feeling."), or you may ask the student how he or she thinks the other person felt about it.

17. What should I do when one student copies the response of another?

Accept the response. You may say, "Would you like to tell us more about...?" so the response can be individualized. Remember that a copied response may indicate avoidance by an individual who does not feel secure. This usually occurs when circle sessions are begun. Wait. Time will gradually establish a feeling of security.

18. How do you stop someone from sharing and sharing and sharing?

Ask the individual a closed-ended question that calls for a succinct response. Another strategy is to interrupt as gracefully as possible so you may reflect on what has been shared so far. Then repeat the topic to enable someone else to respond. From time to time gently but firmly remind the group that everyone has a right to share and that the time is limited.

19. What should I do when I get highly emotional responses to a topic?

This will happen occasionally because we all feel strong emotions at times. The vast majority of the **IMPACT!** topics are upbeat and positive, but some zero in directly on negative emotions. When students respond very emotionally during the circle sessions, be sure to demonstrate acceptance of their feelings, and concern and caring for them. Do not feel compelled to cheer them up or solve their problems for them.

20. What do I do if a student starts crying during a circle?

First and foremost, accept the response positively as a legitimate expression of feeling. Let the student know that it is acceptable behavior. Everyone needs to cry at times. Give students free, warm attention while they cry, and let them cry until they are finished. Tell the group, "Sharon is getting rid of her hurt by crying." If you model this behavior, the other students will behave similarly. If the student wishes to leave the circle, excuse him/her, but make contact again before the end of the class session.

21. What if a student starts talking about something negative that occurred involving another student in the circle?

This problem sometimes arises when the topic is one that can be used to get back at another student, and can be headed off at the beginning of the circle session by reminding students of rule #5, which prohibits gossip. Like any other rule, this one needs to be enforced gently but firmly. Use it to remind students that the circle is a special, protected environment where gossip is not tolerated, and where even the use of names is discouraged. A related issue involves confidentiality. Explain that the students may share with anyone what they as *individuals* say in the circle; however, everything else (anything others say in the circle) is absolutely confidential.

22. What should I do if a student raises family problems as a response to a topic?

Students should be regularly reminded that naming names and sharing embarrassing information is not done in the circle. If a student does share a family problem, accept the statement, but do not pursue it. If the student persists, she or he obviously needs to talk with someone. We suggest that you respond with something like, "I'm a bit uncomfortable discussing that here, but I'll talk with you about it later. Is that all right?" Then be sure to follow through.

23. What should I do about issues raised in a circle such as anger or lying?

Sometimes a student will tell about feeling angry or talk about a time when someone lied and how he or she felt about it. While names should not be mentioned, this is a very acceptable part of a circle session because the student is sharing an experience and the feelings that went with it. However, angry confrontations in a circle are not acceptable. If a confrontation occurs, remind the students that the circle is not meant for confronting one another or putting each other down in any way. Provide an alternative outlet for students who wish to express anger or hostility. For example, you might suggest journal writing that is either private or shared only with the teacher. Or you might do the unit, "Resolving Conflict" to help the students explore ways to deal with their anger.

24. What do you do when a student has lied in the circle?

First, do not confront the student or allow his/her peers to do so. We suggest that you consider the reason for the exaggeration or lie, which is much more important than the lie itself. In reflecting on the reason consider the structure of the circle. Do the students feel they have to share? Are experiences of an unusual nature the only kind of sharing that receives recognition?

Questions About the Process and Content of Circle Sessions

25. Do I have to follow the sequence for circle sessions and activities as laid out in the IMPACT! units?

No. *IMPACT!* is a flexible, open-ended curriculum for teachers of many subject areas and for counselors. The circle sessions have been placed in a suggested sequence but should be interspersed with activities and the distribution of experience sheets, as you see fit.

You may, of course, also delete activities and add others of varying kinds to meet your needs.

26. Is it all right to change the topic when it appears that no one will share?

We prefer that you not. Instead, reflect to yourself on the reasons for the lack of response. Perhaps something is getting in the way of trust-building between you and your students. If you consistently change topics until someone speaks, you are essentially sending this message: "I won't be satisfied until you talk," which stands in direct opposition to the rule of voluntary sharing.

27. How long should I allow a silence in a circle session to last?

Normally, continued silences are not a part of the classroom experience, although short silences do occur during some circle sessions. Consider if the silence is reflective thinking before you interrupt. A general rule of thumb is to allow silence to the point that you observe group discomfort. It may have a catalytic effect if you share your feelings about the silence or begin to respond to the topic yourself as a means of getting things going. If you have tried these things and the silence persists, you may indicate, "Today doesn't seem to be a good day for sharing. The next time we meet for a circle session, the topic will be..." Then stop the session.

28. Will having the circle on a regular basis help my problem students?

If by problem students you mean those who consistently disrupt your scheduled activities by seeking attention and recognition, the circle can help, *if* they abide by the rules during the sessions. The circle is not a panacea. It does provide a time and place for everyone to be given attention and recognition—a space where others will listen. We believe that eventually these factors make a difference in the lives of students and classrooms.

29. What should I do when issues are raised in a circle that relate to cognitive themes in the curriculum?

If the students are interested in the issue, discuss it briefly, preferably as part of the summary discussion. Capitalize on their interest, but keep in mind that the circle is not for instruction. If instruction begins to take place regularly during circle sessions, the students will lose that time for self-expression. When the circle is over, carry out related activities to synthesize the cognitive and affective realms.

30. What should I do when sharing is really just beginning and the time is up?

First of all, be sure to hold the session when there is enough time to follow all the **IMPACT!** circle session procedures. If the time is up before everyone has had a chance to speak, end the circle by expressing your appreciation to the students for listening and sharing. Remind them that soon there will be another chance to participate, and tell them what the topic will be. Then tell the students that those who didn't get a chance to speak today will get their chance the next time the group meets.

31. Is it all right to continue a circle for an additional 10-20 minutes when we are doing a lot of sharing?

One result of an extended time limit may be an implied message: "I am going to continue the circle until everyone shares," which is undesirable. There are other times, however, when the circle has provoked such interest that the students want to continue the discussion. If time permits, continue, but officially end the session first. Twenty to thirty minutes is not magical, but we have found it is generally an appropriate period of time to carry out all the circle session procedures while most students remain actively attentive.

32. Since IMPACT! is an affective program, why do you have summary discussions at the end of every circle session?

IMPACT! is intended to be a confluent education program that prizes students' cognitive as well as affective development. The summary discussion satisfies the need of students to know what they learned from the activity. The cognitive aspects of IMPACT! also help you justify the value of including an affective component in your curriculum, not only to your students but also to administrators, colleagues, and community. In addition to (or instead of) the summary questions listed in each IMPACT! activity, you may create your own that relate your curriculum.

Questions About the Availability and Use of IMPACT! Resources

33. Can I use the IMPACT! materials with college-aged groups and adults?

Yes. You may need to modify some of the activities somewhat, but generally speaking, IMPACT! has been designed for any person beyond age eleven. (Many activities are even appropriate for younger children.)

34. If I have a question or problem, whom should I call or write?

You are always free to call or write to **Innerchoice Publishing**. If you attended a workshop, the trainer who led the workshop is also a resource, as are the other educators who went through the training experience with you. Explore the possibility of organizing an informal group of colleagues to conduct circles and offer one another support and encouragement.

35. How do you respond to the comment, "I don't think I'm qualified to deal with this type of content?"

Each day as you relate to the students in your classroom, you are, in fact, involved with both the affective and cognitive domains. The IMPACT! materials have been developed as guides to help you function more effectively in both realms. In addition to the materials, training sessions are available. The reason we offer training for teachers, counselors, and others is to respond to this concern specifically. These sessions are conducted by experienced trainers and are designed to help you understand the theoretical model underlying the program, as well as have the opportunity to practice the skills essential to its implementation.

In Conclusion: The Two Most Important Things to Remember

No matter what happens in a circle session, without the following two elements it is not really an IMPACT! circle:

1. Everyone gets a turn.
2. Everyone who takes a turn gets listened to.

What does it mean to get a turn? Imagine a pie divided into as many pieces as there are people in the circle. Telling the students that everyone gets a turn, whether they want to take it or not, is like telling them that each one gets a piece of the pie. Some students may not want their piece right away, but they know it's there to take when they do want it.

As the teacher or counselor, you must protect this shared ownership. Getting a turn not only represents a chance to talk, it is an assurance that every member of the circle has a "space" that no one else will violate.

When students take their turn, they will be listened to. There will be no attempt by anyone to manipulate what a student is offering. That is, the student will not be probed, interrupted, interpreted, analyzed, put-down, joked-at, advised, preached to, and so on. To "listen to" in *IMPACT!* is to respectfully focus attention on the speaker and to let the speaker know that you have heard what he or she has said.

In the final analysis, the only way that a circle session can be evaluated is against these two criteria. Thus, if only two students choose to speak, but are listened to—even if they don't say very "deep" or "meaningful" things—the circle can be considered a success.

Cross Curriculum Reference Guide

Each *IMPACT!* activity can be universally applied to grades 7 through 12. Recognizing that teachers and counselors working with students at each grade level are dealing with varied levels of personal development, we encourage adaptation of activities to accommodate student needs.

In the following reference guide, activities have been linked with specific academic areas. With limited alterations or additions, activities can also be adapted for use in academic areas not specified. For example, the circle session entitled "Significant People Who Have Affected My Life" could easily be expanded for Social Studies by including historical figures as significant influences, or "Decision, Decisions!" is adaptable for use in math and science by tying in predictions and probable outcomes.

The reference guide is organized to correspond to the various skill development sections appearing in *IMPACT!* Each activity's page number and title are followed by a listing of the curriculum areas it addresses and in which it can be employed.

PAGE	ACTIVITY TITLE	CURRICULUM AREAS

COMMUNICATING EFFECTIVELY

PAGE	ACTIVITY TITLE	CURRICULUM AREAS
49	Words Are Only Part of It	English, Psychology, Speech, Drama, Consumer Education
51	Language as Pilot	English, Speech, Communications, Consumer Education
53	Putting Those Skills to the Acid Test	English, Speech, Media, Consumer Education
55	Stepping Stones	English, Critical Thinking, Speech, Communication, Consumer Education, Social Studies

MANAGING STRESS

PAGE	ACTIVITY TITLE	CURRICULUM AREAS
106	**When I Like Myself Most**	Values, English, Critical Thinking, Health/Wellness, Career and Family Studies, Communications, Psychology
107	**Significant People Who Have Affected My Life**	English, Critical Thinking, Career and Family Studies, Communications
109	**Helping Someone Learn**	Career and Family Studies, Communications, Psychology, English
111	**Come to Your Senses**	English, Health/Wellness, Career and Family Studies, Psychology
113	**Getting More In Touch With Me**	English, Health/Wellness, Career and Family Studies, Psychology
115	**All the Me's I Am and Have Been**	English, Critical Thinking, Health/Wellness, Career and Family Studies, Communications
116	**A Self-Portrait**	Art, Values, English, Communications, Critical Thinking, Career and Family Studies
117	**Looking At My Many Selves**	Psychology, English, Values, Career and Family Studies

SETTING AND ATTAINING GOALS

PAGE	ACTIVITY TITLE	CURRICULUM AREAS
121	**Something I Enjoy Doing Because It Gives Me a Feeling of Accomplishment**	Values, Communications, Critical Thinking, Health/Wellness, English, Career and Family Studies
122	**Something at Which I'd Like to Succeed**	Values, Communications, Critical Thinking, Health/Wellness, English, Career and Family Studies
123	**Something I'd Do If I Knew I Couldn't Fail**	Values, Communications, Critical Thinking, Health/Wellness, English, Career and Family Studies

MAKING DECISIONS

SOLVING PROBLEMS

RESOLVING CONFLICT

RELATING TO PEERS

TAKING RESPONSIBILITY

EXPLORING CAREERS

TEAM BUILDING

COMMUNICATING EFFECTIVELY

People fail to get along because they fear each other. They fear each other because they don't know each other. They don't know each other because they have not effectively communicated with each other.

Martin Luther King Jr.

Effective communication is critical to social interaction and, via both process and content, most of the units in **IMPACT!** develop communication skills. However, this unit deals directly with the two major components of communication: expression and listening.

While it seems only natural that humans should equitably exchange their thoughts and feelings, many have not acquired the skills necessary to communicate with the understanding and empathy needed to bind relationships. One of the major reasons we experience problems in communication is that we forget that individual experiences are never identical. Yet when we develop a closer understanding of what others experience, we find more agreement than disagreement. In this unit, students have an opportunity to examine their successes and shortcomings in communication, identify roadblocks to effective communication, and develop skills for listening and expressing themselves.

Overall objectives
The students will:
— become aware that active communication is a necessary part of human relationships.
— discuss their communication successes and shortcomings.
— consider the effect of communication on self-concept.
— improve basic communication skills.

Words Are Only Part of It ————

———— Dramatizations and Discussion

Description: Through a sequence of demonstrations, dramatized first by the teacher and then by students, the class examines how emotion is conveyed nonverbally in communication. A summarizing discussion culminates the activity.

Objectives: The students will:
— demonstrate that communication involves much more than the simple transmission of words and ideas.
— discuss how feelings are conveyed in communication.

Time needed: half a class period

Directions: **Prior to class write the following words on the board:**

1. delight
2. confusion
3. surprise
4. worry
5. hate
6. sadness
7. love
8. irritation
9. anger
10. fear

Begin the activity by briefly reviewing the list with the students. Point out that these are just some of the many emotions that people feel. Briefly discuss how communication involves much more than the simple use of words. Emotions get into the act in a number of ways.

Illustrate the point. Silently select one of the emotions listed on the board, and ask the class to guess which one it is while you repeat a tongue twister. Say the tongue twister and, with your tone, inflection, facial expression, body posture and movement, simultaneously convey the emotion you selected.

After the laughter subsides, allow the students to guess which emotion you were trying to convey. Then ask them how they knew. List the clues on the board. The list should include, but not be limited to:

1. facial expression
2. tone
3. inflection
4. posture
5. body movements

(Continued Next Page)

Repeat the tongue twister again once or twice, conveying other emotions from the list. Discuss with the class the specific tones, inflections, facial expressions, body postures, and movements you used to express each one.

Invite the students to demonstrate other emotions. Have volunteers come to the front of the class one at a time and repeat the process. After each demonstration, ask the class to examine the manner in which the emotion was communicated. Ask questions such as:
1. Can you describe the tone and inflection?
2. What did his/her face do?
3. What was his/her posture like?
4. What were the movements of his/her body?

After some or all of the emotions listed have been demonstrated, vary the activity:
1. **Restrict what the performers can do.** First, ask them not to move their bodies in any way, and second ask them to convey the emotion completely nonverbally, depending only on facial expression, posture, and body movement.
2. **Introduce a new tongue twister from time to time:**
   - *Rubber baby-buggy bumpers*
   - *She sells sea shells down by the sea shore.*
   - *Peter Piper picked a peck of pickled peppers.*
   - *How much wood would a woodchuck chuck if a woodchuck could chuck wood?*
   - *Big black bugs bleed blood.*

Discussion questions:

Conduct a class discussion about the nature of nonverbal communication. Use these and other open-ended questions:
— *How do people communicate without words?*
— *Why do you think tongue twisters were used to demonstrate this, instead of important ideas?*
— *Can you hide your feelings when you are communicating with someone? How?*
— *What did you learn from this activity?*

Language as Pilot

A Class Experiment and Discussion

Description: Students simulate an airplane landing on a runway guided by a control tower. They take turns being the pilot of the plane and the air-traffic controller. After trying the experiment several times the class discusses the problems inherent in communicating precise messages.

Objectives: The students will:
— practice communicating clearly and accurately.
— describe communication problems caused by imprecise communication and differing interpretations.

Time needed: half a class period

Materials needed: desks, tables, crumpled paper, and other objects generally available in the classroom

Directions: **Begin by telling the students that you would like them to cooperate in conducting an experiment that relates to language and communication.** Without any further explanation, ask the students to help you build a runway. Construct the runway out of furniture and people. Make it about 15 to 20 feet long and wide enough for a person to walk down. Next, litter the runway with debris, books, papers, pencils, and other small objects which will not cause a blindfolded person to trip or fall.

When the runway is ready, ask a student volunteer to be the pilot of an airplane that will land on the runway. Then ask a volunteer to play the part of the **air-traffic controller** trying to help the pilot land the plane by giving directions over an imaginary radio transmitter. As soon as two students volunteer, ask them to move to opposite ends of the runway.

Blindfold the pilot. Explain that a storm has hit and lightning has knocked out the transmitter of the plane. The receiver is still working so the pilot can *get* messages, but can't *send* them. Indicate that the storm has created havoc on the runway. Debris is all over the place. The control tower must try to land the plane without damage by sending directions over the radio. The visibility is zero, so the pilot must rely only on these messages for a safe

(Continued Next Page)

Language as Pilot

landing. *If the pilot brushes against any of the objects on the runway, the plane is considered crashed.*

Allow several teams of pilots and controllers to attempt to land the plane safely. After each attempt briefly discuss the problems each team encountered.

Discussion questions:

Ask the students to put the classroom back in order and return to their seats for a general discussion. Ask these and other open-ended questions:

— *How can we communicate clear and exact messages?*

— *Did anything like this ever happen to you? Tell us about a time when you had trouble getting a precise message across or correctly understanding someone else's message.*

— *What have you learned about language and communication from this experiment?*

Putting Those Skills to the Acid Test

A Class Experiment and Discussion

Description:	After presenting the students with three hypothetical problem situations, the teacher steps out of the leadership role, allowing the students to decide what to do. Their problem-solving session is tape recorded and then reviewed. A follow-up discussion focuses on communications and decision-making.
Objective:	The students will: —work as a group to solve hypothetical problems. —describe their methods of decision-making and communicating.
Time needed:	one class period
Materials needed:	tape recorder or videotape equipment
Directions:	**Prior to class list three problems on the board that will arouse the emotions of the students; for example:** **1.** The new dress code states that students may no longer wear T-shirts of any kind to school. **2.** All the school's special events will take place during the two weeks when finals will be given. **3.** All assemblies will be cancelled until the litter problem is resolved (or the number of students late to class is reduced).

Introduce the activity. As soon as the class has assembled, tell the students that none of the statements on the board is true, but that you would like them to *imagine* they are true for the next 20 minutes. Ask them to decide what they as a class are going to do about each problem. Explain that they must deal with each issue one at a time, on their own.

Go to a location in the room away from the center of the action, and turn on the tape recorder. (If a tape recorder is unavailable, or if you believe that it will negatively affect your rapport with the class, take written notes. One or two students may also be observer/note-takers.) While the students struggle with, or takes effective advantage of, their freedom, say nothing. After a few minutes, things should start to happen. When three

(Continued Next Page)

Putting Those Skills to the Acid Test

minutes (of the twenty) are left, ask the class to solidify its decisions.

At the end of the 20 minutes, play the tape for the class, or review your written notes with them. If you do the latter, simply reflect to them what you saw happen. Do not critique or evaluate anyone's behavior.

Discussion questions:

Discuss the dynamics of the students' communication and decision-making. Ask these and other relevant questions:
— *How did you get started?*
— *How did not having a leader affect you at first, and what did you do about it?*
— *What was the most difficult thing about the task?*
— *What went well?*
— *What feelings did you have and when did you experience them?*
— *How would you describe your communications?*
— *How did you make decisions?*

Stepping Stones

A Group Task and Discussion

Description: Teams of not more than 10 students are given the task of crossing an imaginary river without getting wet, using baseball bases as stepping stones. The students must cooperate in planning an approach to get everyone across.

Objective: The students will work cooperatively to solve a problem.

Time needed: one class period

Materials needed: nine baseball bases (or any suitable substitute such as cardboard squares or flattened paper bags) and an area (lawn, gym, or multipurpose room) at least 37 1/2 feet long

Directions: Measure off 37 1/2 feet and mark both ends of the space. Group the class into teams of no more than ten and no fewer than seven each. (For example, 31 students could be divided into three groups of eight and one group of seven.) Allow one less stepping stone than there are team members. Subtract 2 1/2 feet from the length of the space for every team member less than ten, as follows:

  9 team members = 35 feet
  8 team members = 32 1/2 feet
  7 team members = 30 feet

Explain to the students that you would like them to imagine that between the two markers there is a raging river. Their task is to get each team member across the river, using the bases as stepping stones.

As each team attempts to cross the river, its members will discover that their task involves trial, error, and team cooperation. They will need to experiment and help one another.

When the first team attempts to cross the river, the other teams may watch. It would be better, however, if each team approached the problem without having seen another team work on it. If this latter procedure is followed, allow teams that have completed the

(Continued Next Page)

Stepping Stones

task to watch the next team(s) attempt it. Laughter and encouragement on the part of observers will make the activity more fun and interesting, but do not allow students to make derogatory statements or sounds.

Discussion questions:

After all of the teams have crossed the river, ask the students:
— *What was the toughest part of this exercise for you?*
— *What part or parts made you feel good?*
— *What did you learn from doing this activity?*

Tape Recorder Dyads

Listening Exercise and Discussion

Description: The listener in this preliminary listening activity mentally records data provided by the uninterrupted speaker. Feedback of data by the listener is then corrected by the speaker. A class discussion follows.

Objectives: The students will demonstrate attentive listening for content.

Time needed: approximately 30 to 40 minutes

Materials needed: chalkboard, chalk, and timer or watch

Directions:

1. **Briefly explain to the students that listening is an integral part of the communication process.** One way to facilitate communication is simply to be silent, giving the person who is speaking a green light to speak without interruptions. The listener further facilitates communication by mentally recording the content of the speaker's monolog.

2. **Divide the students into dyads.** Attempt to pair students who do not know each other very well. Ask them to determine who will be **A** and who will be **B**.

3. **Play two rounds of the activity, as follows:**
   First half of round 1:
   Recording:
   A speaks uninterrupted for two minutes to his or her partner about a topic such as : "The Best Thing That's Happened to Me So Far Today." **B** listens attentively, mentally recording the speaker's data.
   Playback:
   After the speaker's two-minute monolog, the listener is given one-and-a-half minutes to verbally "play back" the data given by the speaker during the "recording session."
   Corrections or additions:
   At the end of the playback, the speaker is given one-half minute to clarify any information the listener didn't understand or to add things the listener forgot.
   Second half of round 1: Reverse roles (**B** speaks, **A** listens) and repeat the entire process (same topic).

(Continued Next Page)

Tape Recorder Dyads

First half of round 2: Person **A** becomes the speaker again. The procedure is exactly the same as for the first half of round 1. However, the topic is changed. A suggestion for the second topic is, "Things I'm Looking Forward to This Semester."

Second half of round 2: Reverse roles (**B** speaks, **A** listens) and repeat the entire process (same topic).

4. **Suggested Topics:**
   One of My Favorite Possesions
   A Secret Wish I Have
   A Person I'd Like To Be Like
   My Idea of a Perfect Saturday Afternoon
   Someone I Trust
   Something I Don't Like Doing

Discussion questions:

After both rounds have been completed, facilitate a discussion by asking these and other questions. Record key responses on the chalkboard for a quick review:

— *How did you feel as the speaker?*

— *How did you feel as the listener?*

— *Did it get easier or harder in round 2 to function like a tape recorder?*

— *Did you learn anything new and interesting about your partner?*

— *Of what value is silent attentive listening to effective communication?*

— *What are some things you can do to show someone you are really listening?*

Tell It Like It Is

A Dyad Sequence and Discussion

Description: Students form groups of eight to twelve, and each student participates in a dyad with every other person in his/her group. A total class discussion culminates the activity.

Objectives: Each student will interact verbally with several other students.

Time needed: one class period

Directions:

Introduce the activity. After observing the manner in which students have been interacting with each other during previous activities, assign them to groups of eight, ten, or twelve. (An even number in each group is essential for this activity to work.) Read the list to the class, and ask the groups to gather in various areas of the room. Then explain that they will be participating in a series of dyads, and when you give the signal for them to change partners, they should pair up with another person in their group, *not* with someone from another group.

Ask the students to choose a partner. Explain that both people will take turns speaking on the same topic. As the first person (**A**) speaks for one minute, the second person (**B**) listens. The listener should ask no more than one question, and it should be to help the speaker express him/herself, not to gain information of personal interest. No questions at all might be best.

Explain also that at the end of the minute **A** and **B** will switch roles, the listener becoming the speaker, and talking about the same topic for one more minute. This will complete the first round, and the students will each find a new partner.

Signal the end of each minute and give clear instructions. Conduct enough rounds so that each student will be paired once with every member of his/her group. (For example, if you have four groups of eight students, conduct seven rounds.) If one student is left over, join this student's group and participate yourself.

(Continued Next Page)

Suggested topics:
  "My Favorite Pastime"
  "My Favorite Food"
  "My Favorite TV Show or Movie"
  "My Favorite Story, Poem, Book, or Magazine"
  "My Favorite Animal"
  "My Favorite Game or Sport"
  "My Favorite Song or Musical Group"
  "My Favorite Subject at School"
  "My Favorite Famous Person"
  "My Favorite Non-Famous Person"
  "Something I'm Looking Forward To"

Discussion questions:

Ask the class to return to their original seating. Facilitate a discussion, using these and other open-ended questions:

— *How did it feel to be the speaker during this exercise?*
— *How did it feel to be the listener?*
— *How did you react to changing partners again and again?*
— *Did speaking and/or listening get harder or easier as you went from partner to partner?*
— *Did you learn anything interesting about yourself that you would like to tell the group?*

Communication Stoppers ——————

—————————————— **Role-Play and Discussion**

Description: The teacher presents a list of behaviors that typically stop or retard communication, and demonstrates them by briefly role-playing each one with a student. A class discussion follows each demonstration.

Objectives: The students will:
—demonstrate common ways of responding to another person that may block communication.
—describe how different ways of responding may affect a speaker.
—discuss what constitutes effective and ineffective communication.

Time needed: one class period

Materials needed: chalkboard and chalk, or chart paper and magic marker

Directions: **Write the following list on the board or chart paper for the students to see when they enter class:**
- Interrupting
- Challenging/Accusing/Contradicting
- Dominating
- Judging
- Advising
- Interpreting
- Probing
- Criticizing/Name-calling/Putting-down

Begin the activity by asking the students to think of a heading or title for the list on the board. Write their suggestions down, and discuss each one briefly. Add the suggested title, "Communication Stoppers," and ask the students if they can imagine how these behaviors might have the effect of hampering communication—or stopping it altogether.

Ask the students to help you role-play each behavior to see what kind of effect it does have on communication. Invite a volunteer to start a conversation with you. Explain to the student

(Continued Next Page)

Communication Stoppers ——————

that he or she may talk about anything that comes to mind, and should attempt to continue the conversation as long as possible, or until you call time.

As the student begins to speak, respond with one of the communication stoppers from the list. Use appropriate gestures, volume, and tone, and make your response as convincing as possible. Continue using examples of that particular communication stopper until (1) the student gives up talking, or (2) the point has been sufficiently made.

After each demonstration, lead a class discussion about the effects of that communication behavior. Ask the discussion questions listed below, and others suggested by the demonstration. *The following elaboration on the communication stoppers includes suggestions for conducting each demonstration, as well as important points to make during discussion.*

- **Interrupting**
  Demonstration: Butt in time and again as the student talks, with statements about yourself and things that have happened to you. For example, if the student says, "I have a dog named...," interrupt with, "Have I ever told you about my dog? You know, he's really a terrific pet..., etc., etc."
  Discussion: Mention how frustrating it is to be interrupted, and how futile it is to continue a conversation when interruptions occur over and over. Interrupting is probably one of the most common, yet assured ways to stop communication.

- **Advising**
  Demonstration: Give lots of unasked-for advice. Use statements like, "Well, if I were you...," "I think you should...," and "Have you tried...." If the student says, "I have a dog named...," respond with, "Dogs are a lot of trouble. Take my advice and get rid or it." or "You should take it to a professional trainer at six months." Etc.

(Continued Next Page)

62 *IMPACT!*   **Communicating Effectively**

Communication Stoppers ———————

Discussion: By giving unsolicited advice, a person immediately assumes a position of superiority. Advice-giving says, "I know better than you do." Advice may also cause the speaker to feel powerless to control his/her own life.

• **Judging**
Demonstration: Evaluate the student and everything s/he says. For example, if the student says, "I have a dog named...," say, "What a good person you are—all dog lovers are fine people." If the student says, "My dog is a poodle," say, "Oh, that's too bad. Poodles are high strung and hard to train."
Discussion: Judging retards communication even when the judgment is positive. Not only does the "judge" assume a superior position, his/her evaluations may so completely contradict the speaker's own feelings that a contest or argument ensues—or further communication seems pointless.

• **Interpreting**
Demonstration: Analyze everything the student says in order to reveal its "deeper meaning." If the student says, "I have a dog named...," say, "You have a dog because you need companionship." If s/he says the dog is a mongrel, respond, "Your self-image wouldn't allow you to have a pedigreed dog."
Discussion: Interpreting and analyzing say that the listener is unwilling to accept the speaker (or the speaker's statements) at face value. Not to mention that the interpretation is frequently wrong.

• **Dominating**
Demonstration: Take over the conversation. If the student says, "I have a dog named...," jump in with, "So do I. My dog is..., and not only that, he..., and so..., because..., blah, blah, blah, etc., etc., ad nauseam.
Discussion: We all know how frustrating and annoying it is to be in a conversation with someone who always has

(Continued Next Page)

Communication Stoppers

something better and more interesting to say than we do. In addition, when one person dominates a conversation, others are forced to use another communication stopper, *interrupting*, just to get a word in.

- **Probing**
  Demonstration: Ask question after question in a demanding tone. If the student says, "I have a dog named..." ask, "Why did you get a dog?" As soon as the student begins to answer, ask, "When did you get it? How much did it cost?" And so on.
  Discussion: Probing tends to put the speaker on the defensive by asking him/her to justify or explain every statement. More importantly, questions may lead the speaker away from what s/he originally wanted to say. The questioner thus controls the conversation *and* its direction.

- **Challenging/Accusing/Contradicting**
  Demonstration: Contradict what the student says and accuse him/her of being wrong. For example, if the student says, "I have a dog named...," say, "No you don't, since when?" If the student says, "I bought him last week...," respond, "You never have any money, so how could you afford to buy a dog?"
  Discussion: Contradictions and accusations put the speaker on the spot, and make it necessary for him/her to take a defensive position. They also say to the speaker, "You are wrong." or "You are bad."

- **Criticizing/Name-calling/Putting-down**
  Demonstration: Make sarcastic, negative remarks in response to everything the student says. If the student says, "I have a dog named...," say, "You jerk, what did you get a dog for? You can't even take care of that mangy cat of yours!" If the student says, "The cat is my sister's." respond, "That's just like you, blaming your little sister for everything."

(Continued Next Page)

Communication Stoppers ———————

Discussion: Criticism diminishes the speaker. Few of us want to continue a conversation in which we are being diminished. Name-calling and put-downs are frequently veiled in humor, but may nonetheless be hurtful and damaging to a relationship.

Discussion questions:

Ask these and other relevant questions <u>after each demonstration</u>:

— *How did you (the speaker) feel?*
— *What effect does this type of response have on the speaker? ...the conversation? ...the relationship?*
— *Has this ever happened to you? What did you say and/or do?*
— *Under what circumstances would it be OK to respond like this?*

The Eyes Have It

Communications Activity and Discussion

Description: Following a brief introductory discussion about eye contact, the students form dyads. In a carefully timed sequence, the students speak to each other without eye contact and with eye contact. A discussion concludes the activity.

Objectives: The students will:
— demonstrate the role of eye contact in communication.
— describe the importance of nonverbal forms of communication.

Time needed: 30-45 minutes

Materials needed: chalkboard, chart, timer, or watch

Directions: **Briefly discuss with the students the importance of eye contact during conversation.** Then ask them to help you create a situation which will give them an opportunity to experience the effects of eye contact (and the effects of no eye contact).

Ask the students to choose a partner and sit so they are facing each other. They should also sit close to each other and as far away from the other dyads as possible to reduce distractions. Ask the partners to decide who will be **A** and who will be **B**.

Top of Round 1: Explain to the students: *For one minute, I want* **A** *to talk to* **B** *about "What I Like About My Favorite Sport or Game" (or some other topic). While* **A** *talks,* **B** *will not say anything and will not look at* **A***. If you are* **B***, look anywhere except into* **A***'s eyes. I'll give you a signal to stop at the end of the minute. Any questions? Begin.*

Feedback: At the end of the minute say: *Stop! Now I want* **B** *to look at* **A** *and for one minute, I want* **A** *to tell* **B** *how you felt when* **B** *wouldn't look at you while you spoke. I'll give you a signal at the end of one minute. Begin.*

Bottom of Round 1: Stop the feedback session after one minute and say: *Now we are going to repeat this procedure.* **A** *will still*

(Continued Next Page)

*be the speaker, and **B** will remain silent. However, this time as **A** speaks, **B** <u>will look at **A**</u>. You will have one minute, and the topic will be the same. Any questions? Begin.*

Feedback: At the end of the minute say: *Stop! Now I want **A** to tell **B** how you felt when **B** gave you eye contact as you spoke. I'll give you a signal at the end of one minute. Begin.*

Round 2: Signal the end of one minute and explain: *Now we'll repeat this procedure once more, only **B** will be the speaker and **A** will listen. I'll signal when each minute is up, and I'll give you directions between stages.*

Follow the same procedure as for Round 1. Ask **B** to speak to the topic, "What I Plan To Do After School Today."

Synopsis:
> **Round 1**
> "What I Like About My Favorite Sport or Game"
> > One minute-A speaks; B gives no eye contact.
> > One minute-A tells B how that felt.
> > One minute-A speaks; B gives eye contact.
> > One minute-A tells B how that felt.

> **Round 2**
> "Something I Want to Accomplish This Week"
> > One minute-B speaks; A gives no eye contact.
> > One minute-B tells A how that felt.
> > One minute-B speaks; A gives eye contact.
> > One minute-B tells A how that felt.

Note: When the partners are not giving each other eye contact (two of the eight minutes). The noise level in the room will increase considerably, because the speakers will be trying to get the listeners' attention, and will be discharging their frustration (almost always by laughing).

(Continued Next Page)

The Eyes Have It ————————————————

**Discussion
questions:**

Facilitate a class discussion about the importance of nonverbal communication. Ask these and other open-ended questions:

— *How did you feel when your partner would not make eye contact with you?*

— *How did you feel when you did get eye contact from your partner ?*

— *How did you feel about giving your partner eye contact?*

— *In what other nonverbal ways do people show they are listening (nodding, leaning forward, interested facial expression, smile)?*

— *Why did the room get noisier when the speakers were not receiving eye contact?*

— *What is the most important thing you learned from this exercise?*

What is a Circle Session?
Teacher Presentation and Discussion

Description:	This presentation conveys to students the reasons for having circle sessions, and what they can expect when they are in one.
Objective:	The students will be able to describe the circle session process and rules, and explain the purpose of each.
Time needed:	10 to 15 minutes
Materials needed:	chalkboard and chalk or chart paper and marking pen
Directions:	The best time to make this presentation is immediately prior to holding the first circle session with this group of students. (For suggestions of ways to assign group membership see, "Leading the *IMPACT!* circle session," located in the section, "Information For Teachers and Counselors.")

Prior to class, put the following lists on chart paper or the chalkboard. Focus the attention of the class on the lists, reading and discussing each one in turn.

Why have a session in a circle?
- A circle has no front, middle, or back.
- No one feels that s/he is in front or behind anyone.
- We're all side by side, and equal to each other.
- We can all see one another.

What is the session for?
To share:
- experiences
- thoughts
- feelings

Circle Session Procedures
1. Setting up the circle (1-2 minutes)
2. Reviewing the ground rules (1-2 minutes)
3. Introducing the topic (1-2 minutes)

(Continued Next Page)

4. Sharing time for circle members (12-18 minutes)
5. Reviewing what was shared (optional 3-5 minutes)
6. Summary discussion (2-8 minutes)
7. Conclusion (less than one minute)

Circle Session Rules
1. Bring yourself to the circle and nothing else.
2. Everyone gets a turn to share, including the leader.
3. You can skip your turn if you wish.
4. Listen to the person who is sharing.
5. The time is shared equally.
6. Stay in your own space.
7. There are no interruptions, probing, put-downs, or gossip.

Explain the following key points:
Circle sessions are a time and place for people to:
- get attention and acceptance
- practice positive communication skills (speaking and listening)
- learn more about themselves and others

Circle sessions are *not* a time and a place for:
- receiving or giving therapy
- solving your problems
- telling others what to think, feel, or do.

Conclusion: Answer any questions that the students have, and conclude the activity.

Note: Do not lead a circle session until you have read "Leading the *IMPACT!* circle session" located in the section, "Information For Teachers and Counselors."

What I Think Good Communication Is

— A Circle Session

Objective: The students will describe the role of effective communication in relating to other people.

Introduce the topic: Say to the students: *Our topic for this circle session is "What I Think Good Communication Is." Almost all of the contact we have with other people involves communicating in one way or another. Sometimes this communication is in writing and other times it involves speaking and listening. Did you know that a good deal of our communication involves body language? We call this non-verbal communication. Think of the things we must do to be good communicators. Take a moment and think about how you would describe truly good communication. Think about what good communication means to all of the people involved in your example, and describe that, too. When you are ready, we can begin to discuss our topic, which is, "What I Think Good Communication Is."*

Discussion questions: When all the students who wish to have shared, ask a number of open-ended questions to encourage a discussion:
— *What are some of the results of good communication?*
— *What can happen when communication is NOT good?*
— *How does it feel when you know that communication between you and another person is good? ...is poor?*

A Way I Let Others Know I'm Interested In What They Say

A Circle Session

Objective: The students will describe specific ways they behave when listening to others that convey their interest in what is being discussed.

Introduce the topic: Say to the students: *Our topic for this session is, "A Way I Let Others Know I'm Interested in What They Say." One way we can let another person know that we are listening and interested in what they have to say is by what we say in response. There are many other things we can do, too. Some of these involve our posture, the way we make eye contact, or whether or how frequently we interrupt them. Think of some of the ways you show other people that you are interested in what they are saying. Also think about how you feel when others listen to you with interest. Select one of the ways you show interest and tell us about it, if you'd like. Our topic is, "A Way I Let Others Know I'm Interested in What They Say."*

Discussion questions:

— *How do you think people feel knowing that you are really interested in what they have to say?*
— *How do you feel knowing that others are interested in what you have to say?*
— *What things can a person do to become a more effective listener or communicator?*

A Time When I Accepted Someone Else's Feelings —————— A Circle Session

Objectives: The students will:
— describe the need all people have to be accepted.
— identify positive and negative feelings that they have experienced.
— describe specific examples of their own pro-social behavior.

Introduce the topic: Say to the students: *It means a lot to all of us to have our feelings accepted. When someone accepts your feelings, it's the same as accepting you. In this session, we are going to turn this idea around and talk about how it feels to be the giver of acceptance. The topic is "A Time When I Accepted Someone Else's Feelings."*

Can you remember a time when you gave attention to someone else and accepted his or her feelings? Keep in mind that accepting feelings may mean accepting feelings that are different from you own, without getting angry or judging the other person. Think of a time when you did this, and tell us about it. The topic is, "A Time When I Accepted Someone Else's Feelings."

Discussion questions: When the students have finished sharing, facilitate a discussion by asking these and other questions:
— *When is it easy to accept someone else's feelings? When is it hard?*
— *Have you ever been unable to accept someone's feelings and not known why? What was going on inside you at that time?*
— *How do you show a person that you accept his or her feelings?*
— *How did the person whose feelings you accepted seem to feel about you?*

A Time When I Really Felt Heard

A Circle Session

Objectives:

The students will:
— describe the importance of listening in the communication process.
— describe feelings generated by being recognized and heard.

Introduce the topic:

Say to the students: *Today our topic is, "A Time I Really Felt Heard." We know that attention is a universal need. Sometimes we do not get it for one reason or another, but when we do our feelings are generally positive.*

Think of a time when you really needed to be heard and someone listened to you. Perhaps you had some kind of a problem that you wanted to talk out, or maybe you had an experience that you wanted to tell someone about. Who listened to you? How did you feel after you had expressed yourself? Think about it for a few moments. The topic is, "A Time When I Really Felt Heard."

Discussion questions:

— *How are people generally affected when their feelings are not accepted?*
— *Do people keep their feelings to themselves because they think they won't be accepted?*
— *When people risk saying how they feel, do others respect them for it? Do you? Why or why not?*
— *How did you feel about the person who listened to you?*
— *How did you feel about yourself?*
— *What happens to communication when people don't listen well?*

Communicating Effectively

Once When Somebody Wouldn't Listen to Me —————— A Circle Session

Objectives:

The students will:

— describe the importance of listening in the communication process.

— make verbal distinctions between attentive, conscious listening and inattentive, unconscious hearing.

— describe the need of people for attention and the consequences of not receiving it.

Introduce the topic:

Say to the students: *Today we're going to talk about a common frustration that occurs in the communication process. Our topic is "Once When Someone Wouldn't Listen to Me."*

Did you ever need to have someone listen to you who wouldn't? Maybe the person you were talking to didn't agree with what you were saying and refused to listen. Or perhaps he or she was busy and didn't want to be bothered. How did you feel? You've probably noticed your little brother or sister, or seen a pet, like your dog or cat, trying to get someone's attention. People and animals can feel lost when they don't get needed attention, and it's especially important for people to be listened to when they need to talk about something. Take a minute to thing about it, and tell us about a time when you had an experience like this. The topic is "Once When Someone Wouldn't Listen to Me."

Discussion questions:

— What similarities and differences did you notice in our feelings about not being listened to?

— What can you do when you're not being listened to?

— Should a person expect to be listened to every time he or she has something to say? Why or why not?

— How did you feel when you are being ignored?

How I Got Someone to Pay Attention to Me ——————— A Circle Session

Objectives:

The students will:
— verbalize the importance of receiving interpersonal attention.
— state the importance of attending as a communication skill.
— identify positive, effective strategies for getting attention.

Introduce the topic:

Say to the students: *Our topic for this session is "How I Got Someone to Pay Attention to Me." When you or I want to communicate with someone, first of all we have to get the person to notice us. We have to do something to get the other person to focus on us. As you have probably noticed, there are many ways to do this. You can do something funny, helpful, destructive, informative, exciting, or whatever, and people will automatically look at you.*

You are invited to share a time when you got someone's attention in a particular situation. Perhaps you tried to get the attention of a person who was a long way away from you in a large crowd. Or perhaps the person whose attention you were trying to get was watching TV or doing something else nearby. Think about it for a few moments. The topic is, "How I Got Someone to Pay Attention to Me."

Discussion questions:

— *Do people really need attention?*
— *Does the way you get attention have anything at all to do with the kind of attention you get or how long the attention lasts?*
— *What do you think a person would be like who never got any attention?*
— *What does giving your attention have to do with good communication?*
— *What did the other person seem to think of your attention-getting method?*

MANAGING STRESS

If we were fully integrated persons, we might refer to ourselves as being "bodyminds" rather than as "having bodies."

Sam Keen and
Anne Valley Fox

Stress is an unavoidable fact of life. When students fail to learn positive ways of dealing with stress, they frequently resort to destructive forms of relief, such as alcohol and drugs. In school, students may be exposed to an impressive array of data about physiology, disease, diet, exercise, drug abuse, and other topics related to stress and health, but still miss a point of great importance—that physical health, mental/emotional health, and stress are interrelated and interdependent. Many different kinds of events and situations can lead to stress, but it is a student's reaction to a situation—not the situation itself—that determines its impact on the "bodymind." This unit is designed to help students identify conditions that typically lead to stress, and to learn to manage their reactions through a variety of pro-social coping strategies.

Overall objectives
The students will:
— understand that physical and mental/emotional health are interdependent.
— identify causes of stress in their own lives.
— learn to monitor their reactions to stress.
— practice stress-management techniques that can be used when sources of stress cannot be eliminated.

Something That Causes Me Stress

A Circle Session

Objectives:

The students will:
— describe causes of personal stress.
— discuss specific things that can be done to relieve stress.
— state that feelings of stress are normal.

Introduce the topic:

Say to the students: *Our topic for this session is, "Something That Causes Me Stress." Do you ever get tongue tied? Feel uptight or on edge? Get a headache or a queezie stomach when you're not sick? Chances are the cause of those feelings is stress. Many different things can cause stress— worrying about a test, feeling angry at someone, or not getting enough sleep, for example. Even good things can cause stress—like the excitement of waiting for a special event. Think of something that causes you stress and tell us about it. What happens to cause the stress, and how does it affect the way you feel, the thoughts you have, and the things you do? Take a few minutes to think about it. The topic is, "Something That Causes Me Stress."*

Discussion questions:

— *Why do people experience stress?*
— *Do the same kinds of things frequently cause you stress?*
— *If you know something is likely to stress you, what can you do about it?*

What I Do When the Going Gets Tough ———————— A Circle Session

Objectives:

The students will:
— identify stressful experiences.
— describe positive ways of handling stress.

Introduce the topic:

Say to the students: *Our topic for this session is, "What I Do When the Going Gets Tough." Most of us have ways to make ourselves feel better when we are stressed. What's one of your ways? What do you do to help yourself when you feel angry, worried, tense, or nervous? Maybe you talk to one of your parents or to a friend about what's bothering you. Or perhaps you take a long walk or bike ride. Spending time alone with your pet may make you feel better. Or perhaps you do something to take your mind off the stressful situation—like watching TV, going to a movie, or reading a book. Tell us what you do, and how you feel when you do it. Let's think it over for a few moments. The topic is, "What I Do When the Going Gets Tough."*

Discussion questions:

— *Why is it important to find positive ways to handle stress?*
— *What are some negative ways in which people try to handle stress?*
— *Do you think fewer people would use alcohol and drugs if they knew how to handle stress in more positive ways?*

I Was So Distressed I Got Sick

A Circle Session

Objective: The students will describe effects of emotional upset on the body.

Introduce the topic: Say to the students: *Our topic today is, "I Was So Distressed I Got Sick." This is something most of us have encountered at one time or another. For example, has someone ever yelled at you, and you ended up with a headache? Have you ever started studying for a tough exam, and found there was more to learn than you thought, and pretty soon your stomach got upset. There are many different situations that cause people to get distressed, and the final reaction or sickness can show itself in many ways. Think of a time something like this happened to you. The topic is, "I Was So Distressed I Got Sick."*

Discussion questions:

— *What did you think was causing your sickness at the time?*
— *How can you prevent these kinds of upsets from hurting your body?*
— *What are some common illnesses that people get because they don't know what to do with their pain and annoyance when they get upset?*
— *Can it work the other way? Can people be feeling sick and then return to healthy feelings because something occurs to make them happy?*

I Did Something for My Body, and It Improved My Spirit

A Circle Session

Objectives: The students will describe a good health habit and how it affects them physically and emotionally.

Introduce the topic: Say to the students: *Our topic for this session is, "I Did Something for My Body, and It Improved My Spirit." Maybe you've seen a cartoon about the person who felt depressed and went out and bought something to improve his or her spirits. That kind of thing works for some people, but others are discovering that when they do things that are more directly related to their physical health, their spirits pick up in a very fulfilling way. Maybe you've had the experience of feeling down and doing something for your body, like taking a jog or a walk, and feeling much better at the end of it.*

We can do other nice things for our bodies, like eating nourishing foods, going on special diets to gain or lose weight, taking naps, going to bed early, sleeping in on Saturday morning, massaging our feet, etc. The list could go on and on. Think of something you've done for your physical self that had the effect of improving your spirit, and tell us about it. The topic is, "I Did Something for My Body, and It Improved My Spirit."

Discussion questions:
— *How much do our bodies affect our minds and vice versa?*
— *What actions can affect our spirits negatively?*
— *What could you do for your spirit that might improve your body?*

Some of the Best Health/Appearance Advice I Ever Heard

A Circle Session

Objectives: The students will describe a health practice they value and observe.

Introduce the topic: Say to the students: *Most of us feel kind of excited when someone shares a secret with us, and today we're going to do that in our circle session. The secrets we share will have to do with becoming very healthy, strong, and great looking and staying that way. The topic is, "Some of the Best Health/Appearance Advice I Ever Heard."*

No doubt you've heard lots of health tips, as well as advice for improving your appearance, and maybe you've followed some of those ideas and found they worked. Think of some advice that you were given by another person, and successfully tried. The person could have been anyone—a doctor, dentist, coach, teacher, parent, or friend. What the person suggested could have been an important, but often forgotten, bit of common sense like the value of flossing your teeth once a day. Or maybe it was something rather exotic like doing Hatha Yoga to improve muscle tone and acquire a sense of inner peace. Think it over. The topic is, "Some of the Best Health/Appearance Advice I Ever Heard."

Discussion questions:

— *Who are the best people to give us good advice regarding health and appearance?*
— *What ideas did you hear that seem worth trying?*
— *Why don't all ideas work equally well for everyone?*
— *Why are some people more interested in their health than others? ...in their appearance?*

A Time I Felt a Lot of Tension and Stress ——————— A Circle Session

Objectives: The students will describe the effects of tension and stress on the body.

Introduce the topic: Say to the students: *Our circle session topic for today is, "A Time I Felt a Lot of Tension and Stress." This is another of those very universal things that all people have probably felt at one time or another in their lives. When we become tense, our bodies react in a number of ways, usually by tightening muscles. Sometimes our stomach, vision, and hearing are affected. Other times we get headaches. When we become tense, sometimes we know it, and sometimes we don't.*

Have you ever discovered that some part of you ached, like your stomach, neck, shoulders, back, or legs, and then realized that an hour or two earlier you were very upset about something? Perhaps you didn't realize just how upset you were when it was happening. Often tension and stress accompany unpleasant circumstances, but not always. For example, when you ride a galloping horse or a roller coaster, your body will undoubtedly be tense and your feelings may be very positive at the same time. The experience can be thrilling and exciting. See if you can remember a time when you experienced tension and stress, and if you will, tell us about it. The topic is, "A Time I Felt a Lot of Tension and Stress."

Discussion questions:
— *When did you become aware of your tension?*
— *What happens to your ability to think straight when you are tense?*
— *What similarities did you notice in how we were affected by tension and stress?*
— *Can you think of ways you can care for yourself after (maybe even during) a tense situation?*

Something I Do for My Own Well-Being ——————— A Circle Session

Objectives:

The students will:
— describe a way they manage stress.
— discuss the importance of taking responsibility for one's own well-being.

Introduce the topic:

Say to the students: *Our topic for this circle session is a very useful one because it gives us a chance to talk about things we do that help us get rid of stress and enjoy life. It's also going to allow us to pick up some good tips from each other on how to be our own best friend. The topic is, "Something I Do for My Own Well-Being."*

Most of us find ways to be good to ourselves, but with all the stress each one of us has to deal with, the more ideas we can get for managing stress, the better. Think about things you do for yourself to be healthy, to relax, play, or feel good in general. Perhaps you have a special time when you go off alone to think calmly and take in pleasant surroundings. Maybe you have a form of exercise you do that helps you get rid of tension and allows you to rest very well afterward. You may enjoy losing yourself in some kind of creative activity that relieves built-up stress. Whatever it is, we'd enjoy hearing about it. The topic is, "Something I Do for My Own Well-Being."

Discussion questions:

— *Who has the most influence on how well or how poorly you manage your stress levels?*
— *What similarities did you notice in the methods that were mentioned?*
— *What new ideas did you get for managing stress?*

Something I Worried About That Turned Out OK ——————— A Circle Session

Objectives: The students will:
— describe a time they worried about something.
— describe ways in which worry can inhibit normal functioning.
— identify ways of avoiding unnecessary worry.

Introduce the topic: Say to the students: *Our topic for this session is "Something I Worried About That Turned Out OK." There are many things in our lives that cause us to become concerned. When we are concerned about something, we usually focus our attention on whatever it is until we are no longer concerned. Sometimes our concern becomes so great that it changes into worry. When we are worried about something, we may find it hard to think about other things that are going on in our lives. When this happens, worry is getting in the way of our leading a normal and productive life. It is producing serious stress.*

Think about something that you have experienced in your life that has worried you very much. It may be something that happened recently or perhaps it occurred many years ago. It doesn't need to be something really big and important. In fact, when we look back on the things about which we worried in the past, they sometimes appear to be insignificant. Whatever it is you choose to share, we'd like to hear about it. The topic is, "Something I Worried About That Turned Out OK."

Discussion questions: After all the students who wish to have shared, ask questions like the following to generate a discussion:
— *How does your body react when you're worried?*
— *What kinds of feelings do you have when you are no longer worried about something, or find that it wasn't worth your worry?*
— *In what ways can over-worry harm us or get in our way?*
— *How often do we worry about things unnecessarily?*

From Panic to Power

Description: The students brainstorm a list of stressors. The teacher then presents a definition of stress, and the class discusses possible courses of action that could be taken in response to each stressor listed.

Objectives: The students will:
— describe causes of personal stress.
— explain how stress works.
— explain how taking action to solve problems can relieve stress.

Time needed: approximately 20 to 30 minutes

Materials needed: easel, chart paper and marking pen, or chalkboard and chalk

Directions: Tell the students that the group is going to spend some time talking about stress—what it is and what can be done about it. Begin by listing on chart paper the stressors that the students mentioned during the circle session, *Something That Causes Me Stress.* Then brainstorm additional stressors to add to the list.

Explain: *Here's a formula that explains stress.* **STRESSOR + PHYSICAL REACTION – ACTION = STRESS.** *When we think we're in danger (of failing, being embarrassed, not getting what we want, etc.), our bodies react just like they would if we were in danger of being attacked by a lion. Adrenaline and hormones start pumping, our hearts beat faster, our muscles tense, and we get set for "fight or flight." Then if we* <u>don't</u> *take action—if we just sit around and worry, for example—all those unused hormones and tense muscles end up hurting* <u>us</u>.

Next, go through the list, one item at a time, and have the students **brainstorm actions they could take** in each type of situation. For example, if they don't understand the current chapter in math, they can talk to the teacher, ask a parent for help, study with a friend, etc.

Empower the students by demonstrating enthusiasm about all the things they can do. Lead them in a rousing "I Can Do It!" cheer after each item is discussed.

(Continued Next Page)

When the stressor is something the students have no control over (like the death of a pet) or little control over (like noisy neighbors), acknowledge that even though they can't "act on" the stressor directly, they *can* use stress reducers. Remind the students of the things they mentioned in the circle session, *What I Do When the Going Gets Tough*, and brainstorm other stress management strategies.

Extension: Act out some of the stressful situations. Concentrate on those in which the students have some control, and encourage them to take turns dramatizing the different courses of action they could take. Lead a discussion after each dramatization.

Stress Breaks

A Movement Activity

Description:	The students take turns leading the class in simple movements that they invent to relieve stress.
Objective:	The students will demonstrate specific techniques for relieving stress.
Time needed:	approximately 15 minutes
Materials needed:	A large circle of chairs—one chair for each student.
Directions:	**Ask the students to sit in a circle.** Announce that the group is going to invent and practice "stress breaks" that can be used at other times to reduce stress.

Explain: *One of best things you can do to relieve stress is exercise. And that doesn't just mean running a mile or playing a basketball game—almost any kind of stretching or moving can help get the tension out of muscles and make the heart beat faster. Think of a movement that you can do sitting down. You can pump your arm up and down, roll your shoulders backwards and forwards; or "run" very fast with your feet.* (Demonstrate several sitting movements for the students.) *We're going to go around the circle and each one of you is going to lead us in a movement for 10 seconds. When it's your turn, show us a movement that <u>no one else has done</u> and we'll all do it with you.*

Get the game started and keep it going at a lively pace. Participate along with the students.

After every student has led a movement, tell the students to stand and move their chairs out of the way. Go around the circle again, this time creating movements that can be done from a **standing position**. Demonstrate a few, like running in place, stretching to the side, etc.

Finally, have each student lead a **"traveling" movement** for 5-10 seconds. Maintain the circle formation. Suggest that skipping, hopping, jogging, etc., can be done using different kinds of arm movements for variation.

(Continued Next Page)

Stress Breaks

Discussion questions:

Note: This activity will generate much laughter and enjoyment. Welcome it, and point out that laughter relieves stress too.

— *When can you use stress breaks outside of class?*
— *What is the value of exercise in relieving stress?*

Extension:

If you have ample space or can go outdoors, do the traveling part of the game in a snake formation, with the leader weaving about and the other students following. Include short "stress breaks" occasionally during class. Have the students take turns leading them.

Four Floors of Fantasy

A Guided Imagery Activity

Description:	The students relax while you guide them through a pleasant fantasy. They then share their experiences in dyads, and a brief class discussion concludes the activity.
Objectives:	The students will: —practice a stress management technique. —describe how imagination can help them relieve stress.
Time needed:	approximately 15 minutes
Materials needed:	watch or clock with second hand, optional cassette tape player and tape of relaxing instrumental music
Directions:	If you have music, start the tape at a low volume so that you can speak over it easily. Use a relaxing tone of voice. Read the following passage <u>slowly</u>, pausing where indicated.

Explain: *You are going to take a ride on an imaginary elevator. Sit or lie in a comfortable position. Be sure you are not touching anyone, and remember not to talk, whisper, or move about during the exercise. Close your eyes and relax your body. Become aware of your breathing (pause 15-20 seconds). Begin counting your breath silently in your mind (pause 45-60 seconds). Now imagine that you are standing in front of an elevator door. You press the button and the door opens, showing you a large well-lighted, empty elevator. You enter it and find that the elevator buttons are labelled as follows: The first button says, "**this room;**" the second button says, "**a peaceful place;**" the third button says, "**a visit with a wise older person;**" the fourth button says, "**a super adventure;**" and the fifth button says, "**a visit with a long-lost friend.**" Choose the floor you would like to go to (pause 15 seconds), and press the button. The elevator door slowly closes and the elevator begins to rise to the floor you selected. The elevator arrives at the floor and the doors slowly open. Go out into the space and explore it. Meet whoever is there; do whatever makes sense for you to do there. (pause at least 60 seconds). Now say good-by to the place you're in, and to anyone who is there. The elevator has remained open for you. Enter it now. Take one last look at the place you have been. Press the button marked*

(Continued Next Page)

Four Floors of Fantasy

"this room." The elevator doors close and the elevator slowly returns you to this room (pause 15 seconds). As the elevator doors open, so do your eyes (pause until everyone's eyes are open). Welcome back!

Have the students pair up. Suggest that they tell their partners as much as they would like to about their fantasies. Allow 2 to 3 minutes for sharing.

Discussion questions:

When the students are finished sharing, ask them:
— *What kinds of feelings did you have during this exercise?*
— *How can you use your imagination to reduce stress?*

Relax and Enjoy Life!

Discussion and Experience Sheet

Description: The students brainstorm a list of ways in which people relax, and a second list describing the reasons people relax. After comparing and discussing the two lists, they complete the experience sheet, "Relax a Little."

Objectives: The students will:
— describe ways to avoid the harmful effects of stress.
— identify specific ways to manage stress effectively.
— discuss how unmanaged stress can be harmful.

Time needed: 30 to 40 minutes

Materials needed: pens or pencils, one copy of the experience sheet, "Relax a Little" for each student, and chalkboard or easel with chart paper

Directions: **Introduce the activity by saying to the students:** *One of the things that people enjoy most is relaxation. Relaxation can involve many aspects, and there are many different ways to relax. Some people relax by doing something athletic like running or engaging in a sport. Other people relax by resting or reading. Still others relax by listening to music they enjoy or being with friends.*

After drawing the attention of the students to the ways people relax, ask them to share some examples of their own. As they do so, write down their comments on the board or chart paper under the heading, "Ways We Relax." Suggest that the students jot down any new ideas they get from the list concerning good ways to relax.

After creating the list, ask the students to think about *why* people relax. Make a list of their comments on the board or chart paper under the heading, "Why We Relax." Help them along by suggesting reasons of your own, particularly reasons connected with some of the feelings that relaxation generates.

Now compare the two lists and point out that by doing the things described on the first list they can generate the feelings described on the second list.

(Continued Next Page)

Distribute the "Relax a Little" experience sheet. Ask the students to think about the things they do—or would like to do—to relax. Have them note these on their experience sheets. Next to each item they list, ask the students to write down how they feel when they participate in that activity. Finally, have the students write down three things that cause them to feel stress and, next to each, record how the stress makes them feel.

Conclusion: After the students have completed their experience sheets, emphasize that by taking the time to do something relaxing when they are experiencing stress, the students can substitute good feelings for bad.

Extension: Encourage the students to start relaxing as a way of effectively managing stress. Point out that developing the habit of relaxing regularly can take a lot of practice. Put a sign up in the room that says, "Feel Good Today—Relax A Little." Each day for two weeks, take a moment to remind students to relax when they experience stress. After two weeks have passed, conduct a circle session using the topic, "A Way I Relaxed to Reduce Stress." (See "Information for Teachers & Counselors" for tips on creating your own circle session topics.)

Relax A Little ———————————

Ways that I can relax:

_____
_____
_____
_____
_____
_____
_____

How I feel when I'm relaxing:

_____
_____
_____
_____
_____
_____
_____

Three things that happen in my life that cause me to feel stress:

1. _____

_____

2. _____

_____

3. _____

_____

How this stress makes me feel:

_____
_____
_____
_____
_____
_____

Because stress causes us to feel badly in many different ways, a very good approach to feeling better right away is to do something that is relaxing. Substitute the good feelings of relaxing for the bad feelings of stress!

SELF-AWARENESS

When I am aware that I experience feelings, thoughts, and behavior, my self-understanding increases. When I become aware that you experience feelings, thoughts, and behavior, my understanding of you increases. And when I learn that you and I are both alike in this way, yet individuals, my respect for us both increases.

The activities in this unit encourage students to focus on their experiences of feeling, thinking, and behaving, and how these experiences interrelate. As they become more aware of this triad of human functioning in themselves, they realize that it exists in others, too. The circle sessions and supporting activities in this unit allow students to share and compare their experiences and reactions with one another. Common human characteristics and individual uniquenesses among the students become apparent. Thus, increased self-awareness leads to a greater awareness of others.

Overall objectives
The students will develop the awareness that:
— everyone is the same in that we all feel, think, and behave.
— everyone is unique in that we all feel, think, and behave in our own ways.
— sharing experiences, feelings, and thoughts with one another in an accepting environment leads to greater human understanding and fulfillment.

One of My Favorite Subjects in School ———— A Circle Session

Objectives:

The students will:
— name a favorite school subject.
— describe how the feelings and attitudes of people are both unique and similar.

Introduce the topic:

Say to the students: *In recent circle sessions, we've been noticing how similar we are to one another in certain ways. The fact that every person has feelings is one of the most significant ways in which we are similar. But, at the very same time, we are all different from one another too. We may all have feelings, but we experience our feelings in our own unique ways. For example, you might really like a certain course or subject here at school, and to someone else it's hard or just plain uninteresting. In fact, that's our topic for this session. It is, "One of My Favorite Subjects at School."*

Think that one over, and tell us about a course or subject you enjoy. When you speak, give us some details. Tell us what is enjoyable about the subject, and when it was you started liking it. Again, the topic is, "One of My Favorite Subjects in School."

Discussion questions:

— *Did you notice any similarities in the courses or subjects we mentioned, or the reasons we enjoy them?*
— *Were there any interesting differences? What were some subjects only one person mentioned?*
— *Is there something wrong with you if you like something no one else likes? ...if you don't like something everyone else likes?*
— *How do we develop our interests and preferences?*

An Ability or Talent I'm Proud Of

A Circle Session

Objectives:

The students will:
— describe an ability or talent.
— discuss the importance of acknowledging one's own strengths and abilities.
— demonstrate appreciation for the abilities of others.

Introduce the topic:

Say to the students: *This is going to be an unusual circle session because we are going to encourage each other to do something most people don't do very often. We're going to take credit for things we're good at. Most of the time people are modest, but today we will ignore any rules of modesty we've learned, which will probably do us good. The topic is, "An Ability or Talent I'm Proud Of."*

It's obvious that everyone has strengths and weaknesses. No one is good at everything and no one is poor at everything. Think for a minute about those things at which you are just naturally good. Think about your special skills. Maybe you excel in an academic area like Math, Science, or English. Or perhaps you have an athletic skill you're proud of. Maybe you have artistic talents, or are good at making things with your hands. You might have inherited your abilities from your parents, or you may be the only one in your family who has them. Think it over for a few moments. The topic is, "An Ability or Talent I'm Proud Of."

Discussion questions:

— *How did we feel telling each other about our abilities and talents? Did it feel a bit like bragging?*
— *What benefits do we get from talking about our strengths and abilities?*
— *How did you feel about each other during this session?*
— *How did you develop your strengths and abilities?*

Something I Like to Imagine ————

Objectives:	The students will discuss their feelings and behavior by focusing first on their creative thoughts.
Introduce the topic:	Say to the students: *Our topic for this session is "Something I Like to Imagine." Did you know that using your imagination is a very healthy and important thing to do? You may find yourself daydreaming and not realize that what you're doing is necessary. You need to daydream and imagine things, even if what you are imaging seems absurd or ridiculous. So think about something you like to imagine. Maybe it's reliving an event from the past or imaging what it would be like to experience something you've never done. Perhaps it's a wish or a creative idea concerning something you'd like to make or write about. Or it could be a wild fantasy of some kind. Whatever it is, we would like to hear about it. The topic is, "Something I Like to Imagine."*
Discussion questions:	After the students have finished sharing, ask several open-ended questions to spark a discussion: — *In what ways do you think daydreaming and using your imagination help you to be creative?* — *What do you think people would be like if they had no powers of imagination?* — *Did you learn something about someone in this session that you didn't know before?* — *What feelings do you experience when you imagine the thing you shared?*

One of My Favorite Pastimes ————

A Circle Session

Objectives:
The students will:
—describe a leisure activity they enjoy.
—describe the importance of leisure.
—discuss how interests and activities are expressions of uniqueness.

Introduce the topic:
Say to the students: *Our circle session topic today is, "One of My Favorite Pastimes." A pastime, of course, is a way you like to "pass" or spend time. In other words, what do you like to do when there is no pressure on you to do anything? What do you prefer to do when the choice is entirely yours?*

Perhaps you are an energetic person and you enjoy sports or games so, whenever you get a chance, you get together with friends and engage in those activities. Maybe you prefer artistic endeavors, like painting, music, or dance. Or perhaps your favorite pastime is just relaxing—reading, watching T.V., or spending time with friends or family. Think it over and tell us what you enjoy doing. The topic is, "One of My Favorite Pastimes."

Discussion questions:
— *Did you notice any similarities in the pastimes we mentioned and why we enjoy them?*
— *Were there any interesting differences? What pastimes were mentioned by only one person?*
— *Why is it important to have leisure? ...leisure activities?*

Something I Enjoy Doing That I Do Well

A Circle Session

Objectives:	The students will share positive things about themselves with one another.
Introduce the topic:	Say to the students: *In this session, we are going to talk about things we like to do and brag a little bit in the process. The topic is "Something I Enjoy Doing That I Do Well." So take a moment to think about something that you are good at, that you would feel OK telling the group about. Perhaps it's something you do away from school that none of us could know about unless you told us, or it could be something you are accomplishing in one of your classes. Tell us about anything that you like to do and do well.*
	Don't be bashful about admitting that you do something well, because we already know that you've got talents and abilities. Everyone does. In this session, you have permission to talk about them. Think for a moment, If you don't feel like talking, just listen; that's fine, too. The topic is "Something I Enjoy Doing That I Do Well."
Discussion questions:	After the students have finished sharing, encourage them to talk about what they learned. Ask these and other questions: — *How did you feel about describing what you do well?* — *Do you think it's OK to do things just for fun, or should everything we do be productive?* — *Did you learn anything that you didn't know before about someone in the circle?*

A Favorite Place of Mine

A Circle Session

Objectives:

The students will:
— describe a place they enjoy being.
— discuss how preferences make each person unique.

Introduce the topic:

Say to the students: *Our topic for this circle session is a very enjoyable one because it encourages us to talk about ourselves and the things we like. The topic is, "A Favorite Place of Mine." So give that some thought.*

Where do you really enjoy being? Perhaps an exciting place comes to mind, or one that's peaceful and beautiful. Maybe the most important thing about a place is who is there with you. Or perhaps when you think of a favorite place you usually focus on feeling relaxed or inspired. The place that comes to mind might be one you've seen in a picture or movie, but haven't yet visited. It might even be an imaginary place. Think about it for a few moments. The topic is, "A Favorite Place of Mine."

Discussion questions:

— *Did you notice any similarities in the places we mentioned and why we like those places?*
— *How do your surroundings affect your mood? ...your thoughts?*
— *Why do we depend on familiar surroundings?*
— *What kind of person regularly seeks new and different surroundings?*

Self-Understanding I've Recently Gained ——————— A Circle Session

Objective: The students will:
— verbalize the importance of self-awareness and understanding.
— describe specific areas of personal growth.

Introduce the topic: Say to the students: *Today we're going to talk about things we've learned about ourselves recently. Our topic is, "Self-Understanding I've Recently Gained."*

By self-understanding, we mean learning something about yourself that you didn't know before—such as why you do things a certain way, or why you react to people or situations the way you do. Maybe you recently figured out why you feel fear or happiness or excitement at certain times. Or perhaps you've had a major breakthrough in understanding why you act the way you do around certain people. Possibly you decided recently what kind of career would be best for you, or what talents you value most in yourself and want to develop. So take a moment to think about this. The topic is, "Self-Understanding I've Recently Gained."

Discussion questions:
— *What similarities and differences did you notice in the kinds of things we've recently learned about ourselves?*
— *How did you arrive at your self-understanding?*
— *What value is there in understanding yourself better?*

When I Like Myself Most —————

A Circle Session

Objective: The students will describe specific areas of personal competence and the feelings of self-esteem derived from each.

Introduce the topic: Say to the students: *Our topic for this session is, "When I Like Myself Most." We are all painfully aware of the times when we are not pleased with ourselves or when we feel something about us could be improved. But we can all become much more aware of those times when we really like ourselves. Think of a time when you feel particularly good about yourself. Maybe you like the way you feel right after you've talked with a friend, or when you are expressing a particular talent or ability. Or perhaps you feel best about yourself when exercising, studying a subject you enjoy, or helping another person. Think about it for a minute, and identify those times when you are aware of feeling very good inside—times when you are glad to be you. Our topic is "When I Like Myself Most."*

Discussion questions:

— *When you like yourself the most, do you think you are more connected to you inner self than you are at other times?*
— *How can we make those times happen more often?*
— *Why is it important to like ourselves?*

Significant People Who Have Affected My Life

Creative Writing and Discussion

Description: After an introductory discussion, students write about one or more people who have been influential, either positively or negatively, in their lives. Students form small groups and share their writings, and then participate in a culminating class discussion.

Objectives: The student will:
— describe people who have influenced them.
— discuss how significant others influence our development.

Time needed: two class periods

Materials needed: writing materials

Directions: **Introduce the activity.** Begin by discussing with the class how people can strongly affect other people's lives. Individuals whom we admire and respect become models. Through their bad examples, other people teach us how <u>not</u> to be.

Explain the writing assignment. Point out that the students will be writing about matters that are somewhat private. Ask them to think and write about one or more people who have significantly affected their lives, positively or negatively. Tell them to describe how each individual affected them. Add that in the cases of people who have had a negative influence, names and relationships should be omitted.

Allow the rest of the class period and about two-thirds of the next class period for writing.

Have the students share their writings in small groups. In the final half or third of the second class period, have the students form dyads, triads, or small groups and share their thoughts about the people who have significantly affected their lives. (Remind them to omit the names and relationships of those people who have affected them negatively.)

(Continued Next Page)

Significant People Who Have Affected My Life ———————————— *(Continued)*

Discussion questions:

Facilitate a total-class discussion, asking these and other relevant questions:

— *How much of who you are seems to be influenced by other people?*

— *If someone influences you, what part do you play in letting it happen?*

— *Can you think of someone who would say you were a significant person in his or her life?*

Helping Someone Learn ———————
—————— A Peer or Cross-Age Tutoring Activity

Description: Students are trained to work as tutors to peers and/or younger children. Meetings are frequently held with the tutors to provide encouragement and information.

Objectives: The students will:
— demonstrate skills working with peers or younger children.
— identify how helping others results in self-growth.

Time needed: a day, a week, or a semester, depending on time available and other commitments

Directions: **Peer tutoring:** Select several capable students in your subject area, and ask them if they would like to help a classmate learn. Assign those students who are willing to a peer who needs assistance. Have at least one meeting with the tutors first, however, to discuss teaching techniques that are effective on a one-to-one basis. Discuss and demonstrate such strategies as the following:
1. Plan with your partner how to approach the material to be learned.
2. Focus on one thing at a time.
3. Accept the learner and be positive.
4. Give information clearly and in bits small enough for the learner to grasp.
5. Listen to the learner's responses.
6. Model the desired skill or knowledge.

Make arrangements for the students to work together during class, and encourage them to get together at other times, too. Frequently hold meetings with the tutors to discuss their problems and familiarize them with teaching strategies and ways of relating positively to their partners.

Cross-age tutoring: Make the necessary arrangements for a number of your students to work with elementary school children who need extra help with various subjects. Volunteers do not need to be among your most able learners. Hold one or two meetings with the tutors to go over the strategies itemized above before allowing them to work with the children. Emphasize the crucial importance of demonstrating respect for the learner.

(Continued Next Page)

Helping Someone Learn ———————

———————————— *(Continued)*

Familiarize the students with various effective teaching strategies. For example, describe this three-step process developed by Maria Montessori:

- First, the learner is presented with a small number of concepts to be learned in a verbal fashion. ("This one is red. This one is blue. This one is orange.")
- Second, the learner is asked to discriminate nonverbally between the concepts. ("Put your finger on the blue one. Put your finger on the orange one. Put your finger on the red one.")
- In the third phase, the learner is asked to give a discriminating verbal response. (Tutor: "What color is this one?" Learner: "It's blue." Tutor: "What color is this one?" Learner: "It's red." Tutor: "What color is this one?" Learner: "It's orange.")

Tell the tutors to pace the steps so that the learners will not be asked to perform at any level until they are prepared to do so. Whenever a learner makes an error at the second or third level, the instructional procedure should be begun again at step one. The tutors may practice the method with each other before working with children, using vocabulary at their own educational level. (This method is very valuable in teaching reading and arithmetic facts.)

Frequently hold meetings with the tutors to discuss their problems and successes, and to acquaint them with additional teaching strategies and ways of relating positively to the children.

Conclusion: When the tutoring program has ended, hold a final meeting with the students. Conduct a circle session with them and have as your topic, "What I Learned As a Tutor."

Come to Your Senses ——————————

————————————— ## A Short Imagery Exercise

Description:	With their eyes closed and bodies in relaxed positions, the students visualize a number of experiences involving their senses, in response to suggestions read to them by the teacher. A discussion culminates the activity.
Objectives:	The students will become aware of feelings and sensations generated by their own imaginations.
Time needed:	20 to 30 minutes for the exercise and follow-up discussion
Directions:	Begin by asking the students to get comfortable in their seats. Then read the following to them very slowly in a relaxed, clear tone. Pause long enough (at least five seconds) between images to allow the students time for focus on each image.

Today we are going to use our imaginations to visualize several scenes that involve our senses. In our minds, we are going to touch, smell, taste, see, and hear things in uniquely personal ways. Afterwards, we'll talk about these experiences.

Relax every part of your body. Let all your tensions just melt away. If you close your eyes you will probably be able to get into this more easily. You'll probably get more vivid images, too. Get in touch with your feet...Feel them from the inside...Now get in touch with your calves...Relax your muscles there... Now relax your thighs... Just let all the tension melt away...Feel your chair underneath you...Just let it hold you up...Be as heavy as you can in the chair... Now feel your hands and fingers... Release any muscle strain you have there...Just let it go...Do the same with your forearms and your upper arms...Become aware of your breathing... Don't force it...Just let it happen by itself... Let go of all the tension in your body... Relax your head and your neck...even your face...Just let yourself relax completely.

Now I would like you to imagine you are in one of your favorite places...It's a very cold day...You have a cup of warm liquid in your hands...Feel the warmth...smell it...Feel the warmth enter your nostrils...Imagine the color and shape of the cup...Now feel a

(Continued Next Page)

cool breeze on your cheek...Taste the warm liquid. It's something that you like to drink...Let it roll around in your mouth, then swallow it...Take another long drink.

Now you are in a field of your favorite flowers...Notice the color of the field...How does it smell?...Pick a flower and smell it...Notice the shape...the color...and the details of your flower...Hand it to someone you care about...What was the expression on the person's face?...in the person's eyes?...Take a flower petal and rub it on your cheek...Stroke it between your fingers...Feel the texture, the thickness, or the thinness.

Now you are swimming...You feel the water streaming through your hair as you glide through it...The water is warm and crystal clear...You pause for a moment and see fish darting about nearby...Now someone you like very much has joined you...Together you swim toward a raft.

When you reach the raft, take a few moments to stretch out in the sun and reflect on your experienc ... Then, when you are ready, come back to this room ...Open your eyes, feeling relaxed and refreshed.

Discussion questions:

Stimulate discussion by asking the following questions:
— *Did you see anything in your mind's eye, and if so, when?*
— *What colors did you see and when?*
— *What sounds did you hear and when?*
— *Did you taste anything? What and when?*
— *What scents did you smell and when did you smell them?*
— *What kinds of things did you feel with your fingers, like temperature, textures, or shapes?*
— *What emotions did you experience?*
— *In what ways do you think imagination helps a person to be creative?*

Note: Occasionally a student falls asleep during an activity of this nature. If you regard such as occurrence as natural and understandable, there will be no negative effect on the student or his/her peers.

Getting More in Touch with Me ——————
—————————— ## A Guided Awareness Exercise

Description: The students close their eyes, relax their bodies, and internally experience some of their own feelings, thoughts, and behaviors at the suggestion of the teacher. A discussion culminates the activity.

Objectives: The students will experience and describe what is going on inside of them physically, emotionally, mentally, and behaviorally.

Time needed: approximately 20 minutes for the exercise and follow-up discussion

Directions: Tell the students you would like to do a guided-awareness exercise with them that will help them focus on themselves and sharpen their self-awareness. Then read the following very slowly in a relaxed, clear tone. Allow plenty to time (at least five seconds) between images:

Get comfortable in your chair and relax your body...Close your eyes and allow whatever images enter you mind to pass through...Just take a look at them...Don't do anything about them...Be aware of the position of your body...How does the chair feel against your back and underneath you?...Feel the chair supporting you...Make yourself as heavy in the chair as you can...Feel the weight of your feet on the floor...Be aware of the space around you...Feel the temperature of the air... Feel your tongue against the roof of your mouth... Be aware of the taste in your mouth...Be aware of temperature of the air as it enters your nose...and as you exhale...Be aware of any muscle tension in your shoulders...upper body...lower body...legs...arms...Be aware of the feelings in your throat...and in your stomach.

Now be aware of your emotions...What are your feelings?...Are you sad?...happy?...curious?...Or maybe you have no special feelings right now...What are you feeling?...Where do you feel emotions in your body? What is the location?...Be aware of what area in your body your feeling covers...What shape is your feeling?...Is it moving?...If so, what kind of movement is it?...What color is your feeling?...Has it changed?...What emotion are you feeling now?...Where is it exactly in your body?

(Continued Next Page)

Getting More in Touch with Me ———

Now become aware of what you are thinking...What thoughts are coming into your head?...Just notice them...and then let them go as though they were a flowing stream...Now take a couple of minutes to notice some more of your thoughts. (Pause for about two minutes.)

Now be aware of what you are doing...Are you moving?... twitching?... smiling?...frowning?...thinking?...relaxing?...What are you doing?

Now keeping your eyes closed, gently come back into the room and become aware of the space around you...Picture the room you are about to open your eyes in...the walls...the floor...and all the other parts of the room...Gently and slowly open your eyes and look at the room and the people in it as though you are seeing it and them for the first time...What comes into your awareness?

Discussion questions:

Culminate this activity by asking the class:
— *What are some of the things that came into your awareness during the exercise?*
— *What emotions did you feel? Where in your body were they located?*
— *How do you feel now?*

Note: Occasionally a student falls asleep during an activity of this nature. If you regard such as occurrence as natural and understandable, there will be no negative effects on the student or his/her peers.

114   *IMPACT!*   **Self-Awareness**

All the Me's I Am and Have Been ———
——————— A Dyad Sequence and Discussion

Description:	In dyads, the students relate to a series of topics dealing with some of the many aspects that make up their person. In a follow-up class discussion, students are encouraged to share what they have learned.
Objective:	The students will identify several different aspects of themselves and describe their feelings about each.
Time needed:	one class period
Materials needed:	chairs or other comfortable seating arrangement; stop watch
Directions:	Ask the students to form dyads. Then ask the members of each dyad to sit close, facing each other. Ask them to decide who will speak first. That person will be **A**, and the other person will be **B**.

Explain that you will be giving them topics to talk about in their dyads. First **A** will talk to the topic while **B** listens for one minute. Then the process will reverse for another minute.

When the class is ready, announce the following topics, making sure to time each minute accurately and signal the students to switch speakers or change topics.

> *When I was five (years old), I felt . . .*
> *When I was five, I liked to . . .*
> *When I was 10, I liked to . . .*
> *When I was 12, I really wanted . . .*
> *Who I am now is . . .*
> *Something I like about you is . . .*

Discussion questions:

After the dyad sequence has been completed, conduct a discussion with the class, asking these and other relevant questions:
— *Did you and your partner share any similar experiences?*
— *How do our experiences as children affect us now?*
— *What new and interesting things did you learn about your partner?*
— *What did you learn about yourself?*

A Self-Portrait

Art Experience and Discussion

Description: The students express their self-image in the art form of their choice. Volunteers display their works of art to the class. A discussion concludes the activity.

Objective: The students will identify and illustrate characteristics about themselves that they want to convey to others.

Time needed: one class period, possibly two

Materials needed: various art supplies, like paints, charcoal, colored pencils, paper, etc.; collage materials, such as scissors, glue, tape, old magazines, photos, etc.

Directions: Explain to the students that you would like them to portray their self-image artistically. Urge them to select any art form that they would like to use to express themselves, e.g., charcoal for sketching, collage, painting, finger paints, and so forth. Stress that they may creatively show as many facets of themselves as they like, in anything from a simple sketch of their face to a complex collage that integrates many aspects of themselves.

Discussion questions: Allow the students to exhibit their works, pass them around, or keep them, as you/they choose. Facilitate a discussion, asking these and other relevant questions:
— *What did you learn about yourself by doing your self-portrait?*
— *Do you think someone would know you better by looking at your self-portrait? In what ways?*
— *What do you see when you look at your self-portrait as if it were of someone else? ...by someone else?*

Extension: Either before or after this activity, duplicate and hand out to each student a copy of the experience sheet, "Looking At My Many Selves."

Variation: Have the students complete their self-portrait outside of class. Begin the activity by sharing and discussing the portraits.

Looking At My Many Selves

There is a part of me that wants to write , a part that wants to theorize, a part that wants to sculpt, a part that wants to teach . . . To force myself into a single role, to decide to be just one thing in life, would kill off large parts of me. Rather, I recognize that I live now and only now, and I will do what I want to do this moment and not what I decided was best for me yesterday.

This is what a man named Hugh Prather had to say about himself in a book he wrote called *Notes to Myself.*

Have you ever noticed how much people can change from time to time — even you? It's as if there are a lot of people inside each one of us. We all have many parts. There are sad parts, happy parts, clown parts and serious parts, pretty parts and ugly parts, smart parts and dumb parts, child parts and parent parts, and adult parts, parts that study and learn, parts that play and laugh, dozens of parts. Take a look at some of your parts. Finish these sentences with as many endings as you can. These are some of the people <u>you</u> are at different times.

Sometimes I like to _____

Sometimes I remind myself of _____

Sometimes I try to be _____

Sometimes I am _____

Here is another way to look at the parts that make up you. At the top of each column put down a word that describes you because of something you do. It might be student, son or daughter, friend, athlete, cook, or whatever. Next, list some of the things you do when you are in that role. Suppose you choose "cook" as your title. You might list recipe reader, organizer, creator or taster, timer, or even dishwasher. Give it a try.

1. _____ **2.** _____ **3.** _____

_____   _____   _____

_____   _____   _____

_____   _____   _____

_____   _____   _____

_____   _____   _____

Was it hard at times to figure out some of your parts? Keep in mind that most people have a hard time looking at some parts of themselves. There are parts we like and parts we don't like. That's natural and human. It helps to know all about ourselves, even if it's hard sometimes. Then we can take full charge of ourselves and change ourselves if we decide to.

You've looked at some of your parts. Now take a close look at who YOU are. Finish these statements with the first words that come to mind. There's no need to take a long time thinking about each one unless you really want to. Don't worry about truth or falsehood or whether they make sense. Just have a good time looking at YOU.

I feel happiest when _____ It hurts me when _____
_____ _____
_____ _____

I am sad when _____ I get angry when _____
_____ _____
_____ _____

I wonder if I _____ I feel satisfied when _____
_____ _____
_____ _____

I trust _____ I feel most loved when _____
_____ _____
_____ _____

Did you like doing this exercise? Parts of it might have been easy and enjoyable, while other parts might have been hard. Were there some items that were tough to complete? That's okay. What you might do now is go back to those hard ones and look at them again. See if rethinking them helps.

SETTING AND ATTAINING GOALS

Persistence for the sake of persistence is not sufficient to attain success. One will not find a bird flying in the depths of the sea, nor a fish swimming amongst the clouds. Therefore, select a right goal, after thorough consideration. Traveling a right route, one successfully arrives at his destination.

The Perrenial Calendar of
I Ching Lunar Commands

The activities in this unit are designed to reinforce students for their abilities, successes, and accomplishments in order to increase their belief in themselves and their eagerness to tackle new challenges. When accomplishments are seen as goals that have been met, future goals readily become the next subject to be addressed. Therefore, the students are encouraged to clarify their present and future goals, examine possible roadblocks to achieving them, and set in motion plans for attaining them.

Overall objectives
   To assist students to:
   — take note of their accomplishments and feel
      deserved pride in themselves.
   — understand that accomplishments are goals that
      have been met.
   — share their short-term and long-range goals with
      one another.

Something I Enjoy Doing Because It Gives Me a Feeling of Accomplisment

A Circle Session

Objectives: The students will describe personal accomplishments and the feelings they generate.

Introduce the topic: Say to the students: *Today we're going to discuss things we're good at. The topic is, "Something I Enjoy Doing Because It Gives Me a Feeling of Accomplishment." Notice that you're asked to brag a little here, and that's OK. You aren't boasting, and you're not comparing yourself to others or putting anyone else down. You're just telling about what you can do that you're proud of. So think about one thing you like to do that gives you a good feeling. This can be something you enjoy doing at school or away from school. It can be something you've only done once, or an activity you engage in frequently. Think about it for a minute. The topic is, "Something I Enjoy Doing Because It Gives Me A Feeling of Accomplishment."*

Discussion questions:

— *What is it about the activity you shared that gives you such good feelings?*
— *How important is it to experience feelings of accomplishment?*
— *Did you learn anything new and interesting about anyone in this session?*
— *What did you learn about yourself?*

Something at Which I'd Like to Succeed —————— A Circle Session

Objective:	The students will: — describe a goal and what they need to do to obtain it. — verbalize the importance of having goals.
Introduce the topic:	Say to the students: *Today's topic is "Something at Which I'd Like to Succeed." It calls for you to think about something you want to accomplish that may be hard for you. It also asks you to think about what is standing in the way of your achieving this goal, and what you can do to overcome these obstacles. If the thing at which you want to succeed is something you have tried and just can't seen to do, what's stopping you? If it's something you haven't tried yet, but would like to, what areas do you need to be strong in before you attempt it? Think about it for a few moments. The topic is, "Something at Which I'd Like to Succeed."*
Discussion questions:	*— How do you think you would feel if you succeeded at this thing?* *— Why is it important to have goals?* *— How does talking about a goal help you reach it? If there is no one to talk to, what can you do?* *— What else did you learn or notice in this session?*

Something I'd Do If I Knew I Couldn't Fail ———————— A Circle Session

Objectives: | The students will
—identify goals.
—describe how fear can get in the way of reaching a goal.

Introduce the topic: | Say to the students: *Our topic for this session is, "Something I'd Do If I Knew I Couldn't Fail." Think of something you would do if you knew you absolutely couldn't fail. Perhaps you'd try out for a team, become a circus clown, put an end to world hunger, make a special friend, or become an honor student. You could do this thing strictly for yourself, or you could choose something that would benefit others too. Take some quiet moments and let your imagination play with the idea of guaranteed success. The topic is, "Something I'd Do If I Knew I Couldn't Fail."*

Discussion questions:

— *What kinds of things did most of us want to do?*
— *What's stopping you from doing the thing you described?*
— *How can you turn your dreams into goals that you will work toward?*
— *What steps can we take to overcome our fears of failure?*

I Made a Plan and Followed Through

A Circle Session

Objectives: The students will
— identify goals that they have achieved.
— describe the importance of planning to goal attainment.

Introduce the topic: Say to the students: *Our topic for today is, "I Made a Plan and Followed Through." Think of a time when there was something you really wanted to do, and it required some planning on your part. You may have wanted a bike or a stereo, and had to save money to help pay for it. Or maybe you wanted very much to pass a test, or get an "A" in a class—and to do it, you had to plan a study schedule. Possibly you wanted to surprise someone with a party or a gift, and you had to prepare carefully to create the surprise. Whatever it was—your plan succeeded. Take a few moments to think it over. The topic is, "I Made a Plan and Followed Through."*

Discussion questions:

— *What was similar about our plans?*
— *What do you think would have happened if you hadn't made a plan?*
— *Was it helpful to hear about all these plans that succeeded? How?*
— *Did anyone need help to reach his/her goal?*

Setting and Attaining Goals

Something I Did (or Made) That I'm Proud Of ———— A Circle Session

Objectives:

The students will:
— identify personal accomplishments.
— describe the feelings generated by accomplishments.

Introduce the topic:

Say to the students: *Our topic for today is, "Something I Did (or Made) That I'm Proud Of." We've all done something, or made something, of which we've been proud. Think of an example in your life, and tell us about it. Maybe the thing that comes to mind makes you proud because other people thought well of you for achieving it. Or perhaps your accomplishment is something no one knows about except you. Perhaps you helped someone who really needed and wanted help, and giving that help made you feel proud of yourself. Or maybe you made something like a perfect fried egg, or fixed something, like a machine, and doing that made you feel proud of yourself. Think for a minute and see if you can come up with something. It can be an accomplishment from your childhood or something you've done recently. The topic is, "Something I Did (or Made) That I'm Proud Of."*

Discussion questions:

— *Who besides yourself was proud of you? How did he or she show it?*
— *How important is it for people to feel proud of themselves?*
— *Have you ever felt it wasn't good to feel proud of yourself? If so, what caused you to feel that way?*
— *How does pride in ourselves help us continue to accomplish things?*

The Odds Were Against Me, But I Succeeded Anyway

Objectives: The students will describe the importance of determination and commitment to achieving a goal.

Introduce the topic: In your own words, say to the students: *Quite often people overcome severe obstacles when they set out to reach a goal, so today, let's talk about how this happens. The topic is, "The Odds Were Against Me, But I Succeeded Anyway." You've all probably heard success stories about people who were determined to do something, even though they knew it was unlikely that they would be able to do it. Maybe something like this has happened to you.*

Can you think of a time when it was really tough for you to do something but you did it anyway? Maybe everyone said you couldn't make the team, but you did. Or perhaps your goal was to do well in a hard class, and through determination and hard work, you got a B or an A. Think about it for a few moments. The topic is, "The Odds Were Against Me, But I Succeeded Anyway."

Discussion questions:

— *How does it feel to know you did something that seemed impossible?*
— *What enables people to overcome odds that are stacked against them?*
— *What's more important for you, succeeding or knowing that you tried?*

Something I Finished That I Had a Hard Time Starting

A Circle Session

Objective: The students will describe thoughts and attitudes that facilitate goal attainment.

Introduce the topic: Say to the students: *Our circle session topic for today is, "Something I Finished That I Had a Hard Time Starting." Do you remember the story of "The Little Engine That Could?" You probably heard it as a child. It was about the little red engine that managed to chug its way over a high mountain because it was sure it could do it. We've all experienced times when we took on something that seemed much too big for us, or when someone else gave us a pretty rough assignment or job. It looked impossible at first, and so it was hard to get started.*

Think of a time like that in your life. Maybe you were given a homework assignment that seemed insurmountable. Or perhaps you were involved in a special project or event that was very involved and complex. Yet, regardless of how difficult it seemed at first, you finished it. Let's take a few moments to think it over. The topic is, "Something I Finished That I Had a Hard Time Starting."

Discussion questions:

— *How did your feelings change from the time you began the task till the time you completed it?*
— *What kinds of attitudes can help a person begin a difficult task?*
— *Sometimes tasks are easy to start but hard to finish. What attitudes help out in these situations?*

Something I Want to Get Done Before Next Week ——————— A Circle Session

Objective: | The students will verbalize a short term goal.

Introduce the topic: | Say to the students: *Today we're going to talk about goals. The topic is, "Something I Want to Get Done Before Next Week." What is one thing that you want to accomplish in the next few days? It could be something that involves another person, like talking over a problem or arranging to get together for the weekend. Maybe you want to earn some money, or even spend some money. Perhaps you want to complete a particular assignment, or try out for a team or play, or take a quick trip somewhere. Think about it and you are likely to find that you've set some kind of short-term goal for yourself over the next few days. Tell us what it is, and how you intend to accomplish it. The topic is, "Something I Want to Get Done Before Next Week."*

Discussion questions: |
— *Why is it important to get things done by a certain time?*
— *What can happen when a goal has no time limit?*
— *When are goals helpful?*
— *When are goals unhelpful?*

A Project I've Got Going Right Now

A Circle Session

Objectives:	The students will: — describe an ongoing project. — discuss the importance of working toward goals.
Introduce the topic:	In your own words, say to the students: *Our topic for this circle session is, "A Project I've Got Going Right Now." You can address this topic in a lot of different ways. For example, your project could be something you are creating. Perhaps you're putting together a bicycle, a quilt, an engine, an article of clothing, an artistic creation, or a musical piece. It could be a problem that you're in the middle of solving, like how you're going to pay for something that you want to buy, or how you can handle a part-time job. It could be a program of self-improvement, too, like going on a diet, or building up your muscles, or improving a specific athletic skill. Looking at life this way, you'll find that you almost always have a project of some kind in progress. What is one of yours? Think about it for a few moments. Our topic is, "A Project I've Got Going Right Now."*
Discussion questions:	*— How do you generally feel when you're involved in your project?* *— Why do you think personal projects are so important to people?* *— How do you think being involved in projects now helps you prepare for the future?*

Something I Want to Do (or Make) Someday That I Haven't Started Yet

A Circle Session

Objectives: The students will:
— describe a long term goal.
— discuss ways of attaining the goal.

Introduce the topic: Say to the students: *Our circle session topic for today is, "Something I Want to Do (or Make) Someday That I Haven't Started Yet." The great Lao Tsze once said, "A journey of 1,000 miles must begin with a single step." What's one of your journeys? Is it a career you'd like to have someday, a place you'd like to go, or a person you'd like to meet or be? Perhaps you want to paint a wonderful picture, become wealthy, or invent something that the world needs. The goal you tell us about could be one you want to accomplish as an adult, or in a couple of years, or over the next few months. Take a minute to think about this. Our topic is, "Something I Want to Do (or Make) Someday That I Haven't Started Yet."*

Discussion questions:
— *How do you feel about your goal right now?*
— *Were there any similarities or differences in the things we shared that you found interesting?*
— *What seems easiest to you, setting long-range or short-range goals? Why?*
— *What value is there in discussing our goals?*

How They Got Where They Are Today

Interview, Report, and Class Discussion

Description: After brainstorming the characteristics of successful people, each student selects and interviews a successful individual with whom he or she is familiar, and prepares a written or oral report describing how that person achieved her/his success.

Objectives: The students will:
— describe characteristics of successful people.
— learn and practice specific interviewing techniques.

Time needed: one week outside of class for interviewing and writing; one class period for voluntary oral reports and a general class discussion.

Materials needed: writing materials, optional student-obtained tape recorders for interviews

Directions: **Begin this activity by asking the students what they think are the main characteristics of successful people.** Answer the question together; then ask the students to think of someone older than they who is successful in his/her occupation or profession. This person could be a friend who is still a teenager, a relative, or an adult who is successful in his or her chosen career.

Brainstorm appropriate interview questions, such as:
1. When do you first remember wanting to be a _____?
2. How did you get started?
3. What kind of training or education did you need?
4. What are some of the other things that are needed for success in your work?
5. What suggestions do you have for young people who want to succeed in a career such as yours?
6. Are there any necessary personal characteristics, such as perseverance, determination, loyalty, honesty, desire to serve people, or ability to get along well with others?

Explain to the students that they may present the information gained from the interview either orally or in writing. For students who choose to deliver their reports orally, allow three to five minutes per report.

(Continued Next Page)

How They Got Where They Are Today

Discussion questions:

As students present their reports, ask the class to jot down key words and phrases that describe important success ingredients in each field. As a class, discuss the process of becoming successful, and what success really means. Here are some suggested discussion questions:

— *How did the people we interviewed become successful?*

— *What did most of the people we interviewed seem to have in common?*

— *What were some characteristics and behaviors these people did <u>not</u> have?*

— *How can success be represented, other than through money, possessions, and a powerful position?*

Stories for Young Children —————

A Creative Writing Exercise

Description:	The students write short stories, fables, or cartoons for elementary-age children about not becoming discouraged when academic and/or life challenges become difficult.
Objective:	The students will describe positive ways of dealing with negative life experiences.
Time needed:	two class periods, one for initiating the activity and beginning the writing, and a second to finish the stories and voluntarily share them with the class
Materials needed:	at least one short example of children's literature; writing materials
Directions:	**Begin by reading aloud a short children's story.** Choose one that would probably appeal to anyone of any age. Briefly discuss the plot, writing style, illustrations, etc.
	Next, explain that you want the students to write a short story or fable for children of elementary school age. The students may also create a cartoon. Explain that you would like the theme of their stories or cartoons to be about <u>dealing with mistakes, problems, criticism, disappointments, or failures</u>. Emphasize that it is important for their stories to encourage the reader, and to help him/her deal with such universal challenges. The objective is to affect the children's attitudes toward these events, not preach to them about how they should always try to be perfect. Urge the students to be creative.
	If possible, make available additional children's stories for the students to use as models.
Discussion questions:	**Allow volunteers to read their stories to the class.** Ask relevant questions to facilitate a discussion about the theme of each story. Here are some samples:

— *What is the value of making mistakes?*
— *How can we learn to approach problems as challenges instead of disasters?*

(Continued Next Page)

Stories for Young Children

— *How do unrealistic expectations often lead to disappointments?*
— *Should we try to control our expectations to avoid disappointment? If so, how?*
— *What feelings does the word "failure" generate?*
— *Why do we tend to remember failures so vividly?*

Extension: Have the students rewrite and illustrate their stories. Make them available to an elementary school, or arrange for interested students to visit a local library during its preschool story hour and read their stories to the children.

Self-Talk That Keeps People from Accomplishing Things

Creative Writing and Discussion

Description: The students select one or more self-destructive messages people sometimes send themselves, and create a short story, playlet, essay, poem, or cartoon illustrating the effects of negative self-talk. In the final 10 minutes of the class period, volunteers read to the class what they have written, and invite discussion.

Objectives: The students will:
— define negative self-talk.
— describe how negative self-talk can inhibit goal attainment.

Time needed: one or more class periods

Materials needed: writing materials

Directions: **Begin by writing the following on the board for the students to see as they enter the classroom:**
I would have done it, except that . . .
If I can't be the best, I won't do it at all.
I might make a mistake.
I'll do it some other time.

Explain to the students that you want them to create a short story, playlet, essay, poem, or cartoon about a specific example of self-talk that can keep people from accomplishing things. They may base their work on one example of self-talk, or on several, and they may use the examples on the board, or think of others. Their creative writing may be about themselves or fictional characters. If they decide to write about people they know, they should use fictitious names.

Emphasize to the students that their creative writing should illustrate how messages that people give themselves cause them to become fearful and inactive. Fear and inaction in turn lead to increased lack of accomplishment, and a negative cycle is begun. On the other hand, the courage to *try* leads to action, accomplishment, pride, and increased willingness to keep on tackling new challenges.

(Continued Next Page)

Self-Talk That Keeps People from Accomplishing Things ———— (Continued)

Before they begin to write, ask the students to close their eyes. Read each example of self-talk to the students, dramatizing the message and briefly elaborating on it. Pause for at least 15 seconds between messages, and suggest that the students recall times when they used the message themselves.

Conclusion: If the students have not finished writing by 10 minutes before the end of the class period, ask them to complete the assignment as homework, or give them class time for writing the next day. In the remaining 10 minutes, ask volunteers to read their creative writing aloud. Follow each reading with a brief class discussion.

Success Bombardment

Group Exercise and Discussion

Description: Students individually list successes they have experienced during different periods of their lives. Each student then describes his/her successes to the other members of a small group, who in turn label the speaker with positive adjectives suggested by his/her success experiences.

Objectives: The students will:
—list four or more successes they have experienced.
—verbally and in writing express their recognition of one another's successes.

Time needed: one class period

Materials needed: two blank sheets of paper, and 12 small self-adhesive labels for each student

Directions: Provide a room large enough to divide any number of students into groups of four or five, with space for them to work independently without disturbing others. Movable chairs or a comfortable floor are necessary.

Distribute 12 self-adhesive labels and two sheets of blank paper to each student. Write the following on the board:

> Before age 6
> Between grades 1 and 4
> During grades 5 and 6
> During junior high or middle school
> During high school (if appropriate)

Tell the students to briefly describe in writing, one success for each of the periods listed on the board. Have them work individually, using one of their sheets of blank paper. Announce that they have 5 to 10 minutes to complete the task.

Ask the students to form groups of four or five. Or announce predetermined groupings (preferably of students who don't know each other very well).

(Continued Next Page)

Success Bombardment

Discussion questions:

Explain the success bombardment process. Tell the students that you want them to take turns sharing their lists in the small groups. *Immediately* after each person has shared his or her list, the other students are to think of <u>at least one adjective</u> that describes the person, and write it on a label. Suggest that they choose adjectives that fit the successes the student described, e.g. *determined, creative, hard-working, brave*, etc. Have them stick the labels to the student's second sheet of blank paper, as s/he holds it up for them.

Allow time for all of the students to share and receive their success bombardments. Then facilitate a total class discussion. Ask these and other questions:
— *How did you feel when you were being labeled positively?*
— *What good does it do to remember our successes?*
— *For which period of time was it hardest to remember successes? Why?*
— *How did people react to your success at the time you achieved it?*
— *What would happen if you <u>asked for</u> positive reactions after every success?*

One of My Goals Is . . .

A Goal-Reinforcement Activity

Description: In triads, the students dramatize examples of the inner dialog people often have with respect to goals. In response to one student's goal, a second student describes doubts and roadblocks, while a third offers encouragement and motivation. A discussion follows three rounds of the activity.

Objectives: The students will:
— describe a personal goal.
— practice dealing with imagined obstacles to the goal.
— identify steps to attaining the goal.

Time needed: approximately 30 minutes: 5 minutes per round, and 15 minutes for directions and discussion

Directions: Locate an area large enough to accommodate groups of three students, allowing ample space between groups.

Divide the students randomly into groups of three. Have them decide who will be **A**, who will be **B**, and who will be **C**. (If one or two students are left over, you can assign additional C's to some groups.)

Explain the procedure to the students: *Person A, you are the "goal-setter," and will state a goal that you want to achieve. Person B, you are the "discourager." You will come up with all the problems, obstacles, and roadblocks that could make achieving the goal difficult. Person C, you are the "encourager." You will offer ideas and solutions for achieving the goal. You will help remove the roadblocks. Offer any good ideas you can think of to help the goal-setter be successful. After a few minutes, I'll call time and tell you to switch roles. We will do three rounds, so that everyone can play all three roles.*

Choose two volunteers and demonstrate the rotation process and the goal-setter/discourager/encourager interaction. Provide examples of goal statements, positive statements, and negative statements.

(Continued Next Page)

One of My Goals Is . . .

Discussion questions:

Lead the activity through three rounds. Circulate, and encourage the students to play their roles with enthusiasm.

After everyone has had a turn in each role, facilitate a class discussion, using these and other questions:
— *What obstacles or roadblocks were mentioned most often?*
— *What were some of the best solutions offered?*
— *Do you think this activity will help you accomplish your goal? How?*

Something I Want

Discussion and Experience Sheet

Description: After an introductory discussion, the students write three goals and identify steps they must take to achieve them. These are recorded on the "Goal Attainment" experience sheet, which is also used to monitor the progress of the students as they attempt to attain their goals.

Objectives: The students will:
—describe how having a goal is the first step to achieving what one wants.
—identify specific steps for attaining goals.
—develop skills in setting practical and achievable goals.
—experience goal attainment.

Time needed: one entire grading period (a quarter, semester, etc.)

Materials needed: pens or pencils, blank note paper, and one copy of the "Goal Achievement" experience sheet for each student

Directions: This is a continuing activity, designed to be used with students over an extended grading period. It will allow them to experience the satisfaction of setting and achieving goals that are important to them, and will teach them an effective goal-setting/attainment process.

Introduce the activity. Explain to the students that a vital trait of successful people is that they set and achieve goals that are important to them. Point out that when we think of goals, we usually picture big, important things like cars, houses, vacations, etc., when in fact, we set dozens of smaller goals each day. For example, each student has something he or she would like to do today.

Ask the students to share some of the things they want or need to do today. As they share, note that there are some things that *you* want to get done, too. Stating these things is the simplest form of goal-setting. All of us have many goals, both small and large, and as we experience their attainment, we also experience success. *Explain to the students that in this activity, they will set some goals and experience the feelings of success that come with attaining them.*

(Continued Next Page)

Something I Want

Ask the students to think about some things that they would like to do better. They may be related to home or school, and they may involve other people, including friends. On a blank piece of note paper, have the students list three things that they would like to achieve. Allow 3 to 5 minutes. Then ask a few volunteers to share their "goals" with the class.

Distribute the experience sheet entitled, "Goal Achievement." Review the experience sheet with the students. Pay special attention to the instructions for writing goal statements. Make sure the students understand that (1) a goal statement is written using only positive words (no "not's," "can'ts," "won'ts," etc.), (2) the goals they set must be for themselves, not others, and (3) goals are written only in the present tense—as though they were happening *right now*, or in the present perfect tense—as though they had *already been achieved*. For example:

I get to class on time. <u>or</u> *I have been getting to class on time.*

Point out that research has shown when goals are written in this way, they are communicated to the brain in their clearest and most understandable form.

Optional: Spend a little time with each student, reviewing his/her goals to make sure that they are attainable, properly written, and within the control of the student to achieve (not dependent on events or people outside the student's control).

After the students have edited their goals and transcribed them to the "Goal Achievement" experience sheet, explain that goals are achieved in steps. *Success is measured as each step is completed.* Point out that the next part of the experience sheet helps them break down their goals into more easily managed steps.

(Continued Next Page)

On their note paper, have the students write down four or five steps they can take that will move them toward each goal. For example, if a student's goal is to be on time to a class for which he or she typically arrives late, the student might commit to these steps:

1. During week one, I am on time to History twice.
2. During week two, I am on time to History four times.
3. During week three, I am on time to History every day.

Allow about ten minutes for the students to complete their steps. While they are writing, offer assistance. This task will be foreign to most students and they will need guidance in formulating the steps.

Optional: Again, you may add significantly to this activity by sitting with each student and assisting in the development of the steps. Your involvement will be particularly valuable in the case of students whose goals pertain to success in your class.

After completing their list of steps, have the students transcribe only the *first step* **to the "Goal Achievement" experience sheet.** Explain that this first step is their immediate focus. Instruct the students to keep their lists, but now continue the review of the experience sheet.

Review the scoring process. Clarify any questions the students have about how their progress is scored, and tell them when you will discuss their progress with them. It is recommended that the experience sheet be reviewed and progress scores recorded weekly. The interval you agree on with students should not exceed ten days.

Tell the students that it is now their responsibility to take the first step toward their goal.

Conducting the achievement reviews: At the first review, ask the students to enter the date of the review and to check either the "Step Achieved" box, or the "Step Not Achieved" box. Then, direct them to enter the "Fraction Achieved" at the bottom of the page. The fraction achieved is the number of steps achieved (numerator) over the number of steps attempted (denominator).

(Continued Next Page)

Something I Want ─────────────

─────────────────── **(Continued)**

Discussion questions:

Invite the students to discuss their results. Ask those who fell short of their objective to think about what they are going to do differently before the next review. Suggest that those who achieved their first step proceed with the experience sheet, by entering the next step they will take in the goal attainment process.

Lead a discussion after *each* achievement review. Ask these and other relevant questions:

— *How do you feel about having achieved this step toward your goal?*

— *If you didn't complete the first step, how did you feel about falling short? Do you think it feels better to succeed?*

— *How can we invite other people to help us achieve our goals?*

Conclusion:

At the last achievement review, ask each student to examine his/her original goals. Although many students will have attained all of their goals, others will have attained only one or two, and some will have fallen short in all three areas. Those who fell short in one or more areas are apt to feel unsuccessful. It is vitally important for those students to know that:

• If they attained even one step (or half a step) toward a goal, they have experienced success.

• Success is *progress*—any amount of it.

• Progress can be as important or even more important to the individual development of the student as actual goal attainment.

Goal Achievement

Goals need to be written in specials ways.

Goals should ALWAYS be—

1. Positive (They contain no negative words.)
2. Personal (They're about us, not others.)
3. Written as though they are happening now or have already happened. (Never write them as though they are "going to" happen.)

Researchers tell us that when we write goals in this way we connect with the part of our brain that tells us what we need to do. Have you ever wanted to make something? If you have, you may remember that after you decided what it was you wanted to make (this was your goal) you started thinking of things you needed to have and other things you needed to do in order to make what you wanted (attain your goal). Not only did you think of all of these things, you were also able to put them into the order in which they needed to be done (the steps you take to achieve your goal). This happened because you used the part of your brain that <u>acts on</u> goals. The more often you set goals in this way, the more you get what you want.

These are the goals I am attaining:

Goal #1 _____

_____

Goal #2 _____

_____

Goal #3 _____

_____

My Goal Achievement Score Sheet . . .

Goal #1 - _____

_____

Steps Toward Achieving My Goal:
_____
_____
_____
_____

Review Date						
Step Achieved						
Step Not Achieved						

Goal #2 - _____

_____

Steps Toward Achieving My Goal:
_____
_____
_____
_____

Review Date						
Step Achieved						
Step Not Achieved						

Goal #3 - _____

_____

Steps Toward Achieving My Goal:
_____
_____
_____
_____

Review Date						
Step Achieved						
Step Not Achieved						

Fraction Achieved						

MAKING DECISIONS

The decision behind the decision is—do you really want to decide.

Decision-making is a very critical and complex area of human functioning. Some of the decisions we make affect our lives on a moment-to-moment basis, and others set our courses for the future. Decision-making involves such things as self-awareness, autonomy, consideration of risk, information gathering, weighing alternatives, and intuition. This unit gives students the opportunity to explore these and other aspects of decision-making by examining choices they have made, and by learning and applying a process for effective decision-making.

Overall objectives
The purpose of this unit is to help students understand that:
— making a decision is taking a risk.
— not making a decision at all is a form of decision-making.
— effective decisions sometimes involve intuition and always involve choosing from among alternatives.
— the more people are aware of their values, attitudes, interests, and abilities, the more alternatives they have to choose from.
— learning decision-making skills increases the probability of having what one wants.

I Had a Hard Time Choosing Between Two Things ———————— A Circle Session

Objectives:

The students will:
— identify choices they have made.
— describe how choosing one thing often means giving up others.

Introduce the topic:

Say to the students: *Our topic for this session is, "I Had a Hard Time Choosing Between Two Things." Every so often something like this happens to all of us. We have to choose one thing over another because we can't have both. Think of a time when you wanted to go to two different places at the same time, or you wanted to buy two things and only had enough money for one. Or describe another kind of situation in which you had to choose between two different things. Think about it for a few moments. The topic is, "I Had a Hard Time Choosing Between Two Things."*

Discussion questions:

— *How did you feel about giving up the thing you didn't choose?*
— *How is making a decision the same thing as taking a risk?*
— *Someone once said that after you make your decision, you need to move out of "what if " and move into "it is." How do you react to this statement?*
— *Did you hear a decision that was best for the person who made it, but would not have been best for you?*

I Didn't Want to Have to Make a Decision ———————— A Circle Session

Objectives: The students will:
— identify decisions they have made.
— describe the consequences of postponing decision-making.

Introduce the topic: Say to the students: *Our topic for this session is, "I Didn't Want to Have to Make a Decision." Think of a time when you felt pressured to make a decision, but didn't feel like you were ready to do it. Perhaps someone urged you to do something you didn't want to do, and you were reluctant to refuse the person, so you put off making a decision. Maybe you didn't want to make a decision because it involved a big risk of some kind. Take a few moments to think of a time something like this happened to you. Describe the situation, but don't mention the names of the other people involved. The topic is, "I Didn't Want to Have to Make a Decision."*

Discussion questions:
— *What did you feel when you realized you needed to make a decision?*
— *How do you feel about it right now?*
— *What happens when you keep postponing a difficult decision?*
— *Is it possible to rush too quickly into a decision?*
— *How much should you know about a situation before making a decision?*

I Thought Over My Decision, and I Stuck to It ——————— A Circle Session

Objectives:

The students will:
— describe a decision and the process they used to make it.
— discuss the importance of identifying and evaluating alternatives when making decisions.

Introduce the topic:

Say to the students: *Today our topic is, "I Thought Over My Decision, and I Stuck to It." Remember a time when you had to make an important decision, perhaps a very tough one. Maybe your intuition told you what would be best right away. But whether you just knew what to do or not, you thought your decision over carefully before acting on it. You thought about all the possible choices you could make and how each choice might turn out. You probably considered how well each option would work and how it would affect other people, too. And after all the study and evaluation, you stuck to your original decision, even though that might have been difficult. If you choose to talk about a time you made this kind of decision, we would appreciate hearing about it. The topic is, "I Thought Over My Decision, and I Stuck to It."*

Discussion questions:

— *How do you feel about your decision now?*
— *Is it possible to make good decisions based on intuition or a hunch? Why or why not?*
— *What can you do to verify that your intuition is correct?*
— *Why is it important to look at alternatives?*
— *How can you go about identifying alternatives? . . . evaluating the possible consequences of each one?*

A Time I Shared (or Didn't Share) in Making a Decision —— A Circle Session

Objectives:

The students will:
— describe decision-making situations and how they were resolved.
— identify some of the benefits and difficulties of shared decision-making.

Introduce the topic:

Say to the students: *Our topic for this session is, "I Time I Shared (or Didn't Share) in Making a Decision." Think of a time when a decision was being made by a person or group, and because the decision was likely to affect you, you were asked for your opinion. Or, think of a time when a decision was being made that would affect you, and you weren't consulted. Perhaps this was a decision that affected you very much. Did you join in the discussion, or was the decision made for you by someone else? Tell us what happened, whichever way it occurred, and how you felt about it. Please don't name the other people involved. The topic is, "I Time I Shared (or Didn't Share) in Making a Decision."*

Discussion questions:

— *What can you do the next time you think you're being left out of a decision that affects you?*
— *When you are in charge of making a decision that involves other people, how will you handle it?*
— *What are some of the benefits of shared decision-making? What are some of the difficulties?*

I Used Good Judgment

Objectives:

The students will:
— describe a decision they made.
— define *judgment* and its role in decision-making.

Introduce the topic:

In your own words, say to the students: *Our topic for this session is, "I Used Good Judgment." The point of this session is to discuss times when we used our judgment to make choices that worked out well for us. No one exercises perfect judgment all the time, but you and I have used good judgment on many occasions. Think of an example. Perhaps you used good judgment in the way you spent some money, or handled a problem, or asked for help in making a difficult decision. Maybe you thought over your decision very carefully, or perhaps you just knew what to do. Regardless of how long it took, or the exact process you used, the results verified that your judgment was sound. If you'd like to tell us about a time when you believe you exercised good judgment, we'd like to hear about it. The topic is, "I Used Good Judgment."*

Discussion questions:

— *How did you feel before you decided what to do?*
— *How did you feel after you decided?*
— *What constitutes good judgment?*
— *If a decision doesn't work out the way you thought it would, does that mean you used bad judgment? Why or why not?*
— *How can a good decision for one person be a bad decision for another?*

I Thought It Over and Then Decided

A Circle Session

Objectives:	The students will: —describe a decision they made. —discuss the importance of giving careful consideration to decisions.
Introduce the topic:	Say to the students: *Today our topic is, "I Thought It Over and Then Decided." Think of a time when you made a decision that you carefully considered first. It wasn't just a snap decision. Perhaps at first you had an intuition or a hunch or you "just knew" what was the best thing to do, but you also thought it over and gathered some facts that supported your intuition. If you would like to, tell us about the decision and what helped you make up your mind. The topic is, "I Thought It Over and Then Decided."*
Discussion questions:	*— How did you feel before and after making the decision?* *— Is it possible to make good decisions based on intuition or a hunch? Why or why not?* *— What can you do to verify your intuition?* *— Someone once said, "When you don't make a decision, that's a decision." What do you think that means?*

Looking Back on a Decision I Made

A Circle Session

Objectives: The students will describe and evaluate decisions they have made.

Introduce the topic: Say to the students: *Our topic for this session is, "Looking Back on a Decision I Made." It's usually very easy for us to look back on something and see how we could have done it differently. That's called hindsight. Perhaps you made a decision once that you wouldn't make again today, or maybe, looking back, you feel proud of yourself for making the decision. Whatever the decision was, and whether or not you think it was a good decision now, if you would like to tell us about it, we would like to hear your story. The topic is, "Looking Back on a Decision I Made."*

Discussion questions:

— *How did you feel about your decision when you made it? How do you feel about it now?*
— *Which decisions were made after gathering facts and thinking things over?*
— *Which decisions were the result of intuition, hunches, or just "knowing?"*
— *Did you learn anything in this session that will be useful to you when you make decisions from now on? If so, what?*

I Had to Remake My Decision

A Circle Session

Objectives:

The students will:
— describe a decision they made that had to be changed.
— describe the importance of gathering information and considering alternatives when making decisions.
— discuss the importance of evaluating decisions.

Introduce the topic:

Say to the students: *Our circle session today has to do with decisions. The topic is, "I Had to Remake My Decision." Just about everything we do requires a decision. Sometimes decisions are so automatic that we don't think about them. Other decisions are made very consciously because we want to know in advance what we are going to do. Styles of decision-making vary too. Some of us take our time and think carefully about all the things that might happen if we decide this way or that. We gather information and consider it carefully before deciding. Others of us have a need to settle things, so we decide as quickly as possible. Being patient is not so easy for us.*

Whether you are the patient type or not, you've probably had to change your mind from time to time. That's because something new comes up, something you didn't know about or consider earlier. Can you think of a time like that? Maybe you decided to buy something and then a friend told you that a different type or brand of the same item was better. Perhaps you made a decision to take a class and you signed up for it, but then read about another more interesting class, and needed to change your schedule. Take a few moments and think of any type of changed or altered decision. Then, if you'd like to tell us about it, we'd like to hear. The topic is, "I Had to Remake My Decision."

Discussion questions:

— *What are the main reasons we remake decisions?*
— *Why do most people prefer to make a decision and then stick to it instead of having to remake it?*
— *What do you think about a person who always seems to be changing his/her mind?*
— *If you change your mind a lot, or have to remake decisions frequently, what can you do about it?*

If I Ignore It, It Might Go Away

Creative Dramatics and Discussion

Description: The students create a short drama illustrating the topic, "If I Ignore It, It Might Go Away." A class discussion follows the performance, and the students respond to questions about decision-making.

Objectives: The students will discuss problems associated with postponing decisions.

Time needed: one class period

Directions: **Introduce the activity.** Explain to the students that you would like three to five volunteers to participate in creating, rehearsing, and performing a short, 2- to 5-minute skit.

Explain the assignment to the volunteers. Tell them that you would like them to demonstrate the meaning of, "If I Ignore It, It Might Go Away," by creating a dramatic situation in which someone refuses to make a decision about something that requires immediate action. In addition to the decision-maker, the actors may play the parts of victims, persecutors, would-be rescuers, and other characters, such as advisors, distractors, and pressurers.

Designate a quiet, private place where the actors can create and practice their skit. Give them at least 20 minutes to prepare for their performance before the class.

Discussion questions: **After the skit has been performed, conduct a class discussion by asking the students:**
— *What did you learn about decision-making from this skit?*
— *How did you feel toward (the character who ignored the necessity to make a decision)?*
— *What can happen when we put off making decisions for too long?*
— *How do you feel about yourself when you put off making a necessary decision?*
— *What can you do to ensure that you make decisions in a timely way?*

(Continued Next Page)

If I Ignore It, It Might Go Away ————

Ask these questions of the creators of the skit:
— *How did you make decisions when you were creating your skit?*
— *What problems did you encounter?*
— *What might you do differently in your next group decision-making task?*

People are Remembered for Their Decisions — Research and Discussion

Description: Students research the life of a living or historical figure, identifying at least one key decision that he or she made that affected the lives of other people. Students share their findings in small groups and conclude the activity with a class discussion.

Objectives: The students will identify and evaluate decisions of consequence made by historical or contemporary figures.

Time needed: approximately 15 minutes to introduce the activity, a week for research and writing, and one class period for sharing and discussion

Directions: **Introduce the activity.** Tell the class about a well-known historical or contemporary personality, describing some of the person's better-known decisions. Tell the students as much as you can about what went into making the decisions. *Or*, provide the students with details and clues concerning each decision and ask them to guess what it was. Discuss the importance of specific decisions from throughout history and how those decisions affect people today.

Explain the assignment. Tell the students you would like them to select a living or historical person who interests them, and research that person's life to find out about at least one key decision he or she made that affected the lives of many other people. Ask the students to see if they can determine whether the decision was the result of careful study, or intuition, or both. Suggest that they not overlook the possibility that the decision was irresponsible, impulsive, irrational, or the result of a premeditated plan to satisfy selfish motives.

Note: If you are studying a particular historical period or country, delimit the assignment accordingly.

Give the students several days to research and write their reports.

(Continued Next Page)

People are Remembered for Their Decisions —————— *(Continued)*

Discussion questions:

Ask the students to share their findings with one another in triads or small groups. Suggest that they follow circle session rules and procedures. After the small-group sessions, conduct a class discussion by asking the following questions:

— *Which decisions were made as the result of careful study, and which ones seemed to be based on intuition? Were any based on both?*

— *How do some of these decisions affect us today?*

— *Did most of these people realize at the time how important their decisions were to the lives of other people?*

— *Which decisions do you admire and respect?*

— *Which decisions seemed wrong, foolish, or irresponsible?*

— *Which decisions do you think were the toughest ones to make?*

— *If these people had to make the same decisions in today's world, what do you think they would do?*

The Silent Circle ———————————

Guided Visualization and Discussion

Description: Students relax, close their eyes, and listen to directions given to them by the teacher. Mentally they recall an event in their lives wherein they now wish they had acted differently. Using their imaginations, they create alternative behaviors that would have worked more effectively. They select one to use should a similar incident occur in the future. A summary discussion concludes the activity.

Objectives: The students will:
— evaluate past decisions.
— make appropriate choices in imagined decision-making situations.

Time needed: twenty minutes—ten minutes for the silent circle and ten minutes for discussion

Directions: Briefly discuss with the students the power of the imagination and the will. Then read to them the following instructions for the silent circle. Be sure to adjust your pace to allow the students plenty of time for inner responses.

Get comfortable in your chair. . . Uncross your arms and legs. . . Close your eyes. . . Take a deep breath. . . As you let it out, think back to an experience you had when you wish you had acted differently. . . Maybe it was a time when someone you cared about was pressuring you to do something. . . Maybe you wish you hadn't said or done what you did. . . Maybe you were silent and you wish you had said something. . . I'd like you to go back to that situation again, remembering where you were, watching yourself as though it were happening on a stage. . . Just silently remember. . . (Pause 15 seconds.). . .Who was there?. . .What were you doing?. . .What were the others doing?. . .What were the people saying to each other?. . . Remember what it was you did that you wish you had done differently . . . Maybe you felt stuck at that point. . . Maybe you felt you had no other choice. . . (Pause 15 seconds.). . . Let that scene become very small in your mind. . . As you let the sounds fade away, begin to create another scene. . . Like a movie director, in your mind create another way you could

(Continued Next Page)

The Silent Circle

have acted. . . How could you have moved and what might you have said. . . Take a few minutes to play the scene out to its conclusion. . . (Pause 30 seconds.). . . Now, I'd like you to freeze that new choice. . . Move it to one side and invite your imagination to create another possibility. . . another way to act in the situation. . . another way to say what you want to say. . . Perhaps you are saying something totally different, surprising even yourself as you move through it. . . See how different the situation is now. . . how different people or things are this time. . . (Pause 30 seconds.). . . Now allow this scene to shift to one side. . . And decide whether you want the curtain to go up slowly or quickly on a third way to play the scene. . . See yourself and the other people as you talk to one another. . . (Pause 30 seconds.). . . While acting the scene to its conclusion, begin to remember each of the three choices you created. . . Now, of the three scenes, select the one that feels best to you. . . (Pause 10 seconds.) . . . This time, in your mind get up out of the director's chair and step into the scene. . . This time you are actually doing it in your mind, not just seeing it. . . See the things around you. . . Hear yourself speaking. . . Intensify each feeling and each new action. . . Take all the time you need to fully experience the entire scene. . . (Pause 30 seconds.). . . Know that you always have a choice to act the way you decide is best. . . Come back to this room when you feel you are ready. . . Listen to the sounds here. . . and wide awake as you open your eyes. . . Turn to your neighbor and say, "You're a creative problem-solver."

Discussion questions:

Discuss the effects and uses of visualization with the class. Discussion questions may include:

— *What can this process do for you?*

— *How can imagining yourself making effective decisions help you make them in real life?*

— *Why do you suppose you were able to create several solutions now and weren't at the time the situation occurred?*

Factoring a Decision ————————

Description: Following a discussion centered around seven statements about decision-making, the students write a descriptive analysis of a recent decision in relation to one of the statements. The students share their conclusions in small groups and a class discussion concludes the activity.

Objectives: The students will:
— define the term decision-making.
— describe and analyze a recent decision.
— discuss factors that affect decision-making

Time needed: one class period

Materials needed: chalkboard and chalk; writing materials for the students

Directions: **Write the following statements on the chalkboard for the students to see when they enter the classroom:**

1. A decision is not necessary unless there is more than one course of action to choose from.
2. Not deciding is making a decision.
3. Learning decision-making skills increases the possibility that I can have what I want.
4. Each decision is limited by what I am <u>able</u> to do. If I cannot drive a car, I cannot choose between walking and driving.
5. The more alternatives I know about, the more I am <u>able</u> to do.
6. Each decision is also limited by what I am <u>willing</u> to do.
7. What I am <u>willing</u> to do is usually determined by what I value (believe in) most.

Introduce the activity. Ask the students to help you define the term *decision-making*. Record their suggestions on the chalkboard and discuss. Through consensus, try to arrive at a simple definition that focuses on the aspect of choice, such as:

Decision-making is when a person selects from two or more possible choices.

(Continued Next Page)

Factoring a Decision ─────────────

Show the students the prepared list of statements. Briefly read through and discuss the statements. Then assign each student a statement. (Number the students off from one to seven and tell them to match their number to a statement.)

Explain the writing assignment. Tell the students that you want them to write about a decision they faced recently and how it relates to their statement. Say to them: *Think of a decision. It can be a big decision like whether or not to get a summer job, or a very small one like what to eat for breakfast. Describe the decision. Then explain how your statement about decision-making relates to that decision. For example, if your decision was to take an elective course in computer drafting next semester, and your decision-making statement is, "The more alternatives I know about, the more I am* <u>able</u> *to do," you might explain that if you didn't know there was a computer drafting class available, you wouldn't have been* <u>able</u> *to make that decision. Or, because you knew that electives were available in computer drafting, computer programming, and computer publishing, you were* <u>able</u> *to do more than if you had only known about the programming class.*

When the students have finished their papers, have them form small groups. Tell the **1's** to get together, the **2's** to get together, etc. Ask them to take turns sharing what they wrote with the group. Encourage them to discuss each person's writing in relation to the group's decision-making statement—*and any other statement from the list that they think applies.* If you like, have the students edit each other's papers. (Rewriting can be assigned as homework.)

Discussion questions:

As a class, discuss what the activity revealed about decision-making. Ask these and other question:
— *Were there any decisions for which the decision-making statements were* <u>not</u> *true?*
— *What did you learn about decision-making from this activity?*
— *How do your beliefs affect decision-making? Your attitudes? Your likes and dislikes? Your previous experiences?*
— *What can you do to increase your alternatives in a decision-making situation?*

Decisions, Decisions! ————————————

—————————— *Experience Sheet and Discussion*

Description:
The class examines a six-step decision-making process, discussing factors related to each step. The students then follow the process in making a decision of their own, and share their experience with a partner. A class discussion concludes the activity.

Objectives:
The students will:
— describe factors related to each step in a decision-making process.
— make a decision, adhering to the decision-making process.

Time needed:
one class period

Materials needed:
one copy of the experience sheet, "Decisions, Decisions!" for each student

Directions:
Distribute the experience sheets. Read through the decision-making steps with the students, examining each one. Here are some ideas to discuss and questions to ask:

- Knowing what is important to you and what you want to accomplish involves such things as likes/dislikes, values, and interests. Most important, it involves having **goals.**

- You can get **information** by talking to people, visiting places, watching T.V., and reading. Once you have the information, you must be able to **evaluate** it. *If two people tell you to do opposite things, how are you going to know which is right? What if neither is right?*

- Look into the future. Ask yourself what would be the **probable outcome** if you chose each of the alternatives available. For example, what would happen if:
  — *you did not go to college?*
  — *you never got married?*
  — *you dropped out of school?*
  — *you became a professional rock singer?*
  — *you decided not to have children?*

  — *How did you make your predictions? What information did you use?*

(Continued Next Page)

Decisions, Decisions!

• When you reach the decision point, **don't procrastinate.** If you've done a good job on the other steps, you can choose the best alternative with confidence. Remember, if you *don't* choose, someone else may choose for you.

• Not every decision requires an **action plan,** but the big ones usually do. The decision to attend a 4-year college in another state won't come true unless you make it. And that means *more* decisions. *Can you think what they are?*

Give the students time to complete the experience sheet. (If you run out of time, let them complete it as homework.)

Have the students choose partners. Ask them to take turns sharing their decision *and decision-making process.*

Discussion questions:

Facilitate a class discussion. Ask these and other questions:
— *What did you learn about decision-making from this activity?*
— *What can happen if you put off making a decision?*
— *Why is it important to know your interests and values when making decisions?*
— *How can having goals help you make decisions?*

Decisions, Decisions!

The decision-making process involves <u>using what you know</u> (or can learn) <u>to get what you want.</u>

Here are some steps to follow when you have a decision to make:

1. Define the decision to be made.
2. Know what is important to you and what you want to accomplish—your goal!
3. Study the information you already have. Obtain and study new information, too.
4. List the advantages and disadvantages of each alternative.
5. Make a decision.
6. Develop a plan for putting your decision into action.

What do you want?

Think of a decision that you need to make in the next month. Define it here:

_____

_____

_____

_____

Now follow steps 2 through 6. Use these spaces for your notes:

Step 2.
_____
_____
_____
_____

Step 3.
_____
_____
_____
_____

Step 4.
_____
_____
_____
_____

Step 5.
_____
_____
_____
_____

Step 6.
_____
_____
_____
_____

Setting Priorities and Managing Your Time

——— Teacher Presentation and Experience Sheet

Description: Following an explanatory teacher presentation and class discussion, the students fill in the first half of an experience sheet. One week later they fill in the second half. The exercise ends with a discussion.

Objectives: The students will:
— prioritize their activities for one week, in writing.
— describe the importance of doing high priority items first.
— discuss the consequences of procrastination.
— discuss the value of making conscious decisions about time use.

Time needed: one class period, and half a class period one week later.

Materials needed: one copy of the experience sheet, "Setting Priorities and Managing Your Time" for each student

Directions: **Introduce the activity.** Briefly review with the students some of the key concepts gained from other activities in this unit related to decision making. Say to them: *We all make decisions every day, primarily decisions regarding how to spend their energy. Some are big, important decisions and others are small and routine. All of us are constantly deciding what to do and when to do it, whether we realize we are making decisions of this sort or not. Those of us who manage to get the really important things done have two very useful skills: (1) setting priorities, and (2) managing our time to act on the priorities we set.*

Write "Setting priorities" and "Managing time," on the chalkboard. Define both terms, getting input from as many students as possible. Then explain how the two terms go together. Say: *When we set priorities, we have to manage our lives so we have the time to accomplish them.*

Ask the students to tell you some of the things they want to accomplish this week. Make a list of the chalkboard. When you have at least 10 activities, examine each one further by asking the student who named it: *How much do you need, or want, to do*

(Continued Next Page)

Setting Priorities and Managing Your Time ———————— *(Continued)*

this? Is it a must? Is it pretty important but not crucial. Or is it one of those things that can wait till some other time?

Code the items "A," "B," or "C." depending of the level of importance described by the student ("A" being most important).

Distribute the experience sheet, "Setting Priorities and Managing Your Time." Go over it with the students. Explain that today they can respond to the first part of the experience sheet, "Set your priorities." In about a week, they can respond to the second half, "Looking back after one week."

Suggest that the students discuss their ideas in pairs or small groups, before working individually to write their responses. Explain: *The experience sheet is designed to help you take a look at the way you make decisions regarding what you do and when you do it. It can help you see which activities are the most important and it can help you <u>do them</u>—even if they're not as much fun as other activities. You'll avoid putting things off, and feel relieved to have those less pleasant, but necessary, tasks completed. And that's very rewarding.*

Answer questions and allow the students to work on the experience sheet for the remainder of the class period. Before adjourning, remind the students that one week from this day you will ask them to evaluate their use of time.

Follow-up, one week later: Ask the students to take out the experience sheet, "Setting Priorities and Managing Your Time," and ask them to complete the second half under the heading, "Looking back after one week."

Discussion questions:

After the students have responded in writing to the questions, hold a general discussion by asking them:
— *How many of you accomplished all of your A tasks?*
— *Did anyone accomplish an A task that you probably wouldn't have accomplished if you hadn't given it an A rating? Let's hear some examples.*
— *Why is an exercise like this useful?*
— *What else did you learn from this activity?*

Setting Priorities and Managing Your Time

Part I: Set your priorities.

A. What do you need or want to do next week?
   List the activities that come to your mind here.

B. Give each activity a priority rating of **A**, **B**, or **C**.

— _____

— _____

— _____

— _____

— _____

— _____

Part II: Looking back after one week.

Here are some questions for you. Answer yes or no.

A. Did you accomplish all your **A** tasks? _____

B. Did the **C** tasks you didn't accomplish really need doing? _____

C. Did you work on your **A**'s first? _____ **B**'s second? _____

   C's third? _____

D. Looking back, how do you feel about what you accomplished?

_____

_____

_____

Learning to set priorities can be a big help to you in the future. You can become a better manager of your time so that the most important things get done. Let's face it: some things aren't as enjoyable as others, but they have to be done sooner or later. By not putting these things off, you will be happier and more successful.

SOLVING PROBLEMS

I have had my solutions for a long time, but I do not yet know how I am to arrive at them.

Karl Friedrich Gauss

This unit focuses the attention of students on another commonality in the lives of people: We all have problems. Additionally, the unit provides opportunities for students to explore effective and ineffective ways to solve problems. Interpersonal considerations such as blaming, advising, and offering suggestions are considered.

Overall objectives
The activities in this unit are designed to help students understand that:
— if you have a problem, you aren't a bad person because of it—everyone has problems.
— the person who has a problem is generally the best one to deal with it.
— the process of problem-solving involves identifiable steps that have proven effective for many people.

I Solved a Problem Effectively ————

A Circle Session

Objective:

The students will:
— describe a problem and its solution.
— verbalize the importance of developing problem-solving skills.
— describe positive feelings associated with successful problem-solving.

Introduce the topic:

Say to the students: *Our topic today is, "I Solved a Problem Effectively." Since this topic focuses on something you did in the past, take a moment to think back. We're not looking for the spicy, intimate details of your personal past. No true confessions, but rather a problem you had, such as a tough school assignment or some other sort of situation like most of us face every day. Think back to how you recognized the problem, how you faced it, and the feelings that went with handling it successfully. Our topic is, "I Solved a Problem Effectively."*

Discussion questions:

— *Was it easy or difficult for you to face this particular problem? What about problems in general?*
— *Why do people sometimes feel ashamed to have a problem?*
— *Did it seem to you that members of this group faced similar types of problems? Did we handle them in similar ways?*
— *How do you feel when you solve a problem effectively?*

I Tried to Solve a Problem Too Soon

A Circle Session

Objectives:

The students will:
—describe how they solved specific problems.
—discuss the importance of gathering information and evaluating alternatives when solving problems.

Introduce the topic:

In your own words, say to the students: *Today's session calls for you to think about a time when you did something that a lot people have done. The topic is, "I Tried to Solve a Problem Too Soon." Sometimes we become aware that there's a problem we're going to have to deal with. Then a nice, easy, pat solution comes to mind, and we go ahead and do it, knowing full well that it won't take care of the problem for very long. Very often we fail to find out as much as we can about the nature of the problem, and in those cases our solution may completely miss the target. Other times we fail to look at the alternatives. We just jump the gun by doing the first thing that comes to mind.. Have you ever done anything like that? When you look back at the situation, can you remember how you felt? If you decide to share, tell us about the situation and how you felt, without telling us the names of the other people involved. The topic is, "I Tried to Solve a Problem Too Soon."*

Discussion questions:

— *When did you realize your first solution was not going to work out?*
— *How long should you wait before deciding on a solution to a problem?*
— *When people tell you not to jump too quickly to a solution, what are they really suggesting you do?*
— *How can you get information that will help you solve a problem?*
— *What can you do when you see that a solution isn't working?*
— *What did you learn about problem-solving from this session?*

I Faced a Problem on My Own

A Circle Session

Objectives:

The students will:
— identify a problem they solved.
— describe the importance of taking responsibility for their own problems.

Introduce the topic:

Say to the students: *Our topic for today is, "I Faced a Problem on My Own." I'd like you to think of a time when you accepted responsibility for a problem. Maybe you could have avoided the problem. Perhaps you even toyed with the idea of ignoring it, in the hopes that it might go away. Perhaps you realized that you could spend your energy blaming someone else for the problem, or dump it in another person's lap. Instead, you chose to deal with the problem yourself. You owned it and you proceeded to solve it. Perhaps you asked someone to give you advice or suggestions, but the point is that you considered it your responsibility. How did you feel when you decided to accept it as your problem, and what did you do about it? The topic for today is, "I Faced a Problem on My Own."*

Discussion questions:

— *How do you feel when you take responsibility for a problem?*
— *Why are problems sometimes hard to face?*
— *What can happen if you don't face a problem?*
— *Is it OK to ask for help when you have a problem? Why or why not?*

Note: This is a complex topic, in some cases difficult for students to respond to. For those students who cannot think of a time when they faced a problem on their own, simply listening will be valuable.

When Somebody Else Tried to Solve My Problem ——————— A Circle Session

Objective:

The students will:
—identify the ownership of specific problems.
—describe the importance of establishing ownership during problem-solving.
—discuss the pros and cons of giving and receiving advice.

Introduce the topic:

Say to the students: *Today we're going to talk about getting advice when you have a problem. The topic is, "When Somebody Else Tried to Solve My Problem." A helpful step in problem-solving is to establish ownership of the problem—to ask yourself if the problem is really yours. Sometimes the answer to that question is that the problem belongs to someone else.*

Let's talk about a time when you had a problem, and you were certain it was yours. Perhaps you didn't know what to do, and maybe you asked someone for advice, or maybe you were simply given some "free" advice. Was the other person's involvement helpful in solving the problem and, if so, how did you feel? Or did you resent the other person's involvement, and find that it was not helpful at all? Sometimes people's advice and solutions to other people's problems turn out well, but sometimes they don't. What was it like for you? If you decide to tell about a time someone's involvement was <u>not</u> helpful, please don't say who the person was. The topic for today is, "When Somebody Else Tried to Solve My Problem."

Discussion questions:

— *How can you tell when you "own" a problem?*
— *How can you tell when a problem is <u>not</u> your own?*
— *What can you do when a problem is jointly owned?*
— *Why do we often reject advice from others?*
— *How can you let a person know that you don't want his/her advice? ...that you do want advice?*

When the Easy Way Out Made Things Worse ——————— A Circle Session

Objective:

The students will:
— describe ineffective solutions to problems they have experienced.
— verbalize the importance of using effective problem-solving skills.

Introduce the topic:

Say to the students: *Today's session calls for you to think about a time when you messed up. The topic is, "When the Easy Way Out Made Things Worse." Sometimes we become aware that there's a problem we're going to have to deal with. Then a nice, easy, pat solution comes to mind, and we go ahead and do it, knowing full well that it really isn't a permanent solution. It's like putting a band-aid on a snake bite. It looks OK but it's just not enough. In fact, it makes matters worse. Have you ever done anything like that? When you look back at the situation, can you remember how you were feeling? As before, if you decide to share, tell us about the situation and how you felt without telling us who else was involved. Today's topic is, "When the Easy Way Out Made Things Worse."*

Discussion questions:

— *When did you realize your easy solution was not going to work out? How did you feel then?*
— *Why do we sometimes seek easy, but ineffective, answers?*
— *What can you do when you realize that you're trying to take the easy way out of a situation?*

Note: This is rather abstract concept and a difficult one for some students to respond to. Taking your turn first may help put them at ease.

When People Try to Solve Each Other's Problems ——— A Circle Session

Objective:	The students will: —evaluate solutions to problems. —describe the importance of solving one's own problems.
Introduce the topic:	Say to the students: *We have been focusing on different aspects of problem-solving. Today our topic is, "When People Try to Solve Each Other's Problems." Think of a time when a person you know became absorbed in someone else's problem. You may have been one of the people involved. Or maybe you were a witness, and saw a friend or relative offer advice or a solution to another person.* *Try to remember whether or not the person with the problem asked for help, and whether or not the advice was really helpful. Did the solution offer long-range benefits for the person with the problem, or was it just an unwelcome interference? Remember, this doesn't have to have been an intimate, personal thing—just a time when one person tried to solve another person's problem. If you decide to share, tell us what happened and how each person reacted, without naming those involved. The topic today is, "When People Try to Solve Each Other's Problems."*
Discussion questions:	— *What was the attitude of the person who tried to solve the other person's problem?* — *How did the person with the problem react when the other person tried to solve it for him or her?* — *Why is it easy for the person who doesn't have the problem to know what should be done about it?* — *Why is it sometimes very hard for a person who has a problem to figure out what to do?* — *If you think you have a suggestion for someone with a problem, what can you say or do?*

When One Person Kept Blaming Another for Causing a Problem —————

A Circle Session

Objective: The students will describe the negative relationship of blaming to problem-solving.

Introduce the topic: Say to the students: *In today's session, we're going to talk about what can happen when we get caught up in the "blaming game." Our topic is, "When One Person Kept Blaming Another for Causing a Problem." Maybe you were involved or maybe you were just an observer, but what we're after today are situations in which it was important to one person to blame another for a problem. A time when the focus was on who <u>caused</u> the problem, not on how to <u>solve</u> it. Common words in situations like this are, "You always..." or "You never..." If you decide to share, tell us about the problem and how one person kept blaming the other (or maybe they both did it to each other), without telling us who the people were. The topic is, "When One Person Kept Blaming Another for Causing a Problem."*

Discussion questions:
— *What good does the blaming do?*
— *What harm can blaming do?*
— *How can we train ourselves to put our energies into problem-solving instead of into anger, frustration, and blaming?*

A Problem I'd Like Suggestions for Solving —————— A Circle Session

Objectives: The students will:
—identify and describe a problem.
—formulate solutions to problems presented by others.

Introduce the topic: Say to the students: *Sometimes when people offer advice it can be an annoyance, especially if the advice isn't asked for. But there are times when suggestions may be helpful. So today our topic is, "A Problem I'd Like Suggestions for Solving." The word "suggestion" usually means you can either accept or reject the idea. However, if you ask for a suggestion, it usually means you have a fairly open mind and will at least consider it.*

Today, each of you is going to have an opportunity to share a problem, one for which you'd be willing to consider some suggestions. When you receive suggestions, you don't need to comment on them. Acknowledge each suggestion by thanking the person who gave it. If you give someone a suggestion, don't worry if it doesn't turn out to be the perfect answer.

The format for today will be a little different. One person will share a problem; then the rest of us will offer alternatives for that person to consider. If your problem involves other people, please don't mention their names. Take a few moments to think it over. The topic is, "A Problem I'd Like Suggestions for Solving."

Discussion questions:

— *What's different about this exercise and having someone give you advice you didn't ask for?*
— *Does just having someone listen as you talk about a problem seem to help? Why?*
— *How did you feel about accepting suggestions from others?*
— *How did you feel about offering suggestions?*

Note: Limit in advance the amount of time allotted to giving solutions for each problem. Explain to the students that this will ensure everyone's having an opportunity to receive help.

Dear Matilda . . .

Description: Students anonymously write letters seeking advice, then exchange letters and write serious and humorous responses. The letters and responses are posted so that other students can read them.

Objectives: The students will:
—write about a real problem.
—describe possible solutions to a problem.
—describe how humor can help in problem situations.

Time needed: one class period for writing letters and beginning to write responses (which may be finished as homework); one-half a class period on a subsequent day for posting and reading the letters/responses.

Materials needed: paper, a collection box (for problems), and bulletin boards for posting letters and responses

Directions: **Introduce the activity.** Read aloud a column from the daily paper to which readers write in with problems and in which the columnist offers advice and solutions. If available, read a spoof on an advice column from a source such as National Lampoon or MAD Magazine.

Ask the students to write a brief letter to Matilda. Assure them that "Matilda" will respond. The letter should consist of a request for advice concerning a real problem, present or past, experienced by the student or by someone the student knows. The letters may be signed by the students with either real or fictitious names. When the letters are finished, ask the students to drop them into the collection box.

Ask the students to reach in the box and draw out a letter. Instruct them to prepare two answers to the letter—one that is serious and sincere and one that is humorous. Allow the students to consult with each other in dyads or triads to generate ideas for thoughtful and amusing responses. The rest of the period can be devoted to writing. Ask the students to sign their (real) names to both responses.

(Continued Next Page)

Conclusion: | **Collect and read the letters and responses.** Collect the sets of letters and, after correcting the responses only, offer the students an opportunity rewrite them. Have the students post their responses on a class bulletin board, along with the letters they address. Give the students time to circulate and read each other's letters and responses.

Consultation with Professionals

Field Trip or Class Visitations

Description: Students plan and take a field trip to a local institution that provides help in solving problems, *or* they invite professionals trained in guidance, counseling, or psychology to visit the class and talk to the students. To culminate the activity, the students discuss and/or write about the experience.

Objectives: The students will:
— identify individuals and organizations in the community that provide professional help.
— interact with two or more professional helpers.
— describe the benefits of seeking professional help for difficult problems.

Time needed: one class period for preparation, one for the trip, two or three for visitations, and about 20 minutes for a culminating discussion

Materials needed: materials that describe the role of psychiatrists, psychologists, and mental health workers in the community, and a description of your school counseling department with a list of the services it provides

Directions: **Introduce the activity.** Discuss with the class the value in our society of having trained professional counselors available to assist people when they want help solving difficult problems. Emphasize that many successful, healthy, and responsible people seek this kind of outside assistance from time to time.

Then decide on one of two possible approaches:

Field trip: Plan with the students a visit to a local hospital, clinic, mental health unit, or similar organization in your community that serves people who seek help solving problems. If there is a drug or alcoholic treatment center in the community, this may be a good choice. In any case, the arrangements should be handled primarily by a team of students. After the destination has been selected, ask the team to locate as much background information as possible, and brief the class.

Brainstorm a list of additional types of information the class would like to gain as a result of the field trip, such as:

(Continued Next Page)

1. What types of services are most in demand?
2. How do people receive these services?
3. How do you go about helping clients with their problems?
4. How long does it take to treat a drinking or drug problem, for example?
5. How much does the treatment cost?
6. Is there any guarantee of success?
7. What about privacy?

Questions to professionals about their careers:

1. What kind of training and experience is necessary to qualify for your position?
2. What general attitudes and abilities should a person have who wants to enter this field?
3. What are the financial opportunities?
4. Other than money, what are the rewards of the job?

Visits from professionals: Begin by asking a school counselor to visit the class to describe the guidance and counseling services offered by the school. In addition to the counselor, ask another professional person, such as a psychiatrist, psychologist, or social worker, to visit the class. Prior to each visitation, formulate a list of questions to ask and allow time for the visitor to answer them. Find out how professional helpers assist people with their problems, and how people decide when their problem is serious enough to warrant asking for professional assistance.

Note: As much as possible, the visitors should be people who enjoy speaking in front of groups and relate well to young people. *Ask the students for their recommendations.*

Conclusion: **Facilitate a culminating class discussion.** Invite the students to express their reactions to the experience, what they learned, what they still have questions about, how they feel about visiting professional helpers, and what they think about the practice of seeking outside help for problems.

Extension: Have the students write about their reactions to the experience.

Steps for Solving a Problem Responsibly —————— A Class Discussion

Description: A series of statements on problem-solving is read by the class. The students are encouraged to discuss their feelings and reactions to each statement.

Objective: The students will describe steps for solving problems.

Time needed: about 20-30 minutes to go over the list of steps together and discuss each item

Materials needed: one copy of the experience sheet "Everybody's Got Problems!" for each student; chalkboard or chart paper

Directions: **Distribute the experience sheets. Read and discuss each step of the problem-solving process with the class. Use the discussion questions listed.**

STEPS FOR SOLVING A PROBLEM RESPONSIBLY
1. **Blaming someone for the problem will not solve it.** If I really want to solve the problem, I will put my energy into working out a solution. Blaming myself or someone else wastes too much time.
   Discussion questions:
   — *Do you agree, and if so, why?*
   — *Does anyone disagree?*
   — *What happens when you get bogged down in the blaming game?*
   — *What happens when you blame yourself?*

2. **I must answer two questions: "What exactly is the problem?" and "Whose problem is it?"** I might find out that it's not my problem. When that happens, the best thing to do is let the person who "owns" the problem, solve it.
   Discussion questions:
   — *Why is it so important to know exactly what the problem is?*
   — *Why does it matter whether it's your problem or someone else's?*
   — *Do you agree that people should let other people solve their own problems?*

(Continued Next Page)

— Have you ever noticed anyone (maybe yourself) get all worked up about a problem that was actually someone else's?

3. **Decide if I want to ask for help.** Maybe I need to talk my problem over with someone who will listen to me.
   Discussion questions:
   — Why is having someone listen to you so helpful when you have a problem?
   — Have you ever needed to be listened to but received a lot of criticism and advice instead? How did you feel?

4. **I need to ask myself: "What are some things I could do about this?"** I need to think of as many reasonable ideas for solving the problem as I can.
   Discussion questions:
   — Why not just do the first thing that comes to mind?
   — Has anyone ever tried thinking of several possible solutions? Was it easy or hard? Was it worth it?

5. **For each idea I came up with, I need to ask myself: "What will happen to me and the other people involved if I try this idea?"** This is extremely important. I need to be very honest with myself. If I don't know how someone else will be effected, I'd better ask.
   Discussion questions:
   — Why is it so important to try to figure out what will happen if each solution is tried?
   — Is it always easy to be honest with yourself?
   — What makes a decision responsible?
   — Have you ever checked with someone to see how he or she would feel if you did a certain thing?

6. **I need to make a decision.** If my solution is a responsible one, it probably will not harm me or anybody else. However, it may require some work.
   Discussion questions:
   — Why is it important that your decisions not hurt anyone else?

(Continued Next Page)

Steps for Solving a Problem Responsibly ———————— *(Continued)*

— *Have you ever made a decision that required a little pain or frustration at the time so that things would be better later?*

— *Can you think of any big problems our society has now that were once easy solutions to problems that used to exist?*

7. **I will follow through in a responsible way.** I will make the decision and stick to it. If the decision doesn't work or causes more problems, I'll start all over again to solve those.
   Discussion questions:
   — *Why stick to a decision?*
   — *What can you do if the solution doesn't work or more problems come up?*
   — *Has anyone ever had to start all over again, trying to work out a solution for a problem? What happened?*

Culminate the discussion: Pass out copies of the "Everybody's Got Problems!" experience sheet. Explain that the steps the students have just discussed are listed on their experience sheets. Encourage the students to read and write on their copies and to keep them as a resource for the next time they have a problem to solve.

Extension: Give a literature assignment, in which the students read a story (anything from a classic such as *Catcher in the Rye* to *The Cheerleader* or a story from Crane's *Fifty Great Short Stories*) and report orally or in writing on the problems faced by the main character and how he or she dealt with them. Or have the students write about a personal problem-solving experience.

Everybody's Got Problems!

Have you ever had a problem and felt as if nobody else could have had one as bad as yours?

Have you ever been so hassled that you completely lost control and blew up?

Or have you ever been so embarrassed or angry about a problem that you just pretended it wasn't really there?

One thing you can be sure of: Just about everbody has felt these things before. We all have problems, and problems do tend to get people upset.

Most people would probably agree that when you've got a problem, you should do your best to solve it. That way, you'll be ready for the next one. But very often that's easier said than done.

The Big Question Is . . .

"What do YOU do when you've got a problem?"

— stop and think, then act
— blame others
— blame yourself
— strike back
— pretend it doesn't exist

— run away from the problem
— bottle up your feelings
— keep on doing the same thing over and over again
— talk it over with another person

Think for a minute about the things you usually do when you have problems.
What are they? _____

_____

_____

Steps for Solving a Problem Responsibly

Being upset about a problem can keep you from thinking clearly . . .

The next time you have a problem try using these steps to help you focus on the problem and see it in a new way . . .

1. **Blaming someone for the problem will not solve it.** If I really want to solve the problem, I will put my energy into working out a solution. Blaming myself or someone else wastes too much time.

2. **I must answer two questions: "What exactly is the problem?" and "Whose problem is it?"** I might find out that it's not my problem. When that happens, the best thing to do is let the person who "owns" the problem, solve it.

3. **Decide if I want to ask for help.** Maybe I need to talk my problem over with someone who will listen to me.

4. **I need to ask myself: "What are some things I could do about this?"** I need to think of as many reasonable ideas for solving the problem as I can.

5. **For each idea I came up with, I need to ask myself: "What will happen to me and the other people involved if I try this idea?"** This is extremely important. I need to be very honest with myself. If I don't know how someone else will be affected, I'd better ask.

6. **I need to make a decision.** If my solution is a responsible one, it probably will not harm me or anybody else. However, it may require some work.

7. **I will follow through in a responsible way.** I will make the decision and stick to it. If the decision doesn't work or causes more problems, I'll start all over again to solve those.

RESOLVING CONFLICT

Peace cannot be kept by force. It can only be achieved by understanding.

Albert Einstein

Conflict is both inevitable and normal. It occurs within and outside us as an unavoidable part of our relationships with others. Sometimes conflicts are unnecessary and destructive; at other times, needed and helpful. The purpose of this unit is to give students the opportunity to recognize how conflicts arise, and to formulate their own creative ways of managing them when they do.

Overall objectives
   The students will:
   — understand that conflicts are a part of life.
   — realize that most conflicts can be managed effectively.
   — learn and practice strategies for resolving conflict.

I Observed a Conflict ——————————

————————————————— ## A Circle Session

Objectives:	The students will: —describe a conflict situation they observed. —discuss the dynamics of conflict. —describe feelings generated in conflict situations.
Introduce the topic:	Say to the students: *Today we're going to talk about conflict situations we've witnessed. Our topic is, "I Observed a Conflict." There probably isn't anyone here who hasn't at some point in his or her life watched some kind of conflict taking place. A conflict can have many forms. It can be a clash of ideas or needs, either inside a person or involving at least one other person. Or it can be a fight or an argument involving some kind of physical or verbal violence or the threat of it. Without actually telling us who was involved in the conflict you saw, or your relationship to them, tell us what happened, if you will. The topic is, "I Observed a Conflict."*
Discussion questions:	— *What are some of the main reasons we have conflicts?* — *What patterns do conflict situations seem to take?* — *Why is it sometimes difficult to think rationally when you get involved in an upsetting conflict situation?* — *Do you think anybody ever wins the kinds of conflicts we have been discussing? Why or why not?*

I Almost Got Into a Fight

A Circle Session

Objectives:

The students will:
— describe a conflict situation that they experienced.
— discuss strategies for handling conflict situations and the feelings they generate.

Introduce the topic:

Say to the students: *Our topic for today is, "I Almost Got into a Fight." You may have heard this saying: "The most important time to keep your temper is when the other person has lost his." This is wisdom, of course, but it's sometimes easier said than done. Everyone gets angry occasionally. Sometimes expressing our anger is healthy, but other times it's important to try to control it. In this session we're going to look at what causes us to lose—or almost lose—our tempers.*

Think of a time when you almost got into a fight. Did someone disagree with you or disapprove of something you were doing? Were you being teased, put down, preached at, lectured to, scolded, or what? Please don't mention the name of the other person involved. The topic is, "I Almost Got Into a Fight."

Discussion questions:

— *What causes us to want to fight?*
— *What actually prevented most of us from fighting?*
— *When is it reasonable to become upset because someone has an opinion that is different from yours?*
— *How, other then by fighting, can we handle our angry feelings?*

I Got Blamed for Something I Didn't Do ——————— A Circle Session

Objectives:

The students will:
—describe a situation in which they were wrongly accused.
—describe effective ways of responding to false accusations.

Introduce the topic:

Say to the students: *Our circle session topic today is a challenging one. It's about one of the most distressing things that can happen to a person. The topic is, "I Got Blamed for Something I Didn't Do." Probably everyone has had this happen at least once and it can certainly be upsetting.*

So give it some thought. Maybe you denied having done the thing you were being blamed for, and your denial was accepted. Or perhaps you denied it, and the other people involved didn't believe you. Whatever happened, if you'd like to tell us about it, we'd appreciate hearing. Tell us what happened, and how you felt, but don't mention any names. Our topic is, "I Got Blamed for Something I Didn't Do."

Discussion questions:

— *Why is it so upsetting to be blamed for something you didn't do?*
— *How can you handle a situation in which you are wrongly blamed?*
— *What does this session teach us about blaming?*

Something I Didn't Mean to Say or Do That Made Somebody Mad ————

————————————————————————— ## A Circle Session

Objectives:	The students will: —describe how they inadvertently caused a potential conflict situation. —discuss different ways words and actions may be perceived/ interpreted by others.
Introduce the topic:	Begin the session by saying: *Today our topic is, "Something I Didn't Mean to Say or Do That Made Somebody Mad." We all say and do things sometimes that make other people mad at us, even though we don't intend to cause that kind of reaction. Can you think of an example from your own experience? Maybe you forgot to thank your grandparent for a present, or neglected to put out the trash, or said something that sounded impertinent, even though you didn't mean it that way—so your parent got mad at you. Or maybe you jokingly used a derogatory name, or put your arm around the wrong person, or forgot to return a borrowed tape—so your friend got mad at you. We can't always control the way others interpret what we say and do. Tell us how you felt and what you did when you realized you had created such a negative reaction. Think about it for a few moments. The topic is, "Something I Didn't Mean to Say or Do That Made Somebody Mad."*
Discussion questions:	*— Why do we so often misinterpret one another's behaviors?* *— Do you think people misinterpret intentionally sometimes? What can you do about that?* *— When something "slips out" that should have remained unsaid, what can you do to repair the damage?* *— What does this topic have to do with communication? ...with conflict management?*

A Time Someone Put Me Down, But I Handled It Well —— A Circle Session

Objectives: The students will describe how they handled a potential conflict situation positively.

Introduce the topic: Begin the session by saying: *Our topic for today is, "A Time Someone Put Me Down, But I Handled It Well." Think about a situation in which you were criticized, ridiculed, ignored, or in some other way diminished, but you managed to maintain your dignity and didn't let it upset you too much. You may have been an adult at the time, or a child. Perhaps you broke something, or made a mistake, or behaved awkwardly, and even though your behavior was unintentional, someone put you down for it. What did the other person say or do? Were there other people present? How did you feel, and what you do to control your reactions? Without mentioning any names, tell us about, "A Time Someone Put Me Down, But I Handled It Well."*

Discussion questions:

— *How do you feel about that person now?*
— *Why do we sometimes enjoy putting each other down?*
— *When seemingly harmless put downs turn into serious conflicts, what can we do?*
— *Why are put downs frequently veiled with humor? For whom are they funny?*

A Time I Was Involved in a Misunderstanding —— A Circle Session

Objectives:

The students will:
—describe how a misunderstanding can lead to conflict.
—discuss ways of effectively handling misunderstandings.

Introduce the topic:

Begin the session by saying: *Today the topic is, "A Time I Was Involved in a Misunderstanding." Think of a time when you got into a conflict with someone, based on a misunderstanding. Maybe you said something that was understood as a put down when you intended it as a joke. Perhaps you didn't call someone, or were accused of talking behind a friend's back, or said something to one person that was misquoted to another. Maybe you made a gesture or a face that was misunderstood and caused someone to react in anger. Or perhaps someone else did something like this and you were the one who misunderstood. Think about it for a few moments. Then tell us about an incident like that in your life, and how you handled it. The topic is, "A Time I Was Involved in a Misunderstanding."*

Discussion questions:

— *When you realize that you have misunderstood someone, what can you do to help clear up the problem?*
— *What can you do when it appears that someone has misunderstood something you have said or done?*
— *What causes us to misunderstand the words and actions of others?*

Something That Really Bothers Me

A Circle Session

Objectives:

The students will:
— describe things that typically annoy and upset them.
— discuss ways of handling irritations and annoyances to avoid conflict.

Introduce the topic:

Begin the session by saying: *Today our topic is, "Something That Really Bothers Me." Most of us can name one or more things that are guaranteed to annoy or upset us. What's one of yours? Maybe you're bothered by people who smoke—or people who criticize smokers. Perhaps you're bothered by loud television commercials, or dirty dishes in the sink, or the sound of chalk scraping across the chalkboard. Does dishonesty upset you? Are you annoyed by people who don't pay attention in class? Think it over, and tell us what bothers you—and how you handle your feelings. The topic is, "Something That Really Bothers Me."*

Discussion questions:

— *Since the thing that bothers you isn't likely to go away, what can you do to control your feelings?*
— *Have you ever become involved in a conflict because of the thing that bothers you? How did it happen?*
— *How much stress do you experience from things that "bother" you? What stress management techniques do you use?*

A Time When Someone Wouldn't Listen to Me —————— A Circle Session

Objective:

The students will:

— describe how poor communication contributes to conflict.

— discuss the importance of listening, to effective human relations.

Introduce the topic:

Begin the session by saying: *Today our topic is, "A Time When Someone Wouldn't Listen to Me." Did you ever want very much for someone to listen to you, but they wouldn't do it? Maybe you tried to explain to your parents why you got a certain grade, or arrived home late, or didn't get your chores done—and they wouldn't listen. Or perhaps you wanted to talk to a friend about something that was troubling you, but he or she was too busy to listen. Sometimes when we find ourselves in conflict situations and try to explain our side of it, the other person refuses to listen. Think of a time something like this happened to you. How did you feel, and what did you do? Please don't mention any names. The topic is, "A Time When Someone Wouldn't Listen to Me."*

Discussion questions:

— *What feelings do you get when you want someone to listen to you and he or she won't?*

— *What can you do to get someone to listen to you?*

— *How does this topic make you feel about listening to others?*

I Got Involved in a Conflict Because Something Unfair Was Happening to Someone Else

A Circle Session

Objectives:

The students will:
—describe a conflict situation that they observed/were involved in.
—discuss problems associated with becoming involved in the conflicts of others.

Introduce the topic:

Say to the students: *Today's topic is, "I Got Involved in a Conflict Because Something Unfair Was Happening to Someone Else." This is something fairly common to us all. Maybe you saw a fight in progress between two people, and one of them was much stronger and bigger than the other. Or perhaps someone had a particular viewpoint on something, and a few other people disagreed, so they ganged up and tried to punish the person for his or her opinion. You became involved because you felt that something very unjust was going on. Can you think of such a time? If you observed the incident, but didn't get involved, just tell us what you saw. Please don't say the names of the people involved or tell us their relationship to you. The topic is, "I Got Involved in a Conflict Because Something Unfair Was Happening to Someone Else."*

Discussion questions:

— *How can you determine when it's right to get involved in someone else's conflict and when it's not?*
— *Why do you think people sometimes become bullies?*
— *What have you learned about conflict from this session?*

A Time I Controlled Myself and the Situation Well —— A Circle Session

Objectives:

The students will:
— describe a conflict situation in which they acted responsibly.
— discuss the importance of self-control in conflict situations.

Introduce the topic:

Say to the students: *Today we have another challenging circle session topic. It is, "A Time I Controlled Myself and the Situation Well." This session gives you a chance to take some deserved credit for handling a difficult circumstance with a cool head. Can you think of a time when you did that?*

Give it some thought. Perhaps you can remember a time when two or more people were upset with each other, or with you, but you were able to remain calm enough to keep the situation from getting out of hand. Perhaps you were afraid that someone might get hurt, so you found some inner confidence and handled things in a way that you're proud of now. Tell us what happened and how you felt, but please don't mention any names. The topic is, "A Time I Controlled Myself and the Situation Well."

Discussion questions:

— *How do you feel now about what you did in that situation?*
— *How do you feel when you lose control of yourself or a situation?*
— *How can you handle a situation well if you are not in control of yourself?*
— *What good ideas did you get for handling difficult situations from this session?*

I-You Messages ———————————

Dyads and Discussion

Description: The students listen to the teacher state the same personal concern in two forms, an "I" message and a "you" message. After discovering the differences between the two, they practice both kinds of messages in dyads. A discussion concludes the activity.

Objectives: The students will:
— identify and describe the differences between accusations and assertive statements.
— discuss the importance of taking responsibility for their own feelings and perceptions.

Time needed: 30 to 40 minutes

Directions: **Introduce the activity.** Begin this exercise by telling the students you are going to speak to them two times about the same subject. Ask them to listen carefully and tune in to themselves and how they feel as they hear the two messages. Then say something like the following, being very careful to begin each sentence with the word, "you":

You students have been dropping papers all over the floor lately. You do it again and again. You don't listen when I ask you not to. You really get on my nerves. *

———————————————————

* The subject does not have to be paper on the floor, which may not be an issue in your classroom. It should concern a problem that the class has to deal with occasionally. One of the messages must be a "you" message, the other an "I" message about the same subject.

———————————————————

Deliver the second message. This time say something like the following, being very careful to begin each sentence with the word, "I":

I've been noticing a lot of paper on the floor lately. I think it makes the classroom look messy. I've mentioned this before, but there is still paper on the floor. I feel frustrated about it.

(Continued Next Page)

I-You Messages

Then ask the students:
1. What was the subject of the first message? ...the second message?
2. How did you feel when I gave the first message?
3. How did you feel when I gave the second message?
4. What was the main difference between the two messages?

Discuss the differences between the two messages. Continue until someone suggests that the major difference had to do with the words, "you" and "I." If the students have difficulty pinpointing the difference, write the messages on the board and repeat them.

When the students have come up with the answer, discuss how amazing, but true, it is that when we deliver a message to someone with the word "I" instead of "you," it's a completely different message. It is straightforward, honest, and easily respected. By contrast, a "you" message is like an accusation. It puts people on the defensive, and they are ready to fight. Very often we get into unpleasant, unnecessary conflicts because we deliver a "you" message when we could just as easily deliver an "I" message—or because someone delivers a "you" message to us.

Write the heading, *"I-You" Messages*, on the board. As a class, construct a brief "you" message. Write it on the board so everyone can see as well as hear how it is constructed. Then turn the "you" message into an "I" message and write it on the board, too.

Ask the students to form dyads. Have them decide who is **A** and who is **B**. Tell them to imagine that **B** just tore a hole in a sweater he or she borrowed from **A**. For <u>one minute</u>, **A** will deliver a "you" message to **B** about what **B** did. (**B** should just listen.) At the end of the minute, stop the students, and then tell **A** to deliver an "I" message to **B** about the same issue.

Stop the students after one minute, and give them directions for the second part of the exercise. Repeat the same procedure, but this time have **B** talk to **A** about losing a book **A** borrowed

(Continued Next Page)

I-You Messages

from **B**. For the first minute, **B** will deliver a "you" message, and during the second minute, an "I" message. (**A** should simply listen.)

Note: The room will become very noisy when the "you" messages are delivered, because the very nature of the message causes the one who is delivering it to become loud and emotional.

Discussion questions:

Conclude the exercise by reconvening the class and asking the students these questions:
— *How did you feel when you were delivering the "you" message?*
— *How did you feel when you were delivering the "I" message?*
— *Which kind of message is easiest to deliver?*
— *How did you feel when you received the "you" message?*
— *How did you feel when you received the "I" message?*
— *Which kind of message is easier to listen to?*
— *What did you learn from this exercise?*

Point out that some people find "I" messages easier to deliver to people who are older or in some kind of authority position. A greater challenge is to deliver "I" messages to friends, family members, and children.

Everyone's Got a Point of View ———

——— Creative Writing, Discussion, and Sharing

Description:	The students listen as the teacher reads "The Maligned Wolf," the story of "Little Red Riding Hood" told from the wolf's point of view. Following a discussion, the class rewrites other classic stories, telling them from the point of view of the villain. The activity concludes with a sharing period in which the students read their stories to one another.
Objectives:	The students will: —describe different perceptions of the same situation. —describe how different perceptions can lead to conflict.
Time needed:	one-and-a-half or two class periods
Materials needed:	The story, "The Maligned Wolf," and writing materials
Directions:	**Begin by defining the word *maligned*:** (Maligned means abused, ill-treated, slandered, assailed, etc.) Then read the story "The Maligned Wolf."

Discussion questions:	After you've read the story, facilitate a discussion with the class by asking such questions as:
	— *Can you remember how you felt about the wolf as a child, when you heard the story, "Little Red Riding Hood?"*
	— *How do you feel about the wolf now?*
	— *How have your feelings changed about the Grandmother, the Lumberjack, and Little Red Riding Hood?*
	— *Can you think of times in your own life when you had very definite feelings about a situation until you heard another side to the story? Who would like to give an example?*
	— *What was the purpose of this story?*
	
	Explain the writing assignment. Following the discussion, ask the students to pick a character from another classic story and rewrite the story from the villain's point of view. Suggested villains/stories are:
	  The Giant in "Jack and the Beanstalk"
	  The Queen in "Snow White"
	  The Spider in "Little Miss Muffet"
	  A Stepsister in "Cinderella"

(Continued Next Page)

Everyone's Got a Point of View ———

Brainstorm additional stories, listing all ideas on the chalkboard. Then ask the students to begin writing. Have the students complete their stories at home, or allow time during a subsequent class period.

Note: Greater creativity and enjoyment may be generated by having the students write their stories in pairs or small groups.

Conclusion: **Have the students share their stories in small groups or with the total class.** If the small-group method is used, remind the students to follow circle session rules and procedures.

Extension:
• Ask the students to convert their stories into short dramas. Conduct a class reaction session following each enactment.
• Ask the students to write about one of the following topics:
  "When Someone Understood My Point of View"
  "When Someone Misunderstand My Point of View"
  "At First I Didn't Understand Someone's Point of View"

The Maligned Wolf ———————— Short Story

By Lief Fearn

The forest was my home. I lived there and I cared about it. I tried to keep it neat and clean. Then one sunny day, while I was cleaning up some garbage a camper had left behind, I heard footsteps. I leaped behind a tree and saw a rather plain little girl coming down the trail carrying a basket. I was suspicious of this little girl right away because she was dressed funny—all in red, and her head covered up so it seemed like she didn't want people to know who she was. Naturally, I stopped to check her out. I asked who she was, where she was going, where she had come from, and all that. She gave me a song and dance about going to her grandmother's house with a basket of lunch. She appeared to be a basically honest person, but she was in my forest and she certainly looked suspicious with that strange getup of hers. So I decided to teach her just how serious it is to prance through the forest unannounced and dressed funny.

I let her go on her way, but I ran ahead to her grandmother's house. When I saw that nice old woman, I explained my problem and she agreed that her granddaughter needed to learn a lesson, all right. The old woman agreed to stay out of sight until I called her. Actually, she hid under the bed.

When the girl arrived, I invited her into the bedroom where I was in the bed, dressed like the grandmother. The girl came in all rosy-cheeked and said something nasty about my big ears. I've been insulted before so I made the best of it by suggesting that my big ears would help me to hear better. Now, what I meant was that I liked her and wanted to pay close attention to what she was saying. But she makes another insulting crack about my bulging eyes. Now you can see how I was beginning to feel about this girl who put on such a nice front, but was apparently a very nasty person. Still, I've made it a policy to turn the other cheek, so I told her that my big eyes helped me to see her better.

Her next insult really got to me. I've got this problem with having big teeth. And that little girl made an insulting crack about them. I know that I should have had better control, but I leaped up from that bed and growled that my teeth would help me to eat her better.

Now let's face it—no wolf could ever eat a little girl—everyone knows that—but that crazy girl started running around the house screaming—me chasing her to calm her down. I'd taken off the grandmother clothes, but that only seemed to make it worse. And all of a sudden the door came crashing open and a big lumberjack is standing there with his axe. I looked at him and all of a sudden it became clear that I was in trouble. There was an open window behind me and out I went.

I'd like to say that was the end of it. But that Grandmother character never did tell my side of the story. Before long the word got around that I was a mean, nasty guy. Everybody started avoiding me. I don't know about that little girl with the funny red outfit, but I didn't live happily ever after. In fact, now us wolves are practically extinct! And I'm sure that little girl's story has had a lot to do with it!

Conflicts I've Managed —————————

Dyad Sequence and Discussion

Description: The students form dyads and discuss a series of topics related to prosocial conflict management strategies. A brief class discussion culminates the activity.

Objectives: The students will:
— describe conflict management strategies they have used.
— discuss the effectiveness of conflict management strategies in different situations.

Time needed: one class period

Directions: **Ask the students to form dyads and sit facing each other.** Tell them to get as far away from other pairs as possible to reduce distractions. Explain that you are going to give them several topics that involve the use of conflict management strategies, and that both partners will speak for two minutes on each topic. Tell them you will call time every two minutes, and urge them not to interrupt each other or ask unnecessary questions. Suggest that they alternate being the first speaker.

The topics:
"I Shared Something I Wanted for Myself"
   (Elaborate, as needed, about the strategy of sharing.)

"A Time Somebody Was Mad at Me, But Calmed Down After I Listened to Him/Her"
   (This topic relates to the effectiveness of active listening at diffusing strong feelings, whereas arguing, criticizing, and blaming generally aggravate them. Elaborate, as needed.)

"A Time I Apologized, But I Didn't Take the Blame"
   (This topic is intended to illustrate that a person can express regret and sympathy, while still making it clear that he or she did not cause the problem. Elaborate, as needed.)

"It Looked As If a Fight Might Start, So We Put It Off"
   (This topic is based on the notion that when one or both persons

(Continued Next Page)

Conflicts I've Managed

in a conflict is tired or overcome by negative feelings, a wise strategy might be to postpone any discussion until a later time. Elaborate, as needed.)

"Instead of Fighting, We Ended Up Laughing"
(This topic addresses the effectiveness of humor, jokes, and clowning in conflict situations. Provide examples, as needed.)

"A Time I Managed a Conflict by Negotiating or Compromising"
(This topic suggests that both parties may be able to win in a conflict situation if they are willing to participate in problem solving, or are willing to *give up* part of what they want in order to *get* part of what they want. Give examples, as needed.)

Discussion questions:

Reconvene the class. In the time remaining, ask several open-ended questions such as these:
— *Which conflict management strategy is easiest for you? Which is hardest?*
— *What is the value of learning conflict management strategies?*
— *What was the most meaningful part of this activity for you?*

Seeing the Same Thing Differently ——

—— Discussion and Experience Sheet

Description: After a short discussion about differences among people, the teacher conducts three rounds of an experiment printed on the experience sheet, "Now You Don't See It. . .Now You Do!" The students then discuss how differing perceptions can cause conflict, and complete the experience sheet by citing an example from their own experience.

Objectives: The students will:
— describe how divergent points of view contribute to conflict.
— discuss how the skill of recognizing and appreciating different perceptions can be used to creatively diffuse conflict.

Time needed: approximately 40 minutes for discussion and the completion of the experience sheet

Materials needed: pens or pencils, a chalkboard or chart paper, a stop watch or watch with a second hand, and one copy of the "Now You Don't See It . . . Now You Do!" experience sheet for each student.

Directions: **Explain to the students that they are going to experience how easily conflicts can arise from the need of people to be right.** In your own words, explain: *Two or more people can be looking at exactly the same thing (e.g., a problem, a question, a statement, etc.) and see it quite differently. This is one of the basic ways in which people are unique. As we grow older, the way we see things in our world is determined more and more by our previous experiences and learnings. The way we say a particular word can be different, just because of the way we learned it. People even tie their shoes and use their knife and fork in many different ways.*

Offer this observation about conflict: *Conflict occurs when people start to argue about the different ways they perceive or see things.*

(**Continued Next Page**)

Generate a discussion by asking these and other relevant questions. As the students consider the questions, be sure to point out that the need to be right about one's point of view or perception is the biggest cause of conflict:

— *What kinds of things do you see or perceive differently from someone else?*

— *What happens when people argue about their different perceptions?*

— *Have you ever thought you were right about something and then learned later that you were wrong? How did it happen? How did you feel about changing your mind?*

— *What do you think is the biggest reason people fight about things?*

Allow a few minutes for discussion, then give a "Now You Don't See It . . .Now You Do!" experience sheet to each student. Ask the students to carefully read the statement, "FINISHED FILES ARE THE RESULT OF YEARS OF SCIENTIFIC STUDY COMBINED WITH THE EXPERIENCE OF MANY YEARS." After they have read the statement, ask the students to count the number of **F**'s it contains. Allow exactly 15 seconds for them to count—then tell them to turn their experience over so that it is face down.

Take a poll. Ask the students to raise their hands if they saw 3 F's. Record the number on the board or chart paper. Then ask for a show of hands from those who saw 4 F's. Record that number. Finally, ask for a show of hands from those who saw 5 or more F's. Record that number.

Point out to the students that even though they were looking at exactly the same statement, they saw it differently from one another. Ask the students to again read the statement and count the F's. Allow 5 seconds—then tell them to turn their experience sheet face down again.

Repeat the poll. Record the number of students seeing 3, 4, and 5 or more F's. Again, point out that even after this second counting, there are differences in perception. Finally, have the students look

(Continued Next Page)

at the statement together. Read it with them and point out each of the six F's as they appear.

Ask the students to complete the experience sheet.

Conclusion: After the students have completed the experience sheet, invite them to try the statement out on their friends and family. Suggest that they have fun with it, while taking advantage of the opportunity to teach others about the concept of different perceptions. Point out that this knowledge not only helps us clarify the origin of many conflicts, but motivates us to better understand and appreciate others for their differences.

Now You Don't See It . . . Now You Do!

Read This . . .

> # FINISHED FILES ARE THE RESULT OF YEARS OF SCIENTIFIC STUDY COMBINED WITH THE EXPERIENCE OF MANY YEARS.

People are different from one another in many ways. How they see things, or what we call their perceptions can be very different even when they are looking at the same thing. This is one important way we are unique from others.

People sometimes disagree, or argue about the different ways they see things. Write down something you argued about because someone else saw it differently:

When I Saw It Differently . . .

_____

_____

_____

_____

_____

RELATING TO PEERS

A friend is one who knows you as you are, understands where you've been, accepts who you've become and still, gently, invites you to grow.

Edwin Markham

Peer relationships are extremely important to secondary students, and this unit addresses some of the more fundamental aspects of the subject. Students are asked to consider times when they were included and excluded by groups, desirable qualities they look for in friends, their own desirable qualities, ways to go about making and keeping friends, and some behaviors to avoid. Through participation in these activities, students also have an opportunity to understand that the need for attention, acceptance, and affection is universal.

Overall objectives:
The students will:
— increase their awareness of the factors involved in developing meaningful relationships with peers.
— explore ways to improve relationships with peers.
— understand that being accepted and included by others are basic human needs.
— identify effective and ineffective ways of getting accepted and included in groups.
— realize that they have the power to affect the feelings of others by including or excluding them from groups and activities.

One of the Best Times I Ever Had with a Friend ——————— A Circle Session

Objectives:	The students will: — describe qualities of effective peer relationships. — identify positive feelings engendered by friendship.
Introduce the topic:	Say to the students: *Our topic today is, "One of the Best Times I Ever Had with a Friend." Most people find that having friends means sharing fun and other kinds of experiences with a person we like. Can you think of a time when you and a friend did something together that was particularly enjoyable? Perhaps you went on a trip together, or played a game, or just relaxed and talked for awhile. What did you do, and how did you feel doing it together? Take a moment or two to think about it. The topic is, "One of the Best Times I Ever Had with a Friend."*
Discussion questions:	— *What was more important—the activity you did or the fact that you did it with a friend?* — *How do you feel when you're with a friend?* — *Why is it that, with friends, good times can be simple—they don't have to involve exciting places and spending lots of money?*

How I Made Friends and It Turned Out Well

A Circle Session

Objectives:

The students will:
—describe positive actions they've taken toward another person.
—identify effective ways to make friends.

Introduce the topic:

Say to the students: *Our topic is, "How I Made Friends and It Turned Out Well." Some people have difficulty making friends, and some have a knack for doing it. Can you remember a time when you made a friend easily? Perhaps there was someone whom you liked and wanted for a friend, and you weren't sure how to go about it. Were you able to figure out an approach that was successful? Or did you give the matter very little thought? Listening to ways others made friends may give us some new ideas. Think about it for a few moments. The topic is, "How I Made Friends and It Turned Out Well."*

Discussion questions:

— *What was something that most of us did to make friends?*
— *Why is it important to have friends?*
— *If your first effort at making friends with a person doesn't work, what can you do to improve your chances the next time?*
— *What are some things you <u>wouldn't</u> do if you wanted to make a friend?*

What I Like Best About the Person I Like Most ———— A Circle Session

Objective: The students will identify desirable qualities and behaviors of friends.

Introduce the topic: Say to the students: *Today our topic is, "What I Like Best About the Person I Like Most." This calls for a description of the behavior of someone very special to you, and you may need to give the matter some thought. What are the things this friend of yours does that you really like? In your relationship with this person, what are the best things that have happened between the two of you? Maybe your friend is always ready to do whatever you want to do, or maybe the generous side of your friend is what stands out. Perhaps you can always count on this person to be honest with you or stick up for you. Or maybe your friend makes life more pleasant for you in little ways. See if you can pick out one way this person pleases you very much. The topic is, "What I Like Best About the Person I Like Most."*

Discussion questions:

— *Can you give us an example of a time when your friend stood up for you or helped you in some way?*
— *Are people born with the qualities and behaviors that we discussed? If not, how can we learn them?*
— *Do really good friends always do things our way? ...always insist on having their way? Explain.*
— *How do you and your best friend handle disagreements?*

How I Handled a Disagreement with a Friend ——————— A Circle Session

Objectives: The students will:
— describe conflict situations involving peers.
— explain strategies for resolving conflicts with peers.

Introduce the topic: Say to the students: *All of us at one time or another have probably disagreed with a friend and had negative feelings as a result. So today let's talk about those times. Our topic is, "How I Handled a Disagreement with a Friend."*

The disagreement you describe may have been a major thing that led to the end of the friendship, or it may have been resolved in such a way that your friendship became even stronger. You can describe a disagreement that happened to you and a friend when you were children, or one that occurred very recently. The disagreement may have built up over a long period, or it may have been a one-of-a-kind situation that cropped up very suddenly. Try to recreate in your mind what happened, and <u>without telling us the name of your friend</u>, describe the situation and what you did. The topic is, "How I Handled a Disagreement with a Friend."

Discussion questions:

— *What are the most common feelings that disagreements generate?*
— *What were some of the main differences you noticed in the situations described?*
— *How do you usually respond to disagreements?*
— *What strategies did you learn from this session that will help you handle future disagreements?*

When Someone Betrayed My Trust —

A Circle Session

Objectives:

The students will:
— describe negative feelings and their causes.
— define trust and explain its importance in relationships.

Introduce the topic:

Say to the students: *Today we're going to talk about the topic, "When Someone Betrayed My Trust." The word "betray" has a lot of meanings. It could mean that someone tricked you, deceived you, or repeated something you told him/her in confidence. Basically, we're talking about a time when you trusted someone and were let down. If this has ever happened to you, it might have made you feel very hurt or disappointed. On the other hand, perhaps you were able to understand why the person did it. Think back on your experiences and see it you can remember a time when your trust was betrayed. Tell us what happened and how you felt, but <u>please don't mention the name of the other person involved</u>. The topic is "When Someone Betrayed My Trust."*

Discussion questions:

— *What did you learn about trust and lack of trust in this session?*
— *Do you think you can trust this person again?*
— *How did you feel when you realized that you had been betrayed or let down?*
— *Did you let the person know you felt betrayed? How?*

Note: This is an advanced topic, and should not be attempted until the students are quite familiar with circles. In addition, it is recommended that the leader begin this session with his or her own experience.

Someone I Learned to Trust ————————

———————————————————— ## A Circle Session

Objectives: The students will define trust and explain its importance in relationships.

Introduce the topic: Say to the students: *Our discussion topic today is, "Someone I Learned to Trust." Have you ever met a person that you immediately felt you couldn't trust, and so at first you didn't give the person a chance? Maybe the person reminded you of someone you didn't like or trust in the past. Of perhaps the person had a physical characteristic or personality trait that you found irritating. Or maybe the person's age, sex, or cultural background bothered you. Whatever the reason, you had to <u>learn</u> to trust this person, and it took some time. Tell us what happened and why you felt the way you did, but don't mention the name of the other person. Think about it for a few moments. The topic is, "Someone I Learned to Trust."*

Discussion questions:
— *What did you learn about trust and about people in this session?*
— *What changed your attitude about this person?*
— *How close or effective can a relationship be without trust?*
— *What can you do to get someone's trust?*

We Made Room For One More ————

————————————————————— **A Circle Session**

Objectives:

The students will:
— describe how they responded to someone's need to be included.
— discuss the need of people to belong and be accepted.

Introduce the topic:

In your own words, say to the students: *Today, we're going to talk about inclusion and exclusion. Our topic is, "We Made Room for One More." Think of a time when you made an effort to include someone. Maybe you and your friends found enough room in the car for an extra person who wanted to go with you to a game or party. Or perhaps you knew someone who really wanted to be part of an organization or group you belong to, and you made an effort to get that person involved. How did you feel? Was this an easy thing for you to do, or did you have to pull some strings? If you had the chance to do it again, would you? Think about it for a few moments. The topic is, "We Made Room for One More."*

Discussion questions:

— *How did the person who was included seem to feel?*
— *How do you feel about having the power to include someone?*
— *Why do we feel the need to belong to groups?*
— *How does it feel to be excluded?*
— *How can a person who is excluded most of the time learn the social skills that groups teach us?*

I Wanted To Be Part of a Group, But Was Left Out ———— A Circle Session

Objectives:	The students will: —describe a personal experience in which they were excluded or rejected. —verbalize negative feelings associated with being left out. —discuss ways of dealing with rejection.
Introduce the topic:	Say to the students: *Today's topic is, "I Wanted to Be Part of a Group, But Was Left Out." Think of a time when you had your hopes set on being with a certain group of people—a club, an organization, or a bunch of friends—but it didn't happen. What were the dynamics of the situation? What happened to cause your exclusion? Perhaps it was an event that had been planned very carefully, or maybe it was just a spur-of-the-moment activity. Did something unexpected come up, or did you kind of know you might be left out? Take a moment and trace in your mind the sequence of events leading up to your being excluded. What feelings did you have when you thought you were going to be with this group? What were your feelings later? The topic for today is, "I Wanted to Be Part of a Group, But Was Left Out."* **Note:** Since this is a challenging topic, consider taking your turn first.
Discussion questions:	*— When you found out you weren't going to be included, how did you feel?* *— What did you feel like doing, and what did you actually do?* *— Was one of the common reactions to not being included a desire to find someone to blame? Does this help?* *— What would help?*

A Time I Felt Like I Belonged

A Circle Session

Objectives:	The students will describe the importance of belonging and feeling accepted.
Introduce the topic:	Say to the students: *Our topic today is, "A Time I Felt Like I Belonged." When we talk about belonging to something, it doesn't always have to be an organized group or club; it can just be a group of friends that gets together to do things we like to do. So think of a time you were accepted or included in a group or an activity that was really good for you. How did it happen, and what did it feel like after you were an accepted member? Did someone do something special to give you a comfortable feeling? What gave you a sense of belonging? Maybe you had a secure feeling just because you were with friends, or maybe something else about the time and place gave you that feeling. The topic for today is, "A Time I Felt Like I Belonged."*
Discussion questions:	— *Was this group or acitivity something for which you had to try out or have certain qualities or abilities?* — *Why is membership in a group important to most people?* — *When is being in a group undesirable?*

A Time When I Preferred Not To Be a Member of a Group

A Circle Session

Objectives:

The students will:
— describe a time when they chose not to be with a group.
— define peer pressure and describe how it is used to maintain groups.

Introduce the topic:

In your own words, say to the students: *We've been talking about what it's like to be included and excluded from activities and groups. Today let's focus on how it feels when we can choose. Our topic is, "A Time When I Preferred Not To Be a Member of a Group."*

When it comes to belonging or not belonging to a group, you usually do have a choice. There may be times when you'd rather not be included. Think about a time when you resisted becoming involved with a group, or left a group after you were already involved. What prompted your actions? Was it the way you were feeling that day, or was there something about the group? Without telling us who was in the group, describe the situation and your feelings at the time. The topic is, "A Time When I Preferred Not To Be a Member of a Group."

Discussion questions:

— *What were the main reasons many of us preferred not to be included as a member of a certain group?*
— *Have you ever become part of a group, without really thinking it over? How does that happen?*
— *How do you get out of a group that you'd rather not be associated with?*
— *What is peer pressure and how does it relate to this topic?*

Famous Friendships ———————

Written Reports and Discussion

Description: The students research the friendship of two well-known individuals and prepare a written or oral report on the relationship. They share what they learned about friendship in a culminating class discussion.

Objective: The students will identify and describe characteristics of successful friendships.

Time needed: approximately three to five periods for research, and two periods for sharing

Materials needed: biographies of famous people of the present or past; magazines such as *Time*, *Newsweek*, and *People;* and newspapers

Directions: First, provide the students with some examples of well-known friendships, such as Ruth and Naomi, Huck Finn and Jim, Adlai Stevenson and Eleanor Roosevelt, Butch Cassidy and the Sundance Kid, John Adams and Thomas Jefferson, Captain Meriwether Lewis and Lieutenant William Clark, Susan B. Anthony and Elizabeth Cady Stanton, and Brian Piccolo and Gale Sayers. Then ask the students to find out about two people who were (or are) friends (historical or modern) and the nature of their friendship. They should get as much information as they can about how the two people met and became friends, what drew them together initially, what kept them together, what their similarities and differences were, and what each individual contributed to the relationship. Suggest that they consider people who were (or are) important in various walks of life, such as sports figures, musicians, politicians, etc.

Discussion questions: After the research and report-writing have been completed, ask the students to share what they learned in small groups. Then conduct a discussion by asking the following questions:

— *What were some of the important things that individuals contributed to their friendships?*

— *Which famous person described in a report would appeal to you as a friend? Why?*

— *What do you think is necessary for people to be friends? What does each have to do to make a friendship work?*

Why I Like My Friend and Why My Friend Likes Me —————— Creative Poetry

Description: The students are given the opportunity to express themselves creatively by writing a poem about a special friendship between themselves and another individual. The poetry may be enhanced by a musical score or an illustration. Volunteers share their poetry with the class.

Objectives: The students will:
— creatively describe what makes friendships work.
— identify positive qualities and behaviors in themselves and their friends.

Time needed: 15 minutes to present the assignment, one or two class periods for writing (if it is not assigned as homework), and half a period for a follow-up discussion

Materials needed: writing materials

Directions: **Begin by reviewing different forms of poetry with the students.** Remind them that poetry doesn't necessarily have to rhyme.

Ask the students to create a poem about friendship. Make it clear to them that the essential ingredients in this creative work are statements about what makes their friend special. They should also say some good things about themselves, explaining why their friends like them.

Provide assistance. If some of the students have trouble thinking about what their friends like in them, ask those students to think about what they and their friend enjoy doing together, what they laugh about, how they happened to become friends in the first place, and what they talk about on the telephone. Suggest that the students make a short list of two columns, one for each person, and see if the lists match at all. Or demonstrate on the board by outlining positive qualities in yourself and one of your friends. (If the assignment is to be graded, allow the students to help establish the evaluation criteria.)

(Continued Next Page)

Why I Like My Friend and Why My Friend Likes Me ——————— *(Continued)*

Conclusion: Ask the students to post their poetry on available bulletin boards in the classroom on a voluntary basis. Since this assignment involves rather personal information, allow them to omit their names if they prefer to remain anonymous.

Extension: Suggest to students with musical ability that they might enjoy creating a musical score to go with their poem or that of another student. Students who enjoy drawing may wish to illustrate their poems. Encourage bilingual or multilingual students to write their poems in a language other than English.

How It Feels To Be Left Out

Creative Writing and Discussion

Description: From the viewpoint of a member of the opposite sex, students creatively write about "How It Feels To Be Left Out." The stories are fictional and focus on the feelings of the person being excluded. Volunteers share their stories with the class and a discussion concludes the activity.

Objectives: The students will:
— describe behavioral choices available in response to rejection/exclusion.
— identify and describe behavioral differences and similarities between the sexes in response to rejection/exclusion.

Time needed: one class period for directions and writing, and another half period for sharing and discussion

Materials needed: writing materials

Directions: **Explain to the students that you would like them to write about the topic, "How It Feels to Be Left Out,"** Emphasize that they will need to use their imaginations, because they are to write from the view point of the opposite sex. Boys will write about a fictional girl's experience, and girls will write about a fictional boy.

In your own words, explain to the students: *Imagine a situation in which a member of the opposite sex might be excluded. Think about how you feel when you are left out of a group or activity that you really want to participate in. How might the situation and/or the feelings be the same or different for someone of the opposite sex? If the feelings would be about the same, what would they be? If the feelings would be different, how would they be different, and what would they be like? You might begin your story when the the person is just starting to think about joining the group or activity. Describe what happens that leads to the rejection, and concentrate on the expression of feelings throughout.*

Ask the students to indicate at the end of their papers whether or not they would be willing to read their story to the class.

(Continued Next Page)

How It Feels To Be Left Out

Discussion questions:

Collect the papers and evaluate them in your accustomed manner, then return them to the students. Suggest that the students rewrite their papers as homework.

At a subsequent class meeting, ask volunteers to read their stories to the class. Facilitate a discussion after each reading, basing your questions on issues presented in the story. Conclude the activity by asking these and/or other general questions:

— *How are the feelings of girls and boys the same in response to rejection? How are they different?*

— *What inaccuracies did you discover in your perceptions of the opposite sex?*

— *What good does it do to try to understand each other's feelings?*

— *What new ideas did you get about rejecting others? ...about handling rejection?*

Getting In at (Name of Your School)

—— Interviews, Investigations, and Oral Reports

Description: Volunteers gather information on extracurricular activities, clubs, and organizations. A report is presented to the class, and the information is made available for student reference.

Objectives: The students will:
— describe the importance of leisure activity to a balanced life style.
— identify opportunities for extracurricular activities in the school and community.

Time needed: about 10 minutes to introduce the activity, 15 to 20 minutes to describe the task more fully to student volunteers (who will then investigate on their own time), and 15 minutes for reporting to the class

Materials needed: index cards, lists of school organizations from the guidance and/or student government office, and information about non-school organizations from local newspapers and outside resources

Directions: **Describe the assignment to the students.** Suggest that it offers a way to check out opportunities for getting involved in various organizations and groups that are doing interesting, exciting things, both inside and outside the school. Discuss the importance of extracurricular/leisure activities.

Form a volunteer committee. Explain that the members of the committee will accept responsibility for gathering information on extracurricular activities, clubs, and organizations. Suggest that they fill out an index card on each organization and, as the cards are completed, post them on a specified bulletin board. Ask them to obtain the following information:
1. Name of the organization
2. Affiliated inside the school ___ or outside ___
3. Types of activities offered
4. Qualifications to join
5. Procedure for joining
6. Sponsor's room number (or leader's telephone number)
7. Time and place of next meeting

(Continued Next Page)

Getting In at (Name of Your School)

As a class, brainstorm other questions related to the special interests of the students. When a number of students express an interest in a specific organization, ask the club president or another officer to visit the class, describe the organization, and answer questions in a 10-minute presentation.

Follow-up: Ask the committee to report back to the class in two weeks. As a class, discuss how the information has been utilized.

Friends ———————————————————————

——————— **Class Discussion and Experience Sheet**

Description: After participating in a short class discussion about why people become friends, the students complete the experience sheet, "What Is a Real Friend?" The activity concludes with a second discussion.

Objectives: The students will:
— describe positive and negative qualities of friendships
— discuss how to make and keep friends.

Time needed: one class period

Materials needed: one copy of the experience sheet "What Is a Real Friend?" for each student; chalkboard or easel pad.

Directions: On the board or easel pad, write the word "**friendships**," and underneath write the headings, "**positive**" and "**negative**" next to each other.

Lead an introductory discussion on the subject of friendship. Begin by emphasizing that there are both positive and negative friendships. Elaborate on the notion that positive friendships are based on the healthy, positive qualities that each person contributes to the relationship, and negative friendships are based on unhealthy, negative qualities and frequently lead to stressful relationships.

Ask the students to name and discuss positive reasons for choosing a friend. List their reasons under the appropriate heading. (You may want to provide the first one or two examples.) Then list and discuss several examples of negative reasons, including some of your own.

At the conclusion of the discussion, distribute the experience sheet, "What Is A Real Friend?" and have the students fill it out. Allow the students to talk among themselves as they work.

Discussion questions:

Lead a culminating discussion. When the students have completed their experience sheets, ask these and other relevant questions:
— *Why do you think people stay in negative friendships?*
— *Why do you think it's important to have positive friendships?*
— *What kinds of things happen in negative friendships?*
— *What kinds of things happen in positive friendships?*

What Is a Real Friend?

Experience Sheet

	YES	NO
1. A friend is someone who knows all about me and likes me at the same time.		
2. A friend is someone who always agrees with me.		
3. A friend is someone who doesn't care how much money I have.		
4. A friend is someone who'll do whatever I say.		
5. A friend is someone who listens to me even if I am talking about my troubles.		
6. A friend is someone who expects me to see things exactly the way he or she does.		

If you said yes to numbers 1, 3, and 5, you have probably had some *real* friends. They knew and liked you in spite of things like whether you were broke. They also cared how you felt. They listened to your feelings. That's how they proved they were friends. If you answered no to numbers 2, 4, and 6, you realize that everybody's different and that's okay. Friends don't have to agree with each other all of the time. And they don't always have to do what each other wants, to prove their friendship.

Think of a friend you had when you were a child:

What did you like about him or her? _____

_____

What do you think he or she liked about you? _____

_____

What was one of the best times you ever had together? _____

_____

Think about someone who is a friend of yours now:

How did your friendship begin? _____

_____

What are some things you like to do together? _____

_____

What is different about your friendship now from the way it was in
the beginning? _____

_____

Have you ever had a friendship that didn't seem good for you? What was it
about the friendship that wasn't good? _____

_____

Other things to think about:

What do you think you would do if you wanted to be friends with someone who spoke a different language?	How do you think you'd make friends with someone who has a vision problem?
What do you think you'd do if a friend of yours started doing something you thought was dangerous?	Or is hearing impaired?

List the most important things you want in a friend.

1. _____   4. _____

2. _____   5. _____

3. _____   6. _____

TAKING RESPONSIBILITY

You are your only master.
Who else?
Subdue yourself,
And discover your master.

The Dhammapada
The Sayings of Buddha

Civilization relies on responsible behavior. We want
students to become independent, to take charge of their
own lives, to realize they have the power to affect others,
and to use this power in considerate, respectful ways.
Yet when we try to teach responsibility, we run the risk
of preaching and admonishing, which rarely develop
self-motivated behavior in students.

This unit is designed to translate the concept of
responsibility from the abstract to the concrete. By
exploring their personal experiences and struggles,
students are likely to arrive at their own conclusions
about the need for responsible behavior, and to develop
workable ideas about how to behave responsibly.

Overall objectives
The activities in this unit will assist students to:
— realize what they are, and are not, rightfully
responsible for.
— appreciate the benefits of responsible behavior.
— develop confidence in their ability to behave
responsibly.

A Situation in Which I Behaved Responsibly ——————— A Circle Session

Objectives:

The students will:
— define responsible behavior.
— describe a situation in which they behaved responsibly.
— discuss the benefits of responsible behavior.

Introduce the topic:

Say to the students: *Today in our circle session, we are going to take some deserved credit. The topic is, "A Situation in Which I Behaved Responsibly." Before we go any further, let's take a couple of minutes to talk about what responsible behavior is and why people think it's so great. Do you have any ideas?*

Listen to the students' comments. Then, in your own words, explain: *The word itself, response-able, says a lot. It means being able to respond, to do something you think is right, not just sit there and do nothing. In other words, when you take care of a situation and yourself, you've behaved responsibly. You can feel proud of yourself. It may have been simple, or it may have been hard, but you did it!*

Think that over. You can probably remember lots of times when you behaved responsibly. See if there isn't one you'd like to tell us about. If there is, we'd like to hear what happened, how you felt, and what you did. The topic is, "A Situation in Which I Behaved Responsibly."

Discussion questions:

— *How do you feel now about the responsible behavior you described?*
— *What rewards do you get for responsible behavior?*
— *What are some of the consequences of irresponsible behavior?*
— *Did you hear any good ideas for ways to behave responsibly that you might not have thought of before?*

A Way I'm Independent

A Circle Session

Objectives: The students will:
— define the term *independence*.
— describe ways in which they are independent.

Introduce the topic: Say to the students: *Today our topic is, "A Way I'm Independent." The word "independent" in this context means that in some part of your life, you have qualified to take responsibility and make decisions, without help from anyone else. Maybe you've found that you can handle a job and school at the same time, or maybe you're quite responsible when it comes to taking care of money. Perhaps you budget your time well, and you don't need reminders anymore about when to do this or that. Whatever way it is that you are now independent, try to remember how you achieved it. Did you have to prove yourself to someone else, or did you develop this independence to please yourself? If you decide to share, tell us how you feel about your new area of responsibility. The topic is, "A Way I'm Independent."*

Discussion questions:
— *How does a person become independent?*
— *How can you become independent in other areas?*
— *Why is it hard for others to accept our independence sometimes?*
— *Do you think there will be times when you'll wish you could go back to being dependent, just for awhile? Why or why not?*

How I Helped Someone Who Needed and Wanted My Help

Objectives: The students will:
— describe incidents in which they played a helping role.
— name some of the characteristics of a helper.

Introduce the topic: Say to the students: *Our circle session topic today is, "How I Helped Someone Who Needed and Wanted My Help." Can you think of a time when someone you knew obviously needed help? Perhaps the person was doing something the wrong way and you could see that. But pride or stubbornness or self-determination wouldn't allow him/her to accept any help. You've also probably experienced times when people really wanted help, but didn't appear to need it. Perhaps they were just a little lazy and wanted your assistance to make things easy.*

But can you think of a time when someone both needed <u>and</u> wanted your help, and you were able to give it? Think about it for a few moments, and tell us about a time this happened in your life. Our topic is, "How I Helped Someone Who Needed and Wanted My Help."

Discussion questions:
— *How do people generally seem to feel when they get help that is both needed and wanted?*
— *What does it take to be a good helper?*
— *What feelings did you have when you realized that you could really help someone?*

An Agreement That Was Hard to Keep

— A Circle Session

Objectives:

The students will:
—describe commitments that were difficult to honor.
—verbalize the importance of keeping agreements.
—discuss what can be done when an agreement is too difficult to keep.

Introduce the topic:

In your own words, say to the students: *Today our topic is, "An Agreement That Was Hard to Keep." Think of a time when it was very hard for you to keep a commitment. You can go either way in responding to this topic. You can talk about a time you kept your commitment, even though it was difficult, or you can describe a situation in which you were unable or unwilling to follow through. Maybe your agreement didn't seem so overwhelming at first, but after you got into it, you found out that it involved a great deal of time or energy. On the other hand, perhaps you knew right from the beginning what you were getting into. Tell us what happened, and how you handled it. The topic is, "An Agreement That Was Hard to Keep."*

Discussion questions:

— *How did you feel about the agreement when you realized it would be hard to keep?*
— *What can you do when you realize you won't be able to keep a commitment?*
— *Should you always avoid making agreements that might be hard to keep? Why or why not?*
— *How does this topic relate to the concept of responsibility?*

I Didn't Do Something Because I Knew It Would Hurt Someone ———

——————————————— A Circle Session

Objectives: | The students will:
—describe a time when they modified their behavior out of concern for another person.
—describe positive feelings derived from showing concern for others.

Introduce the topic: | Say to the students: *One of the most important concepts that relates to responsibility has to do with recognizing your own power to affect other people, and using that power in a respectful way. The topic for this session is, "I Didn't Do Something Because I Knew I Would Hurt Someone."*

Can you think of a time when you knew someone would get hurt if you did something, so you didn't do it? Perhaps it was easy for you to decide not to do this thing, or maybe it was a tough decision because part of you really wanted to do it. Maybe you stopped other people from doing it, too. Perhaps you wouldn't go along with some friends because you realized that somebody would end up getting hurt. Without mentioning names, tell us what you didn't do, and how you felt about your decision. The topic is, "I Didn't Do Something Because I Knew It Would Hurt Someone."

Discussion questions: | — *How do you feel about yourself when you are considerate of other people?*
— *How do you feel when someone demonstrates that he or she cares what happens to you?*
— *When is it right to do something, even though you know it will probably hurt another person?*

My Favorite Excuse ————————

————————————— **A Circle Session**

Objectives:	The students will: — describe an excuse that they frequently use. — discuss how making excuses inhibits responsible behavior.
Introduce the topic:	Say to the students: *We may laugh a little at ourselves in this session. The topic is, "My Favorite Excuse." Do you have an excuse you tend to use a lot for not doing things that other people want you to do? Maybe it's even an excuse you give yourself for things you don't accomplish. Perhaps you thought of your favorite excuse as soon as you heard the topic, but I'll give a little time to think about it. It's what you say to yourself and others when you need to give a reason for not fulfilling someone's expectation. The topic is, "My Favorite Excuse."*
Discussion questions:	*— How do other people usually react when you give your excuse?* *— What similarities did you note in our favorite excuses?* *— How does making excuses relate to taking responsibility?* *— What did you get out of this session?*

When a Stranger Needed Some Help

A Circle Session

Objectives:

The students will:
—describe an experience in which they played a helping role.
—discuss the pros and cons of helping people they don't know.

Introduce the topic:

Say to the students: *Today our topic is, "When a Stranger Needed Some Help." The story of a the good Samaritan is an ancient example of this kind of situation. It's easy to help friends, relatives, or people close to us because we know our help will be appreciated and will probably get some recognition. Helping a stranger is often unrewarding in a direct sense; we may never see him or her again, and we aren't always sure how the person will react to our good intentions. In fact, we may be putting ourselves in a dangerous situation. Still, something inside us causes us to want to help a stranger who's in trouble.*

Can you think of a time when you helped a stranger? The stranger may have needed directions or help with some packages. Perhaps he or she was being threatened or hurt. Some people admire others who have gone out on a limb to help someone they didn't know. Others say it's stupid. What were your feelings as you considered whether or not to help this person? Take a few moments to recall what happened. The topic is, "When a Stranger Needed Some Help."

Discussion questions:

— *What similarities did you notice in our feelings before and after helping these people?*
— *What are some of the riskiest considerations when helping strangers?*
— *How would you feel if you were the stranger in trouble, and no one would help you?*
— *What is your reaction to reported incidents of someone being raped, mugged, or murdered in the vicinity of witnesses who were afraid to get involved?*
— *Besides risk, what are some other considerations of helping?*

I Put Off Something I Wanted for the Sake of Someone Else

A Circle Session

Objectives:	The students will: —describe an incident in which they helped someone. —discuss possible motives of helping behavior.
Introduce the topic:	Say to the students: *The topic for this session is, "I Put Off Something I Wanted for the Sake Of Someone Else." We often hear that people are basically selfish and out for themselves. "Look out for number one!" "God helps those who help themselves." "Survival of the fittest," etc. But we all know of instances in our own lives and the lives of others when help was given without any expectation of reward. Sometimes we help complete strangers whom we may never see again. We may even offer help at some risk to our own safety and comfort. What is it that motivates us at these times?*
	Try to remember an incident in which you helped—or tried to help—someone else and had to give up something in order to do it. Maybe you gave up some of your own pleasure or ran some kind of personal risk. You may have provided help alone, or in cooperation with family, friends, or some other group. Take a minute to think about it. The topic is, "I Put Off Something I Wanted for the Sake of Someone Else."
Discussion questions:	— *What motivates people to help one another?* — *What value is there in working as a member of a team or group to help someone?* — *What conditions make it hard to give up what you want so that someone else will benefit? What conditions make it easier?*

Where I Think Humankind is Headed

A Circle Session

Objectives:	The students will: —describe their feelings and concerns about the future of the human race. —discuss global issues facing humanity.
Introduce the topic:	Say to the students: *The topic for this session is, "Where I Think Humankind is Headed." Perhaps you've heard it said before, "Man, alone amongst animals, is created incomplete, but with the capacity to complete himself." This is a quotation from the Talmud. What do you think of our progress to complete ourselves? In most of our circle sessions in this unit we've been discussing good things that one human being—you by yourself or as a member of a group—has done for other human beings. We've described many wonderful instances of helpfulness and kindness. However, we know that there is a lot of cruelty and greed in the world, as well. There is also much violence and injustice.* *As you look at the world around you, and the way individuals, societies, and systems act toward one another, the way they compete or cooperate with each other, how do you see the trend running? Think back to what you know of history and where humankind has been in the past. This may help you think about the future. Are you optimistic or pessimistic about the future of humankind? Think about it for a minute. Today's topic is, "Where I Think Humankind is Headed."*
Discussion questions:	*— What similarities did you notice in our thoughts and feelings?* *— If you could describe the way things are going between people of this world as a season of the year, would it be Spring, Summer, Autumn, or Winter? Why?* *— If you were to describe where you think humankind is headed as water, what term would you use to describe the water: "calm,'" "rough," "stormy," "river," "creek," "ocean," "pond," "lake," etc? Why?* *— What do you think are the main issues facing our world?*

Something I've Done (or Could Do) to Improve Our World

A Circle Session

Objective: The students will describe ways in which they can contribute to the betterment of the community/world.

Introduce the topic: Say to the students: *The topic for this session is, "Something I've Done (or Could Do) to Improve Our World." Can you think of a time when you did something that you felt really helped, even in a small way, to improve the world we live in? Perhaps you improved a condition of some kind on your street or in your community. Maybe you helped change something that you thought was wrong. Or perhaps you did something to help the ecology–like making careful use of resources like water and electricity, or treating animals with care. Whatever it is, we would like to hear about it. If you can't think of something you've already done, perhaps you can think of something you would like to do in the future, either independently or with a group. Our topic is, 'Something I've Done (or Could Do) to Improve Our World"*

Discussion questions:
- *How are feelings of apathy developed?*
- *How can we create an atmosphere in this community/country that will encourage people to take action to improve things?*
- *How do you feel when you do something that helps improve our world?*

The Rules I'd Like to Live By —————

———— Creative Thinking, Writing and Discussion

Description: The students are divided into small groups to draw up constitutions for a model society. Then each group shares its rules with one other group.

Objectives: The students will:
— develop and describe rules of conduct for living in a fictional society.
— discuss positive and negative considerations of having governments.

Time needed: two class periods for directions and group meetings; a third class period for small group sharing

Materials needed: writing materials

Directions: **Divide the class into an even number of small groups, not exceeding six members each.** Explain that each group has been stranded on a desert island with no hope of rescue. Food is plentiful and there is unlimited drinking water. Their task is to draw up a list of rules to be followed in the following areas:
    A. What will be considered basic human rights?
    B. How will decisions be reached?
    C. What if someone dissents?
    D. How will justice and injustice be determined?
    E. How will property be divided?
    F. How will work be allocated?
    G. Who will educate the children and how?

Tell the students that they should select someone to write down the rules that the group agrees upon. Tell the students they will have the rest of the period and all of the next one to develop their rules. Then let them begin.

Conclusion: **In the next class session, ask the groups to share their rules with one other group.** Ask the students in the combined groups to sit in a large circle and select a leader to conduct the sharing session. The leader's job is to make sure that only one person speaks at a time. Tell the students that the session will last

(Continued Next Page)

The Rules I'd Like to Live By ———

————————————————————————— *(Continued)*

approximately 30 minutes. Urge them to divide the time equally between the two groups, and signal them at the halfway point.

Extension: In a fourth class period, have a guest speaker talk to the students. Choose a person who has lived in a community, such as Synanon, a kibbutz, a religious community, a commune, etc. Ask the speaker to describe the community's rules and how they were established, and to tell the students about the values of the community, which the rules were designed to support.

Note: This activity is very effective when used as an introduction to a history unit focusing on the Constitution of the United States (or another republic).

254   *IMPACT!*   **Taking Responsibility**

Music That Stirs My Soul

Musical Interpretation

Description: In the first of two class periods, the students listen to musical compositions that have the effect of inspiring action and/or unity toward a cause or ideal. In the second, they share their own inspiring musical selections. The students discuss the effect each piece of music has on them, immediately after hearing it. A general discussion concludes the activity.

Objectives: The students will:
— describe the emotional effects of specific musical selections.
— discuss the ability of music to motivate and inspire.
— discuss the enthusiasm and excitement that can accompany participation in an ideological cause.

Time needed: one class period for directions, initial listening, and discussion, and a second session for additional listening and discussion

Materials needed: Prepare for this activity by acquiring musical selections that have inspired action and/or unity in the past: national anthems, "The Battle Hymn of the Republic," "We Shall Overcome," "Onward Christian Soldiers," "Last Night I Dreamed the Strangest Dream" (by Pete Sieger), "Ode to Joy" (choral selection from the last movement of Beethoven's Ninth Symphony), marches, fanfares from the Olympics, etc.; phonograph, tape recorder, compact disk player, or musical instruments.

Directions: **Introduce the activity.** Discuss with the class how people have used music throughout history to motivate themselves and others to do something to help change the world for the better (or for the worse).

Play the musical selections you brought to class. Briefly explain the background and history of each. After each selection ask the students to make comments regarding their emotional/visceral reactions by asking:
1. How did this selection affect you?
2. How did you feel inside as you listened to it?
3. What thoughts or urges did you have as you listened to it?

Music That Stirs My Soul ——————

Ask the students to bring selections of their own to the next class session. These may be on tape, CDs, or records. They may also be sung and/or played "live" in the classroom. A brief explanation by the student should preface each selection.

Limit each piece to a reasonable amount of time (two or three minutes), but be flexible if the class wants to hear a particular selection again. As in the prior class session, discuss the feelings that each selection stimulates. Point out that, historically, such stimulation had a beneficial effect on the world in some instances, and that the results were clearly not beneficial in other instances.

Discussion questions:

Conduct a culminating discussion. Some suggested questions are:
— *How can great changes in the world be accomplished without mobilizing enthusiasm?*
— *When is enthusiasm not a good thing?*
— *What other art forms have the capacity to stir the soul?*

Extensions:

• Teachers with some background in Physical or Health Education might want to investigate why stirring music makes the heart beat faster, i.e., the physiological effects of heightened emotions, the flight or flight reaction, the role of adrenalin in circulatory regulation, heart rate, breathing, etc. Pulse rates could be taken before, during, and after hearing some of the selections.

• Encourage the students to express their reactions to some of the musical selections nonverbally through works of art, body movement, and creative writing.

Freedom and Responsibility ———————

——— A Class Reaction Session and Discussion

Description: The teacher reads aloud several brief stories and, after each, the students write notes to themselves about the responsibilities of the people involved. The students discuss their reactions to one of the stories in triads. A discussion concludes the activity.

Objectives: The students will:
— define what is responsible behavior in three situations.
— discuss the meaning of freedom and its relationship to responsibility.

Time needed: one class period

Materials needed: writing materials

Directions: **Read the following quotation to the class and discuss its meaning:**

> *Freedom is a partial, negative aspect of responsibility which is richer and more complete in meaning. We may become free from the immediate and yet remain irresponsible. We cannot become responsible, however, without also becoming free.*

> John Wild
> *Existence and the World of Freedom*

Tell the students you are going to read them several brief stories. Explain that each story is followed by some thinking questions. Ask them to listen to each one very carefully and, after you've read the story and its accompanying questions, write some brief notes to themselves about how they see the situation. Their notes should relate to:

1. Who is responsible to whom.
2. What the individuals should do in order to behave responsibly.
3. Any specific question asked.

(Continued Next Page)

The Stories:

Judy and the Orioles

The Orioles girls' softball team has been practicing after school at the park and winning most of its Saturday games. Judy is the best pitcher. The most important game of the season is coming up next weekend, a three-day holiday. It will determine which teams make the finals. Everything is going fine until Judy tells the girls on her team that for months her parents have been planning a camping trip for that weekend, and they expect her to go with them. The members of the team become angry and upset. They try to convince Judy to stay and pitch, but she says she's free to do as she pleases.

- *Who is responsible for what? ...to whom?*
- *Is Judy responsible to the team, to her parents, or to herself?*
- *Are Judy's parents responsible to the team?*
- *Is it the coach's responsiblity to persuade Judy's parents to cancel the trip or allow Judy to stay?*
- *Was it Judy's responsibility to check the schedule and see that her parents were informed?*
- *How much freedom should Judy have in this situation to decide what to do?*

Tony's Father Quits

Tony's father has been a responsible worker on the same job for 15 years. Because of this, Tony has had the typical advantages of an upper-middle-class student—clothes, money, and just about any other reasonable thing he needs or wants. Then one day Tony's father suddenly announces that he hates what he's doing for a living. He says he can't take another day of it, quits his job, and goes on unemployment.

For years Tony has assumed that his father would buy him a new car for his 16th birthday and send him to Hawaii for the summer, but neither of those things will be possible now. In fact, his father tells him there will be no more allowances, and if he wants money for anything other than basic things like food, he will have to work for it himself. Tony protests. He insists

(Continued Next Page)

that his father owes him an allowance, the car, and the trip. He says he assumed these were his rights all along. He also tells his father he has no right to quit his job without checking with the rest of the family first. Tony's father says Tony is confused. He tells Tony he is free to do what he wants.

- *What basic responsibilities does Tony's father have to Tony and the rest of the family?*
- *Does he really have the freedom or the right to quit his job?*
- *Is he responsible to Tony to give him an allowance, buy him a car, or send him to Hawaii?*
- *What are his (the father's) responsibilities to himself?*
- *Is Tony responsible as a family member to be kind and understanding during a difficult time in his father's life?*

Krontz Faces Pollution Charges

Samuel Krontz owns a factory. Years ago his factory made large profits, but he and the board of directors invested the money unwisely and lost almost all of it. Now the business has a lot of competition; costs of production and salaries for workers are rising. The corporation is barely able to stay alive. Besides that, the factory is old, and there is not enough money in the corporation to tear it down and build a new one. The possibilities of getting a large enough loan to do the job are very slim because of the corporation's bad deals in the past. Despite all these troubles the factory does provide employment to 2,000 workers.

Several years ago, Mr. Krontz started getting a lot of complaints about the smoke pouring out of the factory's smokestacks. Combined with the smoke from other factories in the area, the smog is so bad that on some days people can't see further than a block in the city. The smog is causing their eyes to burn, and it's being blamed for the deaths of many people in the city with respiratory problems. Since those first complaints, more and more people have become upset about the pollution. Mr. Krontz doesn't know what to do. He's sure there's no way he can build a new, modern factory that wouldn't put out so much smoke. If he shuts the factory down, 2,000 people will be out of work.

(Continued Next Page)

- *Should Mr. Krontz be free to do whatever he wants?*
- *To whom is Mr. Krontz responsible, the people in the city and neighboring cities, the 2,000 workers and their families, or the corporation's board of directors and stockholders?*
- *What would be the most responsible thing for him to do?*
- *Should he try to get a loan to rebuild the factory, even though he's sure he won't get enough?*
- *Should he close the factory?*
- *Should he keep things as they are?*
- *Should he seek other solutions?*

Ask the students to form triads and share their reactions to the stories. Suggest that they select one story to discuss in depth, rather than attempting to discuss all three in a cursory manner. Remind the students to follow circle session rules and procedures, and not to expect total agreement. Their goal is to allow each triad member enough time, without interruptions, to explain who s/he sees as being responsible to whom, and what constitutes responsible behavior in each situation. Allow about 15 minutes for triad interaction.

Discussion questions:

Engage the whole class in a culminating discussion. Some suggested questions are:
— *What did you agree on in your triad?*
— *What differences of opinion did you have?*
— *Why is it important for people to understand to whom they are responsible?*
— *When do we have a right to be responsible to ourselves?*
— *What makes behavior responsible or irresponsible?*
— *Did anyone in any of these stories misunderstand the meaning of freedom?*

Extension:

Instead of reading the stories to the class, work with a group of students to create and rehearse three short skits that dramatize the stories. Have the group present their skits to the class, and carry out the rest of the activity as suggested.

How Would You Handle This Situation Responsibly? ——— Writing and Discussion

Description: The students write about real situations in which it was difficult to decide what was the most responsible thing to do. In a subsequent class period, they brainstorm ways of handling the situations. Then, after reviewing guidelines for responsible behavior, they evaluate the suggestions, deciding which are responsible and which are not.

Objectives: The students will:
—describe a personal experience involving the issue of responsibility.
—define responsible and irresponsible behavior in relation to real situations.

Time needed: two class periods

Materials needed: writing materials

Directions: **Introduce the activity.** Ask the students to think of situations they have faced when it was hard to decide what was the most responsible thing to do. Discuss a few examples, *including one from your own experience.*

Explain the writing assignment. Ask the students to write about one personal experience of this nature, *without putting their names on their stories.* Announce that they will have the rest of the class period to complete the writing. Students who finish writing their stories before the end of the class period may write about a second experience.

At the end of the class period collect the stories. Prepare for the next class period by reading all the stories to yourself and selecting four or five to review aloud. The best kinds of stories to select are be ones that:
  • reflect typical binds that the students can relate to.
  • provide sufficiently detailed information to give the reader/ listener most or all pertinent facts.

(Continued Next Page)

How Would You Handle This Situation Responsibly? ——————— *(Continued)*

Begin the second class period by reading one of the stories. Emphasize that the identity of the student who wrote the story is not important.

Have the class brainstorm possible ways (either responsible and irresponsible) to handle the situation described in the story. Write at least ten suggestions on the chalkboard.

On a second chalkboard, list ideas concerning what constitutes responsible and irresponsible behavior. Ask the students to forget the story for a minute or two, and just think about behavior in general. In this discussion, be sure to refer to:
1. the rights of individuals to meet their own needs.
2. the importance of not harming others.
3. how (**1.**) and (**2.**) can be responsibly resolved when they conflict.

Conclusion: **Return to the suggestions for handling the situation described in the story.** Ask the students which are responsible and which are not. Circle the suggestions that the students generally agree are responsible. If time remains, follow this procedure with the other stories you have selected.

Extension: In a couple of weeks, conduct an informal discussion, asking the students to share recent personal experiences in which they consciously pondered alternatives before doing what seemed best.

The Way I See It

Research, Written Reports, and Discussion

Description: The students investigate a current or historical event or interview an adult in a responsible position. Their task is to give serious thought to what constitutes responsible and irresponsible behavior, using these sources as grist for the mill. The students share their conclusions in small group interaction sessions, and a general class discussion culminates the activity.

Objectives: The students will:
— define responsible and irresponsible behavior in specific situations.
— discuss the benefits and challenges of responsible behavior.

Time needed: 20-30 minutes to present the activity, a week (possibly more) for research, and one class period for small-group interaction sessions and a culminating discussion.

Materials needed: a biography of a famous (or infamous) individual who lived in the past, and a current newspaper or news magazine; writing materials

Directions: **Bring the biography and newspaper or news magazine with you to class.** Tell the class in your own words about the person described in the biography, emphasizing his/her behaviors. Then open the newspaper or news magazine and summarize an article that concerns the conduct of individuals and/or nations. In neither of these presentations label anything "responsible" or "irresponsible." Rather, describe fully what the people and/or nations did, allowing the students to reach their own conclusions.

Next, ask the class: *Did anything I've been describing from either the biography or the newspaper or news magazine strike you as being responsible or irresponsible? If so, what?*

Allow as many students as wish to, the opportunity to respond. Briefly add your own opinions as you see fit.

(Continued Next Page)

The Way I See It ———————————

Explain to the class that their assignment is to choose one of the following three options and write a report of at least l00 words:

1. Using a biography, investigate the actions of a famous or infamous person from the past.
2. Using a current newspaper or news magazine, learn about what an individual or a nation has recently done.
3. Interview an adult in a responsible position to learn about his/her duties. (Any position in which a person is in charge of what happens to other people is a responsible position.)

In each case, the report should constitute the opinion of the writer. The students should explain what behaviors they see as responsible and irresponsible that the person (or nation) has done or routinely does. The students may also add what they would do if they were the person (or nation) in question.

After the reports have been completed, ask the students to share their evaluations in small groups of four to six. Allow them about l5 to 20 minutes, and suggest that they follow circle session rules and procedures.

Discussion questions:

The remainder of the period may be devoted to a general class discussion. Some suggested questions follow:

— *What similarities did you notice in what most or all of us saw as being responsible behaviors?*
— *What kinds of things did most of us see as being irresponsible?*
— *When is it easy to be responsible?*
— *What rewards do you get for behaving responsibly?*
— *What boomerangs can occur with irresponsible behavior?*

These People Did ———————————————

——————— Research, Creative Writing, and Drama

Description: In small groups, the students read biographies of people who have changed the world for the better. They then plan, rehearse, and perform scenes dramatizing significant moments in the lives of those people. Discussion follows each scene and a general discussion concludes the activity.

Objectives: The students will:
— research the lives of people who have contributed significantly to the betterment of the world.
— describe how people contribute through community/world action.

Time needed: one class period for directions, assignments, and planning; one to two weeks for individual research; one to two periods for planning and rehearsal of dramatizations; and one to two periods for performances and discussion.

Materials needed: biographies and simple props for the performances

Directions: **Introduce the activity.** Discuss with the students how the world has often been made better by what a single individual has chosen to do, often against strong opposition or general apathy.

Describe the assignment. Tell the students that during the next week (or two) their assignment will be to read books or articles about such a person, and then write a short dramatic scene or sequence about a significant incident in that person's life.

The following individuals are all 19th or 20th century American reformers, easily researchable, and by almost anyone's standards, altruistic and idealistic:
> Robert Owen
> Lucy Stone
> John Peter Altgeld
> Susan B. Anthony
> Julia Ward Howe
> Frederick Douglas
> Dorothea Dix

(Continued Next Page)

These People Did ———————————————

Elizabeth Cady Stanton
Amos Bronson Alcott
William Lloyd Garrison
Harriet Tubman
Dag Hammerskjold
Clara Barton
Ralph Nader
Anthony Comstock
Samuel Gridley Howe
John Muir
Jane Addams
Martin Luther King
Sojourner Truth
John Humphrey Noyes

Add names of your own to this list and urge the students to do likewise. (There are many excellent reference books with short biographies of people who changed the world for the better.) Also list organizations such as the United Nations, UNICEF, the Sierra Club, and other public interest groups that work to effect social and political changes that benefit large numbers of people.

The students may work in groups of two to six to conduct their research. When the groups have been established, ask them to select one student to act as coordinator. Suggest that assignments be planned and allocated to avoid duplication of effort, and a reasonable amount of time allowed for individual research and reading.

Develop the dramatizations. In a later class session, have each group meet separately to plan and rehearse a three- to four-minute dramatic scene illustrating a key incident in the life of the person researched. The presentations should include a short introduction that will tell the other students something about the person whose life is being dramatized, what the person accomplished during his or her lifetime, etc.

Allow one or two class periods for the presentations.

(Continued Next Page)

These People Did

Discussion questions:

Write the names of the people and organizations researched on the board (or have the research groups design a poster with a picture of the person, or the symbol of the organization, and a list of achievements). After each presentation discuss the following points with the class.

— *What motivated this person (or organization) to take action?*

— *What were some of the obstacles encountered?*

— *How were the obstacles overcome?*

— *Did the person (or organization) during his/her own life feel that he or she had accomplished something that had really changed the world?*

— *What have you learned about community action from this activity?*

Special Note:

The following activities are designed to introduce students to the idea of Community Outreach and Volunteerism.

If you choose to involve students in these activities, we recommend that you plan to do all three activities in the order they appear.

A World of Opportunity

Class Discussion and Experience Sheet

Description: Following a class discussion concerning the role of volunteer service, the students conduct individual research and interviews to gather information about problems/issues that need to be addressed in the nation and community, and identify existing volunteer organizations in the community.

Objectives: The students will:
— describe volunteer efforts in which they have participated.
— describe the importance of volunteer community service.
— identify national and community problems that need to be addressed.
— identify volunteer organizations/agencies in the community.

Note: This is the first in a series of three activities focusing on community involvement. It should be followed by the activities, "Choosing to Contribute" and "Becoming Involved."

Time needed: approximately 15 to 20 minutes for an introductory discussion and 2 to 3 days for completion of the experience sheet (outside of class)

Materials needed: chalkboard and chalk; one copy of the experience sheet, "A World of Opportunity" for each student

Directions: **Ask for a show of hands from students who have been involved in some type of volunteer work.** Call on a few individuals and ask them to briefly describe a specific project in which they participated. Keep notes on the board, including a list of organizations that are mentioned, such as scouts, boys/girls clubs, environmental groups, civic or political action groups, health agencies, church/temple, etc. Ask each student to describe any personal benefits derived from the experience.

(**Continued Next Page**)

A World of Opportunity

Discussion questions:

Next, referring to some of the examples that were shared, **facilitate a discussion regarding the necessity and importance of voluntary action.** Keep track of important points by writing them on the board. Here are some questions you might ask:

— *Why do we need to collect food and clothing for the homeless? Isn't it the job of our welfare system to take care of people in need?*

— *Why can't the paid staff at the Heart Association (Cancer Society, Kidney Foundation, United Way, etc.) raise funds and provide services without help from volunteers?*

— *What roles have volunteers played following major oil spills? What would have happened without them?*

— *What motivates people to become volunteer fire fighters, take part in political demonstrations, or reach down and pick up other people's trash?*

Distribute the experience sheets. Explain to the students that the purpose of the experience sheet is to help the class become more aware of how volunteer efforts are needed—and utilized—in the world, the nation, and the community. Go over each of the activities and make sure that the students understand what they are to do. Provide suggestions as needed. Announce a due date for completion of the experience sheet and have the students record the date in the space provided. Allow a couple of days or a weekend.

In the next activity, "Choosing to Contribute," the students will share and summarize the information they gather. The following activity, "Becoming Involved," will guide the students as they organize, implement, and evaluate a volunteer effort of their own.

A World of Opportunity

Some people think that there's a paying job for everything that needs to be done in our world. Not so. If it weren't for volunteer efforts, hundreds of problems would go unsolved, and thousands (perhaps millions) of people would have to do without the things they need to live decently—or to live at all. Help your class identify some of the problems that can be partially solved through volunteer community service. Complete these activities and share the information with your classmates.

*S*urvey three adults. Ask *each person* these questions:

1. *What is the biggest problem facing our nation today? What can each one of us, as an individual, do about it?*
2. *What are the two biggest problems facing our community today? What can each one of us, as an individual, do about them?*

National Problems	What We Can Do
1. _____	_____
_____	_____
_____	_____
2. _____	_____
_____	_____
_____	_____
3. _____	_____
_____	_____
_____	_____

(Continued Next Page)

Community Problems	What We Can Do
1. _____	_____
_____	_____
_____	_____
2. _____	_____
_____	_____
_____	_____
3. _____	_____
_____	_____
_____	_____
4. _____	_____
_____	_____
_____	_____
5. _____	_____
_____	_____
_____	_____
6. _____	_____
_____	_____
_____	_____

(Continued Next Page)

Look through the newspaper. Find an article that describes a problem facing the world, the nation, or your community. It could be related to pollution, hunger, human rights, homelessness, crime, education, health care, efforts to find a cure for a specific disease, or some other issue. **Read the article carefully and summarize the problem here:** _____

_____

_____

Name three things that individual citizens could do *voluntarily* that would help alleviate the problem.

1. _____

2. _____

3. _____

In the space below, write the names of three volunteer organizations or agencies in your community. Briefly explain the purpose of each one.

Here are some suggestions: Use the telephone directory and ask people you know. Call the United Way, which represents many volunteer agencies. Don't guess the purpose of an agency. Telephone the agency and ask the person who answers to explain the purpose to you.

Organization 1: _____

Purpose: _____

Organization 2: _____

Purpose: _____

Organization 3: _____

Purpose: _____

Bring your completed experience sheet to class on _____. Be prepared to share what you have learned with your classmates.

Choosing to Contribute —————

——— **Sharing, Discussion, and Consensus Seeking**

Description: In small groups, the students share and discuss the results of their interviews and research (homework from the previous activity). They then brainstorm ideas for community involvement projects and select three to recommend to the entire class. The class discusses the ideas and selects one (or two) to implement.

Objectives: The students will:
— identify ways that they can become involved in the community.
— select one (or two) community involvement projects for the entire class.

Note: This is the second in a series of three activities focusing on community involvement. It should be preceded by the activity, "A World of Opportunity," and followed by the activity, "Getting Involved."

Time needed: one to two class periods

Materials needed: the completed experience sheets entitled, "A World of Opportunity;" chart paper, masking tape, and marking pen or paper and pencil for each small group; chalkboard and chalk

Directions: If it is your customary procedure, collect and check the experience sheets; however, do not grade them. Give them back to the students before starting this activity.

Ask the students to form small groups of five to eight. If they belong to established circle session groups, these will be ideal. Direct them to bring their completed experience sheets with them to the groups. Ask each group to choose a recorder. Make sure the recorder has either chart paper, masking tape, and marking pen *or* paper and pencil. If chart paper is used, have the recorders tape the paper to the wall for backing.

Explain to the groups that you want them to share the information recorded on their completed experience sheets. There were three separate tasks to complete. Suggest that they take one task at a time, and follow circle session rules and procedures while sharing. Tell the recorders to keep abbreviated, but careful notes on what each person says.

(Continued Next Page)

Choosing to Contribute ────────────

────────────────────── *(Continued)*

When the groups have finished sharing, go around the room
and ask each recorder to quickly summarize the findings of
his or her group for the rest of the class.

Next, enthusiastically invite the students to think of ways that
the class could become constructively involved in the community. Offer these and/or other examples to help the students
generate ideas: *organizing a tutoring program for younger children, collecting cans for recycling, holding a car wash to raise
money for a particular organization, passing out organ-donor
cards and telling people about their importance, visiting elderly
people in retirement/nursing homes, organizing neighborhood
watch groups, creating and performing a series of anti-smoking or
anti-drug/alcohol skits, etc.*

Explain that you want each group to identify and describe
three separate projects that the class could organize and carry
out in the community. Suggest that the projects should meet
these criteria:
• address an identified community need.
• call for a reasonable time and energy (not monetary)
  commitment.
• be something that the majority of the class would enjoy and
  commit to.

Suggest that the groups brainstorm as many ideas at they can think
of, and then, through **consensus**, select the best three. Provide
these rules for brainstorming:
• Set a time limit of 5 to 10 minutes for brainstorming.
• Think of and record as many ideas as you can, being creative
  and not worrying about whether or not the ideas will work.
• Do not evaluate any ideas, either positively or negatively, during
  the brainstorming process.
• When the time is up, stop the process and go back and discuss
  each idea.
• Eliminate unworkable ideas and narrow down the list.
• By consensus, select three ideas that best meet established
  criteria.

(Continued Next Page)

IMPACT! ────────────────────── **Taking Responsibility 275**

Choosing to Contribute

(Continued)

Discussion questions:

Have the recorders post their group's ideas, or write them on the chalkboard.

As a class, read and discuss each idea. Look for ways to combine similar ideas, and eliminate any that are unworkable or do not have the interest of the students. Finally, **select one idea** to implement as a class project (if the class is large, you might prefer to implement two projects).

Conclude the activity by asking the students to discuss how well they worked together in their small groups. Ask these and other questions:
— *How successful were you in following circle rules and procedures?*
— *What was the leadership like in your group? Did one or two people dominate or was leadership shared?*
— *What process did you use to select your three ideas?*
— *If you were asked to complete this kind of group task again, what would you do differently?*

The next activity provides guidelines for organizing and implementing the selected project.

Getting Involved ⸻

⸻ Planning and Implementing a Class Project

Description: This activity is designed to help the students plan, implement, and evaluate the community involvement project selected in the previous activity.

Objectives: The students will:
— clarify the goals and objectives of the project.
— identify and describe steps to accomplishing the goal/objectives of the project.
— assume responsibility for implementing the project.
— evaluate the project.

Note: This is the last of three activities focusing on community involvement. It must be preceded by the activities, "A World of Opportunity," and "Choosing to Contribute."

Time needed: approximately 1 to 2 class periods for planning; 1 class period for evaluation and follow-up

Materials needed: chalkboard and chalk; paper and pencils, and journals (optional) for the students

Directions: **Decide in advance whether or not you will facilitate the planning of the project.** Keep in mind that the students will probably learn more from the process—and perhaps feel greater commitment to the project—if they provide their own leadership. If you decide to let them handle it, be prepared to step aside at the appropriate time, thenceforth serving as a consultant.

Write the name of the class project on the board in large letters for the students to see when they enter the room. Announce that today the class is going to plan the project. Two different planning processes are described below. Choose one, combine the two, or use your own preferred method. If you intend to relinquish leadership at some point, you might want to outline this information on the chalkboard or a guide sheet.

(Continued Next Page)

A. A Linear Planning Process

Formulate a goal statement, incorporating the name or a brief description of the project. For example, the goal statement might be, "To collect items for recycling," or "To provide an after-school tutoring service for elementary students who are having problems with reading."

Formulate a series of objectives that must be met in order to achieve the goal. An objective, in this case, is a milestone on the way to the goal that is specific, measurable, and has a time-line. For example, the first objectives to the above goals might be:

— *By 11/3, obtain information and guidelines from at least three recycling plants.*
— *By 11/3, identify a total of nine elementary teachers in three different schools who will provide children and guidance for tutors.*

Break down each objective into specific steps that must be taken. For example, steps involved in the second objective above might be:

— *List names and locations of elementary schools in the area.*
— *Contact the principal at each school and explain the project to him/her.*
— *Obtain names of likely teachers from the principal.*
— *Visit the teachers, or write them a short letter explaining the project and what they would need to do if involved. Ask for a commitment.*
— *Decide which schools and teachers to include and notify them.*

Assign one or more students to be responsible for each step. Set a deadline for the completion of each step.

(Continued Next Page)

Make sure that attention to student requirements, such as **parent permission, transportation**, and **materials/tools** is included in the planning process.

B. A Visual Planning Process
Formulate a goal statement. Follow the procedure described above.

Make a mind-map of the project. A mind-map is a graphic representation in which the project is pictured or symbolized in the center of a page (or the board), and the major components of the project (roughly equivalent to objectives) are shown as branches emanating from that central point. Subcomponents (roughly equivalent to steps) emanate from the main branches. A mind-map has an organic tree-like look. It can continue to grow in any or all directions as the plan is refined. There is no right or wrong way, no correct or incorrect order, for making a mind-map.

Note: For further information on mind-mapping, see (among others) *Use Both Sides of Your Brain* by Tony Buzan (E.P. Dutton, New York, 1974), *The Brain Book* by Peter Russell, or *Super-Teaching* by Eric Jensen (Turning Point for Teachers, Del Mar, California, 1988).

Make assignments and set deadlines. Add these to the mind-map too.

Implement the project. You might want to ask each student to keep a journal throughout the project.

(Continued Next Page)

Getting Involved ———————————

Follow-up: | **Evaluate the project.** After the project is completed, hold a follow-up meeting to discuss outcomes. Here are some questions to ask the students:
— *What were some of the high points/low points of the project?*
— *How did you benefit from the experience?*
— *Who in the community was helped by the project?*
— *Should the project be continued? If so, how might that be accomplished?*
— *What would you do the same (or more of) next time? What would you do differently?*
— *How did you work together as a team? What did you learn about cooperation, planning, etc.?*
— *What kinds of community involvement would you like to try in the future?*

A week or so after the project is concluded, hold a **circle session** so that the students can share what they learned/gained from the experience. The topic of the circle might be, "An Important Thing I Learned While (Participating in the Recycling Project)," or "Something I Learned About Myself While (Tutoring Children)."

EXPLORING CAREERS

I want to be all that I am capable of becoming

Katherine Mansfield

It is vitally important that students be encouraged to view themselves from as many different perspectives as possible before they begin to look at career options. As they gain insight into their capabilities and limitations; interests and disinterests; and skills and preferences, they can more clearly and objectively see career choices as exciting and challenging, rather than as overwhelming mysteries that seem unattainable or out of reach.

Overall objectives
The students will:
— assess personal aptitudes, interests, and abilities.
— choose alternatives and make decisions to plan and pursue tentative educational and career goals.
— relate careers to the needs and functions of the economy and society.
— identify types and levels of work performed across a broad range of occupations.
— apply skills to locate, understand, and use career information.

A Skill or Talent of Mine that I Could Use in a Job —————— A Circle Session

Objectives: The students will:
— assess personal aptitudes, interests, and abilities relative to career possibilities.
— apply skills to plan or revise a career plan.

Introduce the topic: Say to the students: *Our topic for this session is, "A Skill or Talent of Mine that I Could Use in a Job." We all have skills and talents that we use every day. Some of these skills and talents are important not only to students, but to employees in many different jobs. Perhaps you work well with people. Or maybe your strongest talent lies in dealing with information. Maybe you make friends easily, or handle confrontations tactfully and diplomatically. Perhaps you are good at solving math problems, or organizing materials. Do you like to build or repair things? Do you draw, sing, play a musical instrument, or dance well? All of these skills and talents are useful in certain jobs. Some are useful in many jobs. Tell us about a talent or skill you have and how you could use it in a job. Think it over for a few moments. The topic is, "A Skill or Talent of Mine that I Could Use in a Job."*

Discussion Questions:
— *Which skills and talents were mentioned most often?*
— *Which skills and talents are needed in almost every kind of job?*
— *How can knowledge of your skills and talents assist you in planning a career direction?*

A Job I Would Really Enjoy

A Circle Session

Objectives:	The students will: —describe a job they would enjoy doing. —demonstrate positive attitudes toward work and learning. —relate educational achievement to career opportunities. —relate careers to the needs and functions of the economy and society.
Introduce the topic:	Say to the students: *Our topic for this session is, "A Job I Would Really Enjoy." There are probably many jobs you would enjoy doing. Think of one, and tell us why it appeals to you. Maybe you know you would like to be a park ranger because you love the outdoors and are interested in conservation. Perhaps you're certain you would enjoy being a robotics engineer because you have already successfully built three robots. Maybe you are fascinated with the structure of cities, so you think you would enjoy being a city planner, an architect, or an urban geographer. Maybe independence or travel are your top priorities, so you think you would enjoy being a travel writer. Perhaps you want to contribute to society by developing new sources of energy, so you hope to become a physicist. Think about it for a few moments and then tell us what job you would enjoy and why. The topic is, "One Job I Would Really Enjoy."*
Discussion Questions:	— *What similarities and differences were there among the things we shared?* — *Which of the jobs mentioned would require education beyond high school?* — *How did some of the jobs mentioned meet an important need of society?* — *What skills would be needed in all of the jobs that were mentioned?*

A Job I Think I Would Dislike

A Circle Session

Objective: The students will identify a job or career they don't want to pursue, and describe why it is wrong for them.

Introduce the topic: Say to the students: *Our topic for this session is, "A Job I Think I Would Dislike." We all want to be happy in our jobs. Consequently, we develop opinions about jobs that we think would <u>not</u> make us happy, jobs we would dislike. Can you think of a job you're almost positive you wouldn't want to have? Maybe you wouldn't want to be an accountant because to you the job sounds boring and repetitive, and you would have to work at a desk all day. Perhaps you wouldn't want to be a management consultant because you would have to travel a great deal, and continually work with strangers. Maybe the job of construction worker is not for you because it can be dirty and physically challenging. Maybe you would turn down the opportunity to become a nurse because nursing is a relatively low-paying profession. Take a few moments to think about it. The topic is, "A Job I Think I Would Dislike."*

Discussion Questions:

— *What is the major difference between the job you dislike and one you like?*
— *How were our dislikes similar? How were they different?*
— *How essential to the economy is the job you dislike? How essential is it to society?*
— *What would it take to make you like the job you described?*

A Job I Would (or Would Not) Like To Do Alone — A Circle Session

Objectives:	The students will: — choose alternatives and make decisions related to tentative education and career goals. — identify preferred working conditions.
Introduce the topic:	Say to the students: *Our topic for this session is, "A Job I Would (or Would Not) Like To Do Alone. Some people are very happy working alone; in fact, they prefer it. It allows them to concentrate and be more creative or productive. Other people like to be part of a team. They prefer to share the workload, enjoy the social contacts, and appreciate receiving regular creative input from co-workers. Think of a career area in which you could work <u>either</u> alone or with others, and tell us which you would prefer. For example, an artist can paint alone, or work for an advertising agency with many other people. A computer programmer can work in an office at home, or with a team of other programmers at a large company. A gardener can work alone maintaining small, private yards, or with several assistants, landscaping large apartment buildings. If you could choose, which way would you have it, and why? Take some time to think about it. The topic is, "A Job I Would (or Would Not) Like To Do Alone."*
Discussion Questions:	— *What kinds of jobs might best be done alone?* — *What are some of the advantages of working with others? ...alone?* — *If you preferred to work alone, but your job required you to work with others, how could you handle the dilemma?*

A Job Society Really Needs

A Circle Session

Objective: The students will understand how societal needs and functions influence the nature and structure of work.

Introduce the topic: Say to the students: *Our topic for today is, "A Job Society Really Needs." Almost all jobs fulfill societal as well as personal needs. For example, society needs to have doctors to help care for the sick and injured, contractors and carpenters to build homes, refuse collectors to remove trash, engineers to design bridges, teachers to instruct, and pilots to fly planes. But what is a job that society* really *needs right now? Based on events that are happening in our city, nation, and world, what jobs seem particularly essential? Think about it for a few moments. The topic is, "A Job Society Really Needs."*

Discussion Questions:

— *How would society be affected if some of these jobs were not filled?*
— *Why are some jobs more crucial than others?*
— *Do you think people are compensated better financially for jobs that society really needs? Give an example.*
— *Name a job you think is unnecessary in our society? Why is it unnecessary?*

If I Could Do Anything, with No Limits

A Circle Session

Objectives:

The students will:

— describe what career they would choose if their possibilities were unlimited.

— describe the relationship of career to lifestyle and vise-versa.

Introduce the topic:

Say to the students: *Our topic for this session is, "If I Could Do Anything, with No Limits." Too often, we place limits on ourselves. Sometimes those limits are realistic, but often they are not. We block ourselves because of perceived rather than real limitations. One way to discover what we really want in our lives, both personally and professionally, is to consider what we would do if we had no limitations at all. What would you want your job to be if you didn't have to worry about money, education, or training? Maybe you would be a ski instructor and live in the mountains so that your family could grow up in a natural environment. Perhaps you would like to raise horses or take care of sick animals, if you didn't have to worry about buying a ranch or paying for veterinary school. If you didn't have to worry about supporting yourself, maybe you would write a novel, or become an inventor, or work full time raising funds for the homeless. Tell us about the lifestyle and profession you would want if <u>anything</u> were possible. Take a few moments to think it over. The topic is, "If I Could Do Anything, with No Limits."*

Discussion Questions:

— *How much does a person's job determine his/her lifestyle?*

— *Does lifestyle determine career, or does career determine lifestyle? How?*

— *What happens when we place arbitrary limits on ourselves?*

— *How can you plan a career that is compatible with your desired lifestyle?*

Discover Your Skills ────────────

Experience Sheet and Discussion

Description: The students brainstorm and code a list of personal activities, skills, and likes/dislikes. Next they choose their best, worst and favorite school subjects. A class discussion makes connections between their choices and possible careers/jobs.

Objectives: The student will:
— assess personal aptitudes, interests, and abilities relative to career possibilities.
— relate educational achievement to career opportunities.

Time needed: one class period

Materials needed: pens or pencils, and one copy of the experience sheet, "Activities, Skills, and Likes" for each student

Directions: **Begin by writing the headings, Activities, Skills, and Likes above three separate columns on the board.**

Point out that people engage in numerous activities every day. Inherent in each activity are skills that must be employed in order to accomplish the activity. For example: Skiing is an activity that requires the skills of **balance**, **coordination**, and **spatial perception**. What we like about skiing may be the **scenic beauty** of the mountain, the **company**, **exercise**, **competition**, etc. Using the columns on the board, develop two or three other examples, listing the skills and probable likes inherent in each.

Distribute the experience sheets. Explain that you want the students to each develop a personal activity list, following the example on the board. Suggest that they try to fill the column with activities. As they work, individually assist the students to identify the skills involved in their respective activities. Then walk the class through the coding process. Explain: *In the first column, write "O" if the activity takes place <u>outdoors</u>, "I" if the activity takes place <u>indoors</u>, or "O/I" if the activity takes place either outdoors or indoors. In the second column, write "A" if you do the activity <u>alone</u>, "O" if you do it with <u>others</u>, or "A/O" if you can do it either alone or with others. In the third column, write "L" if you <u>like</u> the activity and "D" if you <u>dislike</u> the activity.*

(Continued Next Page)

Next, have students list their required and elective subjects in the column provided. Again, assist them with the coding process, by explaining: *Look over the list carefully and choose your <u>best</u> subject. Place a plus mark beside it. Next, decide which is your <u>worst</u> subject and indicate it with a minus. Finally, choose your <u>favorite</u> subject and place a star beside it. If your favorite subject is also the one at which you do best, that subject will have two marks beside it. Think carefully when making your choices. Don't confuse your feelings for a course with your feelings for the teacher of the course—they are not the same.*

Finally, ask the students to write "why" statements for their best, worst, and favorite subjects. For example:

- *My best subject is Math because I learn math concepts easily and get A's on all my tests.*
- *My worst subject is Art because I don't draw well and, compared to talented kids in the class, my work always pulls a C.*
- *My favorite subject is Physical Education because I'm on the track team and I love to run.*

Discussion questions:

Allow 3 to 4 minutes for volunteers to share discoveries from their lists. Then lead a class discussion.

— *What kinds of activities did you list?*
— *What skills are inherent in your activities?*
— *What skills did you list that you haven't developed yet? Are you working on them? How?*
— *What kinds of jobs might utilize these skills?*
— *How many of you seem to prefer outdoor activities? ...indoor activities?*
— *How many of you seem to prefer independent activities? ...group activities?*
— *How might these factors affect your choice of a career?*
— *What surprised you the most about your list of skills?*
— *What relationships do you see between your list of activities and your list of courses?*

Discover Your Skills ───────

─────────────── **Experience Sheet**

O/I	A/O	L/D	Activities	Skills	Likes

(Continued Next Page)

List Required Subjects and Electives

	Best	Worst	Favorite

My best subject is _____ **because**

_____

_____

My worst subject is _____ **because**

_____

_____

My favorite subject is _____ **because**

_____

_____

When Money Counts

Research and Discussion

Description: The students list jobs they might like to have in the future. Then, utilizing the *Occupational Outlook Handbook,* they gather information about salaries, training requirements, job outlook, and related jobs. A discussion follows.

Objectives: The student will:
— apply skills in locating, understanding, and using career information.
— identify types and levels of work performed across a broad range of occupations.
— relate careers to the needs and functions of the economy and society.

Time needed: one to two class periods

Materials needed: paper, pens or pencils, and copies or reprints of *Occupational Outlook Handbook,* (If not available in your library or career center, the Handbook may be obtained by writing to Superintendent of Documents, U.S. Government Printing Office, Washington, DC 20402.)

Directions: **Begin by asking the students what careers or jobs they think they might like to have in the future.** Elicit several responses. When students mention categories instead of specific jobs, jot the categories down on the chalkboard. For example, *law* is a category within which there are many different jobs, only one of which is *lawyer* (and there are many different types of lawyers). Likewise, teacher, artist, and business manager might be considered categories. Teaching skills, for example, are used by school teachers at all levels, college professors, corporate and military trainers, health professionals, fitness trainers, recreational specialists, salespeople, etc. Urge the students to be open to examining the enormous variety of specific jobs within any one category.

Next, working individually, have the students make a list of careers or jobs they might like to have.

(Continued Next Page)

When Money Counts ————————————

————————————————— (Continued)

Introduce the students to the *Occupational Outlook Handbook.*
Explain that the handbook lists thousands of job titles, along with
the salary range, education/training requirements, and current/
projected outlook (demand) for each job. Show the students how
the handbook is organized. Help them to use the handbook to
locate the careers/jobs on their individual lists, writing down the
salary, education/training, and outlook for each job. In addition,
suggest that for every job on their list, they find <u>two related jobs</u>
of which they were previously unaware, and add these to their list,
too.

**Discussion
questions:**

When the students have completed their examination of the
handbook and finished their information search, conduct a discus-
sion about their findings.   Ask questions like the following:
— *What <u>new</u> jobs did you identify?*
— *Which jobs require the most education/training?*
— *What relationship did you discover between education/training
and salaries?*
— *What kinds of jobs seem to have the best outlook? ...the worst
outlook?*
— *What was the most unusual job title you saw?*
— *What need or function does the job of _____ fill in
society?*

Picture This . . . —————————————————

Brainstorming and Discussion

Description: After listing characteristics about themselves in four areas (values, goals, family goals, and skills), the students select preferred conditions from four lists of job characteristics. Based on a comparison of the personal and occupational information generated, the students select two compatible jobs/careers.

Objectives: The student will:
— make decisions and choose alternatives in planning and pursuing career goals.
— understand the interrelationship of life goals and careers.

Time needed: one class period

Materials needed: one copy of the experience sheet, "Picture This" for each student; information generated from the activity, "When Money Counts"

Directions: **Begin by explaining that when we have a picture of the kind of lifestyle we desire, we can better develop and direct our career plans.**

Pass out the "Picture This" worksheet. Go over the directions on side one. Elicit some examples of values, goals, family goals, and skills. List them on the board. Give the students time to complete side one. Circulate and offer assistance to individual students, as needed.

Ask the students to turn their sheet over. Note that while side one asked for characteristics about the students, side two lists characteristics of jobs. Tell the students to circle one or two items in each category to get a picture of conditions under which they prefer to work.

Have the students pair up and take turns sharing the information generated with a partner.

(Continued Next Page)

Picture This . . .

Discussion questions:

Finally, have the students compare the job information gathered through the activity, "When Money Counts" with the choices made in this activity. Tell them to identify the <u>two jobs/careers</u> that appear to best satisfy these combined criteria. When the students have made their decisions, lead a class discussion.

—*What connections did you discover between your personal goals and your job goals? ...your family goals and your job goals? ...your skills and your job goals?*

—*What career choices look promising?*

—*What are some important issues to consider when making career choices?*

—*Which of your choices appeared to be in conflict?*

Picture This . . .

Directions: In each category, list things that are true *for you*. List things you <u>value</u>, like travel, exercise, beautiful surroundings, friends, etc. List future <u>goals</u>, like graduating from college, owning a home, buying a particular car, etc. List <u>family goals</u>, such as when (and if) you want to marry, have children, etc. Finally, list some of your <u>skills</u>, <u>aptitudes</u>, and <u>interests</u>.

Values	Goals
Family Goals	**Skills, Aptitudes, Interests**

(Continued Next Page)

Now Picture This . . .

Directions: In each category, circle two or three items that describe the job conditions *you* prefer.

Rewards

High Pay
Excitement
Commissions
Responsibility
Recognition
Adventure
Security
Risk
Flexible Time
Emotional Satisfaction
Other _____

Level of Responsibility

No Decisions
Some Decisions
Decision Maker
Own Boss
Work for Someone
Team Effort
Creativity
Limited Stress
Power
Freedom
Other _____

Place

Indoor
Outdoor
Office
Home
Shop
Warehouse
Garage
Hospital
School
Church
Factory
Other _____

Working with

No one else
Many others
Adults
Children
Senior Citizens
Animals
Information
Things
Hands
Art
Machines
Other _____

What Do I Want to Be When I Grow Up? —————— Research

Description: The students research the two jobs/careers selected in the previous activity and record the information on the accompanying worksheet. A class discussion culminates the activity.

Objectives: The student will:
— relate educational achievement to career opportunities.
— research, evaluate and interpret information about career opportunities.
— apply skills to locate, understand, and use career information.

Time needed: one to two class periods

Materials needed: *Dictionary of Occupational Titles,* various career materials from the library, previous completed worksheets, and two copies of the worksheet, "Gathering Career Information" for each student

Directions: **Review the steps taken and information gathered in the previous career activities.** Announce that in this activity, each student will gather in-depth information about the two career choices made in the activity, "Picture This."

Discussion questions: **Distribute the worksheets.** Note that some of the information called for on the sheet has already been obtained in previous exercises. Show, and/or list on the board sources for obtaining additional information. Circulate and assist the students while they complete the worksheet. When the students have finished, lead a class discussion.
— *How likely are you to pursue one of the careers you researched?*
— *What information surprised or concerned you?*
— *What will be the most difficult part of obtaining your career goal?*
— *Are you more or less interested in this career now that you have a greater familiarity with it?*

Gathering Career Information ———

Choose a job title for one career choice. Fill in "Job Title." Then, answer the questions about the job as completely and specifically as you can with the available resources.

Job Title _____

1. List specific duties performed in the job.

   _____

   _____

   _____

2. Where is the job performed? (Indoors, outdoors, office, factory, etc.)

   _____

   _____

   _____

3. What makes the job particularly appealing to you?

   _____

   _____

   _____

4. What kinds of rewards does the job offer?

   _____

   _____

   _____

5. How much education or training is required for this job?

   _____

   _____

   _____

6. Where could you receive the necessary training or education?

   _____

   _____

   _____

7. What are the physical requirements, if any?

_____

_____

_____

8. What is the approximate starting salary? ...the approximate mid-career salary?

_____

_____

_____

9. Will the number of jobs available in this field by the time you are prepared to enter the job market be low, moderate, or high?

_____

_____

_____

10. What special talents or abilities are required for the job?

_____

_____

_____

11. What can you do <u>now</u> to begin preparing for the job?

_____

_____

_____

12. What high school classes will help you prepare for the job?

_____

_____

_____

13. In what geographical areas of the state/nation/world is the job available?

_____

_____

_____

Expertly Speaking ————————————

———————————— ## Interviews and Discussion

Description:	The students plan and conduct interviews with two workers in the career fields of their choice. A class discussion follows the interviews.
Objectives:	The student will: — research, evaluate and interpret information about career opportunities. — choose alternatives and make decisions to plan and pursue tentative educational and career goals.
Time needed:	30 to 35 minutes of class time, and varying amounts of time outside of class
Materials needed:	two interview worksheets for each student
Directions:	**Introduce the activity by saying to the students:** *One valuable way to gain insight into a career is to interview someone who is already doing the job you're interested in. Such a person can offer information not easily found in resource materials. Many employment counselors and career experts recommend this approach. Since most people like to talk about themselves as well as help others, they are often willing to give informational interviews to students.*

Students who already know someone working in their field of interest can contact that person. If they do not know someone, suggest that they consult a teacher, fellow students, parents, professional organizations, unions, employment offices, the librarian, the Chamber of Commerce, service clubs such as Rotary, Lions, etc., or the yellow pages of the telephone directory.

Elicit from the students suggestions concerning how to contact prospective interviewees. Here are some examples:
- State your name and school clearly.
- Describe the purpose of your call.
- Describe the reason for the interview.
- Schedule a specific time for the interview.
- Obtain directions, if necessary.

(Continued Next Page)

Expertly Speaking ———————————

(Continued)

Discussion questions:

Remind the students that business and professional people usually maintain busy schedules and that, on the day of the interview, they should:
- Plan to be prompt.
- Dress appropriately.
- Terminate the interview at the agreed upon time.
- Introduce themselves, shake hands, be polite, maintain eye contact throughout the interview, and do more listening than talking.

Following the interviews, allow class time for sharing and discussion. Ask questions such as the following:
— *Which aspects of the job were in keeping with the information you gathered through your research? ...which differed?*
— *What was the most interesting piece of information you learned from the interview?*
— *How has your attitude about this job changed?*

Note: Designate class time for writing thank-you notes to the interviewees.

Expertly Speaking ───────────

─────────────────── **Interview Worksheet**

Name: _____

Job Title: _____

How many years have you worked in this profession? _____

Describe your educational background and preparation. _____

_____

_____

Would you do anything differently if you had an opportunity to live your

educational years over again? If so, what? _____

_____

_____

What do you feel would be the best approach for me to prepare for this career?

_____

_____

_____

How does this career fit into the needs and functions of the economy and

society? _____

_____

_____

What is the best and the worst aspect for you about this job? _____

_____

_____

Did you work in any other job/career prior to this one? If so, what, and did it

lead to this one? _____

_____

_____

Do you feel you will experience a career change before you retire? If so, what

would the change be? _____

_____

Getting From Here to There ————————

————————————————— **Research and Sharing Groups**

Description:

Using various resource materials, the students estimate the cost of selected colleges and technical/trade schools, complete an income-expense worksheet, and explore sources of financial aid.

Objective:

The students will research, evaluate and interpret information concerning the expenses of post high-school education, and the financial resources available to meet those expenses.

Time needed:

two class periods, several weeks apart

Materials needed:

a variety of college catalogs (both 2- and 4-year); brochures and catalogs from technical schools, business schools, and branches of the military; samples of bulletins and financial-aid information from all types of colleges and vocational/technical schools; and one copy of the experience sheet, "Getting From Here to There," for each student

Distribute the experience sheets. Go over them with the students. In your own words, say: *Based on your research, you have a pretty clear picture of the education and/or training needed for the career you desire. Whatever career choice you make will probably require money, and that can be discouraging if your resources are limited. Examine the catalogs and brochures to gain a clearer picture of the costs of education and/or training. Then, using the experience sheet for your notes, figure the expense of tuition and fees, books and supplies, room and board, transportation, and personal expenses such as clothing, laundry, entertainment, etc. Add up all expenses to reach an approximate total figure. Then estimate your income from all sources. Subtract your income estimate from your expense estimate. The balance is the amount that you must finance through scholarships, loans, or employment.*

(Continued Next Page)

Encourage the students to read about different sources of financial aid. Explore with them various options available for financing an education. Here are some examples:

- **Scholarships** and **grants** that do not have to be repaid. Some are based on financial need, others on scholastic achievement, athletics, or special ability in the arts.
- **Loans**, which must be paid back, usually with interest. Educational loans frequently have lower interest rates; repayment begins after graduation.
- The **military** offers opportunities for education and training, both during and after a period of enlistment.
- Full or part-time **employment**. Completing an education this way takes longer, but does not entail the repayment of loans.

Extension: Have each student request information and application materials from at least three sources of financial aid. Help them choose sources that are appropriate to their tentative college/technical school choices. On a specific date, have the students bring their materials to class and share them. Group the students according to whether their information primarily addresses the military, 4-year colleges, community colleges, or technical/trade schools. Following a discussion period, have each group report its findings to the class.

Getting From Here to There ——————

Experience Sheet

Looking through catalogs and brochures, examine two colleges or trade schools you could attend to obtain your career goal. Using the figures you find, fill in the two columns for each with the approximate amounts for the items listed to determine the cost of one year's schooling/training. Then, estimate your sources of income and fill in the blanks.

Estimate of Yearly Expenses	College/ Trade School	College/ Trade School
Tuition & fees	$	$
Books & supplies		
Room & Board		
Transportation		
Personal		
Entertainment		
Miscellaneous		
TOTAL	$	$
Sources of Yearly Income		
Savings	$	$
Parent contribution		
Summer work		
Other		
TOTAL	$	$

<u>Subtract total income from total expenses to determine the amount of financial aid needed.</u>

How Most People Get Jobs!

A Networking Activity

Description:	The students are visually and orally presented with a story in which a person uses her networking skills to get a job. Groups of students role play the story and three other networking situations. Finally, the students research the incidence of networking by completing the experience sheet, "How Did You Get Your Last Job."
Objectives:	The students will: —explain and demonstrate the use of networking to reach employment goals. —define networking and state why it works.
Time needed:	45 minutes to one hour
Materials needed:	one copy of the experience sheet, "Does Networking Really Work?" for each student; the following chart drawn on a large piece of chart paper or on the chalkboard:

Maria	**Tom**	**Mr. Harris**	**Mrs. Gomez**
Wants a part-time job. Enjoys small children.	Needs transportation 5 miles a day to his job in Putville.	Owns a pizza shop. Needs a delivery person.	Wants to sell a dining room set.
Dave	**Susanna**	**Bob**	**Dennis**
Sandy	**Terri**	**Jack**	**Jan**
Joe	**Sal & Nancy**	**Angie**	**Lee**
Makes two deliveries each day to Putville, morning and afternoon.	Got married last month. They need a dining room set.	Has two small children. Needs a baby-sitter.	Has a car and needs a part-time job.

(Continued Next Page)

How Most People Get Jobs!

Directions:

Ask the students if they have ever heard the word "network-ing," and talk with them about its meaning and importance. Explain that when researchers asked thousands of people how they got their jobs, sixty to eighty percent answered by saying they received help (a tip, good advice, recommendations, etc.) from friends, family members, former co-workers, etc. The word *networking* may be a bit overused, but it's a handy one. It means *soliciting the assistance of other people to reach a personal goal.* Explain that the activity the students are about to do illustrates how networking is done. Later, the students will conduct their own research to establish how well networking works in the real world.

Introduce the chart and explain: *Here's how a network works. The people in Rows 1 and 4 have wants and needs. But they don't even know each other. The people in Row 1 only know the people in Row 2. The people in Row 2 only know the people in Rows 1 and 3. The people in Row 3 only know the people in Rows 2 and 4. The people in Row 4 only know the people in Row 3. So, in order for the people in Rows 1 and 4 to find each other, they have to get help from the people in Rows 2 and 3.*

Using the chart as a visual aid, and drawing lines from Maria to Dennis to Terri to Angie, read the students the following story about Maria, the first person in Row One:

Maria is a senior in high school and is looking for a way to earn some extra money. She really likes small children and would enjoy babysitting, but she just moved to the area and doesn't know very many people. One day, Maria meets Dennis in the hall. He lives in one of the other apartments on her floor. He says, "Hi," and they begin to talk.

Dennis is married and in his twenties. Maria asks him, "Do you and your wife have any children?"

"No, we don't," he responds. But Maria doesn't give up. She asks him if he knows anyone with children who might need a baby-sitter.

(Continued Next Page)

Dennis thinks for a minute and says, "Yeah. I have a sister, Terri, who lives two blocks away. She doesn't have kids either, but a lot of people in her building do and she knows them. I'll tell her to call you, okay?"

Maria thinks for a moment. She likes what she is hearing but she wants to keep control of this situation herself. She smiles and says, "Thanks. Would it be okay with you if I called her myself?"

"No problem," says Dennis.

Maria asks Dennis to wait for a moment. She darts back into her apartment and quickly returns with pencil and paper. She writes down Terri's number and thanks Dennis warmly.

"Good luck," says Dennis. "Let me know what happens."

"I sure will," Maria answers. Then she goes inside and calls the number. She hears a young woman's voice and asks, "Is this Terri?"

The woman says, "Yes, it is. Who is this?"

Then Maria says, "Terri, my name is Maria Martinez and I live in the building your brother Dennis lives in. Dennis and I were just talking and he gave me your name and number. I'm new to the area and I'm looking for some babysitting work. Dennis said you don't have any children but you live in a building with some families that do. Do you have any friends in the building I might call to see if they could use a baby-sitter?"

"What a coincidence!" says Terri. "I sure do. My friend, Angie, in the next apartment just asked me yesterday if I knew anyone who might be able to baby-sit for her three nights a week when she goes to class. I'll tell her to call you. What's your phone number?"

(Continued Next Page)

Maria realizes that it's a good idea to give Terri her phone number, but she knows that Terri might not see Angie for a few days, or she might even forget. "My number is 452-8977." she says. Then she adds, "This is great! Do you, by any chance, have Angie's number? I'd really like to call her myself."

Well, it all works out fine. Maria calls Angie and starts babysitting for her two days later. For the next year she baby-sits for Angie and lots of Angie's friends. And it all started the day she had that little talk with Dennis out in the hall.

Discuss the story with the students. Ask them:
— *What did Maria do well?*
— *What mistakes could Maria have made that she didn't make?*
— *Would you say Maria used polite persistence? Why?*

Pick four volunteers and have them act out the story in front of the class.

Then pick three more teams of volunteer actors, with four people on each team. Have them create extemporaneous dramatic presentations of the other three situations shown on the chart.

Hold a final discussion. Ask the students the following questions:
— *What are the key ideas this activity teaches us?*
— *Have you ever networked before, maybe without even realizing at the time that you were networking? If so, how did it work?*

Distribute the experience sheet, "Does Networking Really Work?" and read it over with the students. Work out a realistic time frame for canvasing job holders. Set a date for tallying the results as a class.

(Continued Next Page)

How Most People Get Jobs!

After the class has tallied its findings and calculated the percentages, point out to the students: *These results show how many people got jobs with the help of other people. Some of them did it skillfully; others probably were not so skillful.—yet networking worked. Imagine how much higher the networking percentage would be if everyone knew how to network skillfully. That's what we've been learning how to do!*

Does Networking Really Work? ———

Experience Sheet

Experts who have conducted surveys report that 60% to 80% of the people in the workforce have obtained their jobs through networking. These people received help from other people. This is a very impressive percentage and some people have trouble believing it.

Why not join the other students in your class and conduct a survey? Canvas some people you know. Each time you get a response, check the line below that best matches what the person tells you.

Approach as many people with jobs as you can and ask them, "How did you get the job you have now? Did you...

See an ad in the paper and answer it?_____

Go to an employment agency?_____

Write a letter to the company and send along your resume?_____

Get a tip, suggestion, or a recommendation from a friend, relative, neighbor, or some other person? _____
_____

Get your job some other way? How?"

_____
_____
_____
_____

(Continued Next Page)

Tally your results.

Write your totals on the lines below. When your teacher tallies the results in class, write in the class totals in the parentheses.

How many people did you canvas?_____ (_____)

How many got their jobs through each of these categories:

     Ads_____ (_____)   Agencies_____ (_____)

     Letters_____ (_____)   Networking_____ (_____)

     Other_____ (_____)

Now do some math.

Figure out the percentages in each category based on the results for the entire class.

The highest percentage went to:_____ with _____ percent.

The second highest percentage went to:_____ with _____ percent.

The third highest percentage went to:_____ with _____ percent.

The lowest percentage went to:_____ with _____ percent.

Use this space for your notes:

Team Building

> *What energy is to the individual, synergy is to groups. When team concepts are applied to group formation, the result is not only the effective use of energy, but also the creation of new energy.*
>
> H.B. Karp, Ph.D.

Ironically, while industry is abandoning worker isolation as an effective avenue to productivity, schools still cling to it. For the most part, students are expected to work alone rather than in teams, and to compete, rather than cooperate. Yet when they leave school, your students will work in environments where they will move from one problem-solving team to another, and from one program to another on a regular basis. By having your students work in teams now, you are helping them prepare for this reality.

These activities bring team building to the here and now of your classroom. Students learn to observe and help one another, share leadership and responsibility, experience the synergy of creative problem-solving, and share in the collective pride of team achievement.

Overall objectives:
The activities in this unit will assist students to:
— understand how teams develop
— examine their own behavior in team situations.
— make decisions about what constitutes more and less effective behavior in team situations.
— practice decision making and problem solving in teams.

My Favorite Team ——————————————

A Circle Session

Objectives:

The students will:
— describe the importance of teamwork to accomplishing group goals.
— describe qualities and behaviors that contribute to effective teamwork.

Introduce the topic:

Say to the students: *Today we're going to talk about teams and the qualities that seem to make them successful. Our topic is, "My Favorite Team."*

Think of your favorite team and tell us what it is and why you like it. Maybe your favorite team is one to which you belong, such as a school athletic team, cheerleading team, chess team, or a project team in one of your other classes. Or perhaps your favorite team is a professional baseball, football, soccer, or hockey team. You can choose a team that exists today, or one that you belonged to when you were a child. You can also describe any group of people that acts like a team, even though the group isn't usually called a team. Tell us what you think makes your team a good team. You might want to mention what the team has accomplished, or describe how individual members of the team contribute to its success. Think about it for a few moments. The topic is, "My Favorite Team."

Discussion Questions:

— *What is a team?*
— *What did most of the teams we mentioned have in common?*
— *Must a team have a purpose or goal? Why or why not?*
— *How are teams usually organized?*
— *What are some of the qualities of a good team member?*

Connect!

A Preliminary Team Experience

Description: Working silently, teams of students attempt to assemble eight identical squares from puzzle parts distributed randomly among them. An Observer notes the behaviors of each team and describes his/her observations at the conclusion of play. All players participate in a culminating discussion.

Objectives: The students will:
— coordinate their actions to solve a problem.
— identify specific cooperative and competitive behaviors and describe how they affect completion of a team task.

Time needed: approximately 40 minutes

Materials needed: construction paper or tag board (one color only) with which to make a set of puzzle pieces for each group of players (see "Preparation," below); table and chairs for each group of players

Preparation: Start with <u>eight</u> 8-inch by 8-inch squares of construction paper or tag board for <u>each</u> team. Individually cut each square into three to five smaller pieces (see illustration). Place all of the pieces in an envelope.

Directions: **If the entire class is playing, ask the students to form teams of five to eight.** Have each team sit around a table, and select one member to be its Observer. Announce that all other team members are players.

Take the Observers aside and say to them: *Your job is to stand beside the table while your team is playing the game and notice what happens. Be prepared to describe such things as how well the group works together, who shares puzzle parts and who does not; whether members concentrate only on the puzzle in front of them or watch the progress of all the puzzles; cooperative vs. competitive behaviors; any conflicts that occur and how they are resolved.*

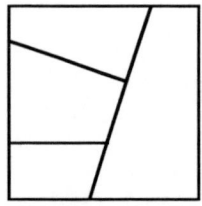 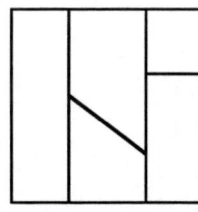 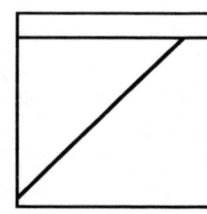 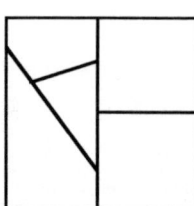

(Continued Next Page)

Read aloud the following rules of play:

1. Your task is to assemble eight squares of **EQUAL** size.
2. There will be **NO** talking, pointing, or other nonverbal communication.
3. A player may pass puzzle parts to any other team member <u>at any time</u>.
4. You may **NOT** take, ask for, or indicate in any way that you *want* another team member's puzzle pieces.
5. There is no time limit. The game is over when you have finished the task.

Distribute the puzzle pieces randomly among the players. Give each player approximately the same number of pieces.

Give the signal to start play.

At the conclusion of play, have the Observers give feedback to their team. If several teams are playing, have the Observers do this simultaneously. Advise the teams to follow circle session rules, i.e., to listen carefully, and not to interrupt, argue with, or put down the Observer in any way.

Discussion Questions:

Assemble all of the teams and encourage them to talk about their experience. Ask these and other open-ended questions:

— *What did you learn from your Observer?*
— *What was the object of the game?*
— *Which kind of behavior was most effective in this game, cooperative or competitive? Why?*
— *What are some of the effects of competitive behavior on a team? ...of cooperative behavior?*
— *If you could play the game again, how would you change your own behavior?*
— *What did you learn from this experience?*

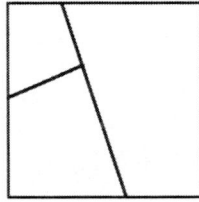 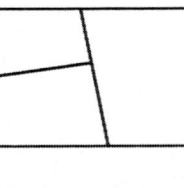 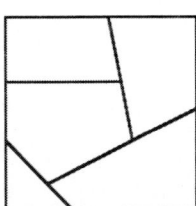 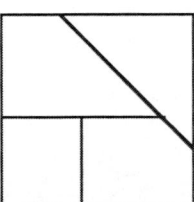

The Spirit Club ———————————————

A Group Simulation

Description: Students participate in an imaginary group decision-making situation in order to learn more about what happens in similar real-life situations. Some students are given specific roles to play; others play themselves; still others act as observers. A discussion and debriefing concludes the activity.

Objectives: The students will:
— work as a group to reach a decision.
— describe how roles played by individuals affect group dynamics and task completion.
— identify individual "agendas" and describe how they affect the group.

Time needed: one class period

Materials needed: one set of nine 3-inch by 5-inch **Role Cards**, each printed with a role description, as follows:

1. **Information Giver:** You point out facts, ask questions, and give information.
2. **Evaluator:** You encourage the group to talk about the pros and cons of each suggestion. You secretly decide that you will support the idea that is best supported by facts and information.
3. **Clarifier:** You try to make sure everyone understands every idea and suggestion.
4. **Topic Switcher:** You keep getting off the subject.
5. **Facilitator:** You help others participate and suggest ways to share ideas.
6. **Harmonizer:** You try to ease tension and settle any conflicts that occur.
7. **Leader:** You want to be the leader of the group, and attempt to take charge of the meeting.
8. **Clown:** You get bored, and start telling jokes to try to make the task more fun. You secretly hope the money will be used toward a trip to Disney World.
9. **Dropout:** You think the faculty advisor and school administrators should make the decision. You say so, and then back off.

(Continued Next Page)

The Spirit Club

Directions:

Choose from 10 to 15 volunteers to participate in the simulation game. Have them move their desks or chairs into a circle near the center of the room. Have the remaining students form an outer circle, and announce that they will be observers. Instruct the observers to take notes so that they can describe what they see to the class in a debriefing session, later. Suggest that they pay attention to both **content** (*what* happens) and **process** (*how* it happens).

Read the task to the players. Say: *You belong to the Spirit Club here at school. The club sponsors dances and other special events. It pays for these events by selling soft drinks, hot dogs, and snacks at games, concerts, and other school functions. This year, the club has made a lot more money than expected. After all expenses and special events have been paid for, there is still $4,000 left. Your task, as a member of the finance committee, is to recommend to the entire club how the extra money should be used. The club's faculty advisor has said that s/he will support any responsible decision the finance committee makes.*

Randomly distribute the role cards to the players. Tell them to memorize their role and then put the card away or give it back to you. Caution them not to divulge their role to other players. If any players have questions about their roles, assist them privately. Instruct those without role cards to play themselves.

Convene the meeting, playing the part of the faculty advisor. Answer any questions the committee members have about the task, and then announce that you have an errand to run and will return in 30 minutes. Take your place among the observers.

(Continued Next Page)

The Spirit Club ———————————————

**Discussion
Questions:**

At the end of 30 minutes, stop the meeting and lead a debriefing session. Use these and other open-ended questions to debrief the players. Then ask the observers to describe their observations. During any remaining time, facilitate a total class discussion.

— *How did you feel in your role?*

— *What problems did you have playing your role?*

— *What behaviors were most helpful to the group?*

— *What behaviors were least helpful?*

— *What would have helped the group reach a decision more easily?*

— *How did the "hidden agendas" of some group members affect the process?*

— *How was this like real group situations you've experienced?*

— *What did you learn from this activity?*

Variation: Design a situation more in keeping with the interests and experiences of your students. The role definitions and discussion questions are generic; only the hidden agenda of the "clown" will need to be changed.

A Role I Play in Groups ————————

A Circle Session

Objectives:

The students will:
—identify specific roles they play in group situations.
—describe how roles help and hinder a group's progress.

Introduce the topic:

Say to the students: *Today, we're going to talk about some of the things we typically do and say in group situations. The topic is, "A Role I Play in Groups."*

We all have many different roles in life. We are children to our parents, role models to our younger brothers and sisters, students at school, and employees at our jobs. In group situations, we take on still other kinds of roles. These roles are often related to what we want to see happen in the group. For example, if you want everyone in a group to be happy, you may play the role of Harmonizer. If you enjoy making decisions, you may take on the role of Leader. If you are in a bad mood, you may become the group's Antagonist. Are you usually quiet in groups? Are you a person who asks lots of questions? Do you tend to clown around a lot? Recall a group you were part of recently, or a club whose meetings you attend, and tell us about your role in that group. Think about it quietly for a few moments. The topic is, "A Role I Play in Groups."

Discussion Questions:

— *Why do people play different roles in groups?*
— *What determines whether a role is "good" or "bad"?*
— *In what kind of situation would the role of Clown be helpful to a group?*
— *In what kind of situation would the role of Harmonizer <u>not</u> be helpful to a group?*
— *How can you become more aware of the roles you play in groups?*
— *If you don't like a role you often play, how can you change it?*

Alphabet Names ———————————————

———————————————— **Achieving Group Synergy**

Description: Working first alone and then in small groups, the students brainstorm famous names to match given sets of initials. They compare their performance and commitment levels under the two sets of conditions.

Objectives: The students will:
— compare the feelings, performance, and commitment levels experienced when performing a task alone and in small groups.
— describe how individual motivation affects individual performance.
— describe how individual and group motivation affects group synergy.

Time needed: approximately 45 minutes

Materials needed: individual writing materials, and one sheet of chart paper and magic marker for each small group

Directions: **Have each student take out a sheet of paper.** Instruct the students to list the letters of the alphabet from "A" through "Z" in a vertical column down the left side of the sheet.

Randomly select a sentence from any document and read aloud the first twenty-six letters in that sentence. Tell the students to write these letters in a second vertical column to the right of the first. Every student should end up with the same twenty-six sets of letters.

Tell the students that they now have 10 minutes to individually record the names of famous people whose initials correspond with the twenty-six sets of letters. The people can be politicians, authors, inventors, film stars, musicians, etc. Only one name may be recorded for each set of initials. Announce that the maximum score is twenty-six points, one for each legitimate name.

At the end of 10 minutes, have the students exchange and "grade" each other's papers. Allow a few moments to verify any questionable names. Then have the students call out their scores while you jot them on the board. Circle the high score and ask the students to see who can be the first to compute and call out the average score. Write it on the board, too.

(Continued Next Page)

324 *IMPACT!*   **Team Building**

Alphabet Names ———————————

Have the students form teams of five to eight. Give each team a sheet of chart paper and a magic marker. Have each team choose a recorder. Announce that *working together as a team*, the students have 10 minutes to develop a second list of famous names. Have the recorder list the letters of the alphabet in a vertical column on the chart paper; then read the first 26 letters from a newly selected passage of text.

Call time after 10 minutes and check the lists. Record the team scores and average score on the board. Compare them with the individual scores. Then lead a discussion, focusing on the differences in motivation, frustration, enjoyment, and achievement experienced working individually and in teams.

Discussion Questions:

— *How did your individual score compare with your team score?*
— *What feelings did you have working individually? ...working with a team?*
— *How well did your team work together?*
— *Which did you experience most when working individually, a sense of competition or collaboration? Why?*
— *Which did you experience most when working with a team? Why?*
— *Were you more motivated to think of names when you were working alone or as part of a team? Why?*
— *What did you learn from this activity?*

Variations: Tailor the task to your subject area. For example, if you are teaching history, require that the students list only historical names. If your subject is geography, omit one of the columns of letters and require that the students list geographical names. In science, have the students list elements, compounds, names of rocks, or parts of the body.

Becoming a Team ———————————————

——————— ## Presentation, Role Play, and Discussion

Description:	Volunteers role play four stages of group development as the teacher presents them. A discussion follows.
Objectives:	The students will: — identify four stages of group development. — describe the characteristics of each stage. — evaluate the development of a real-life group.
Time needed:	one class period
Directions:	**Begin by asking the students to help you define the word** *team.* Say to them: *Six students who sit at different desks, work on individual assignments, and receive separate grades are not a team. When they sit around a table and work on a project together, however, they start becoming a team.*

Try to reach consensus on a definition. For example:

> *A team is a group of people working together, or doing some activity together.*

Ask the students to imagine a scenario with you. Say to them: *Suppose I call six of you aside and tell you that you are now the official stress-management team for the class. I think stress interferes with learning, and your job is to figure out ways to reduce stress in the classroom. I want you to get started right away. Do you become an team instantly? No. You have to* develop *into a team. Along the way, you will probably go through several stages.*

Choose six volunteers to play the part of the stress-management team. Have them act out the stages of group development as you present them.

Explain the following stages, one stage at a time. Make notes on the board. Then have the actors role play that stage. (Coaching suggestions are in italics.) Stop the action after 2 or 3 minutes and go on to the next stage.

(Continued Next Page)

Becoming a Team ─────────────────────────

STAGES OF GROUP DEVELOPMENT

STAGE 1: The team looks for <u>leadership</u> and <u>directions</u>.
You look at each other and ask, "What are we supposed to do?" You feel somewhat confused. Maybe you ask your teacher for help, but for the most part, you realize you're on your own.

STAGE 2: The team starts to <u>organize</u>. <u>Conflicts</u> emerge and are settled.
You try to figure out all the different parts of the job. For example, you have to decide what kinds of activities reduce stress, who will lead them, how often they will be done, what equipment and materials are needed for each activity, etc. In the process of getting organized, you sometimes disagree about who should do things and how they should be done.

STAGE 3: <u>Information flows freely</u> and members <u>feel good</u> about the team.
The team is organized and conflicts are settled. You find yourselves working together extremely well.

STAGE 4: The team can <u>solve problems</u>. Members are <u>interdependent</u>.
The team seems to be able to tackle anything. Creative ideas are abundant. Members work alone, in pairs, or as a total group with equal success. Every member of the team is valued and is depended upon by every other member.

Discussion Questions:

After the dramatizations, ask these and other open-ended questions to facilitate discussion:
— *Why do groups have to develop?*
— *What kinds of things might help a group move to higher stages?*
— *What kinds of things might slow a group down or prevent its development?*
— *What happens when a group can't get past stage one? ...stage two?*
— *Think of a real-life group or team you belong(ed) to. What stage of development did it reach? How could you tell?*

Extension:

Have the students identify a group or team to which they belong(ed) and describe its development in writing. Explain that the group can be a scout club, church group, athletic team, or just a group of friends. Require that the students support their conclusions.

Looking for Leadership —————————

————————— **Presentation and Discussion**

Description: | The students listen to several scenarios involving group or team situations and decide what kind of leadership is being provided in each scenario. Throughout the activity, the teacher facilitates a discussion about leadership and leadership styles.

Objectives: | The students will:
— define leadership as a process and a shared responsibility in most groups.
— identify five styles of leadership and describe how they work.
— describe circumstances under which different leadership styles are needed.

Time needed: | approximately 30 minutes

Directions: | **Begin by writing the following statement on the chalkboard:**
Leadership is a <u>process</u>, not a person.

Ask the students what they think the statement means. Facilitate a discussion about leadership and what leaders do. Be sure to make these points:
• Every group/team needs leadership.
• Leadership does not necessarily mean "a" leader.
• In many groups, leadership is <u>shared</u>.
• A leader <u>influences</u> other members of the group/team.
• A leader gets the team, or individual members of the team, to do things that move the *whole* team in the direction of its goal.

Point out that, just as there can be several leaders, there can also be several kinds of leadership. Write the following list of terms on the board:
> **Providing leadership by:**
> 1. giving <u>directions</u> and <u>information</u>
> 2. giving <u>encouragement</u> and <u>praise</u>
> 3. <u>participating</u> and <u>facilitating</u>
> 4. <u>delegating</u>
> 5. offering <u>vision</u> and <u>inspiration</u>

(Continued Next Page)

Read the following scenarios to the students. After each scenario, ask the students to identify (from the list) the type of leadership that is being provided. Take a few minutes to discuss each type (style) of leadership, perhaps asking the students to think of examples from their own experience when that style was used/needed. Discuss the people and conditions that would benefit most from each style of leadership. Use the discussion questions below and add some of your own.

SCENARIOS

• The student council is in the process of establishing a memorial scholarship fund. It has several donations already and needs to decide how to invest the money for maximum safety and profit. Brian, the student body president, appoints Cindy and Tom to study the issue and make recommendations to the council. Cindy and Tom are both good in math and economics, and Cindy works part time at a bank. (providing leadership by <u>delegating</u>)

• The school newspaper team is putting out a special edition next Tuesday. Maria, Chris, and Jim are using word processing to type their stories. They want to type the stories in a format that will make it easy for Carl to do the page layouts. However, they don't know anything about computer page-layout programs. So Carl tells them how to format the stories and explains why it will help him do the page layouts. (providing leadership by giving <u>directions</u> and <u>information</u>)

• The school band has won many awards and competitions. Eric, a saxophone player, has been talking to the other band members about entering a competition in Germany. He tells them about all the fun they'll have and says money shouldn't be an obstacle because there are lots of ways to raise funds. Lately, Eric has been distributing passport applications, and wearing lederhosen to school every Friday. The rest of the band is starting to take the idea seriously. (providing leadership through <u>vision</u> and <u>inspiration</u>)

(Continued Next Page)

Discussion Questions:

- The class is working on a project about global warming that is due in two days. Ruben, Jennifer, and Michael are in charge of charts and illustrations. They are doing some great computer drawings, but will have to stay late at school to complete them. They could substitute some quick hand drawings or xeroxed diagrams from a magazine, but are having trouble making a decision. Sylvia sits down with them. She listens, asks questions, and helps them decide what to do. (providing leadership through <u>participation</u> and <u>facilitation</u>)

- Kim is the stand-in for Melinda, who has the lead in a school play. Two days before a big performance, Melinda injures herself in P.E. and the drama coach tells Kim that she will have to play the lead. Kim knows the lines, but doesn't feel nearly as convincing in the part as Melinda was. During rehearsals, she becomes discouraged and wants to quit. Robert, a fellow actor, says to her, "Hey, you can do it. We really need you tonight." Robert sticks close to Kim for a while and tells her she's doing a good job. (providing leadership by giving <u>encouragement</u> and <u>praise</u>)

— *If you know how to do something but are not motivated to do it, what kind of leadership would be most likely to help?*

— *How do you feel when someone tries to give you directions for something you already know how to do?*

— *How do you feel when someone delegates a job to you that you have no idea how to do? How can you ask for the leadership you need in such a situation?*

— *What makes leadership by vision and inspiration work?*

— *When does it help to have someone sit down and actually work <u>with you</u> to complete a task or solve a problem?*

A Time I Provided Leadership

A Circle Session

Objectives:

The students will:

— identify situations in which they provided leadership to others.

— describe how different types of leadership can help a group achieve its goals.

Introduce the topic:

Say to the students: *Our topic today is, "A Time I Provided Leadership." You don't have to be elected chairperson or president in order to be a leader. All of us provide leadership to others at one time or another.*

When you take on the role of leader, you are trying to influence an individual or group to move in the direction of a goal. Can you think of a time when you did that? Perhaps you were a member of a committee that was confused about its job, so you did some investigating and clarified the task for everyone. Maybe your friend was tired and discouraged about a tough assignment, but you said that you were confident your friend could do it. Or maybe you were on an athletic team that wasn't doing very well, so you gave everybody a pep talk. Have you ever drilled someone on his/her spelling words so that your team could win an oral quiz? Have you ever realized that your club or team needed some equipment or refreshments and sent someone off to get them? Have you ever stood up in a bogged-down meeting and suggested what the group should do next? These are all examples of leadership. Take a few moments to think about it. The topic is, "A Time I Provided Leadership."

Discussion Questions:

— *How did you feel when you were providing leadership?*

— *What does it take to be a leader?*

— *If more people assumed leadership more often, how would we benefit?*

— *When is it a good idea to have one designated leader?*

The Plop...and Other Types of Group Decisions

Description: After a presentation on group decision-making, the students dramatize seven types of group decisions, taking their examples from literature, history, current events, or their imaginations. A discussion follows each dramatization.

Objectives: The students will:
— identify, define, and dramatize seven types of group decisions.
— describe the probable consequences of different types of group decisions.

Time needed: approximately two class periods

Materials needed: a handout for each student describing the different types of group decisions (optional)

Directions: **Explain that one of the most important things a group or team does is make decisions.** Remind the students of the stages of group development (covered in the activity, "Becoming a Team"). Point out that during stage two, when a group is getting organized, it usually makes many decisions—what has to be done, who is going to do it, etc.—and that decisions continue throughout the life of the group.

On the board, list the following types of decisions and discuss each. If you have prepared a handout, distribute it.

- **The Plop**
  One member suggests a decision. There is silence. No one says anything, so everyone thinks the decision is accepted—or doesn't know what to think!
- **Self-authorization**
  One member makes a decision and pushes it on the others. For example, s/he says "I think we should take a break now." S/he gets up and starts to do just that—and everyone else follows.
- **Default**
  This is when *no* decision is made. Sometimes there's not even any discussion. So whatever happens to get done ends up being "the decision." Naturally, no one can remember making it.

(Continued Next Page)

- **The Handshake**
  Two or more members decide on something before a meeting. Then they sort of slide it through at the meeting. One suggests the idea and the other jumps in with, "Hey, that's a great idea. That's what we'll do."
- **Baiting**
  In this case, members are pressured not to *disagree*. For example, someone says forcefully, "This project has to be completed by next week. Surely no one's going to argue that." And no one does.
- **Voting**
  This category includes majority rule, 2/3 rule, polling, and secret balloting. Whichever method is used, the idea that gets the most votes wins.
- **Consensus**
  After listing several ideas and talking about each of them, the group chooses an idea that everyone agrees to try.

Divide the class into seven teams. Assign a decision type to each team. (To randomize the process, have representatives draw their assignment from a box.)

Have each team plan and rehearse a dramatization showing its type of group decision in action. Suggest that the teams limit their dramatizations to 3 minutes in length. To enrich the assignment, allow enough time for research, and require that the decisions be taken from literature, history, or current events. (Or delimit the assignment even further, depending on your subject area.)

After each performance, discuss the decision dramatized. If the dramatization depicts an actual event, talk about the consequences of the decision. Use the questions below and think of others.

Discussion Questions:

— *How are group members apt to feel after this type of decision has been made?*
— *What are the consequences of making this type of decision?*
— *Which type of decision making has the best chance of satisfying everyone?*
— *Which type of decision making would probably work best in an emergency?*
— *Which type of decision making takes the most time?*
— *When is a secret ballot a better choice than a show of hands?*
— *If you don't like a group's decision-making process, what can you do?*

Team Problem Solving

Description:	The students work in teams to solve a problem, using what they have learned about teams, problem solving, decision making, and communication. All aspects of the process are left to their discretion. They present their problems and solutions to the class.
Objectives:	The students will: — work in teams to solve a problem. — describe their individual and collective behavior and how it affected the team's progress.

Note: This activity gives your students an opportunity to put into practice everything they have learned about teams and team building. For best results, complete the preceding activities before attempting this one.

Time needed:	two or more class periods (varies depending on the complexity of the problems assigned)
Materials needed:	several problems for groups to solve, developed in advance and printed on 5-inch by 8-inch cards. Problems may relate to your subject area, or to social or environmental problems that exist in your classroom or school. Here are some examples:

> **Math:** Teach a new math concept, math game, or puzzle to the rest of the class.
>
> **English:** Rewrite the Gettysburg Address, modernizing the language while maintaining the theme.
>
> **Marketing:** Improve the design of an existing product and develop an ad or jingle to sell it.
>
> **Environment:** Design a realistic incentive program that will reduce littering on school grounds by 50%.
>
> **Health:** Develop and lead the class in a guided visualization to music or a slow stretching routine for classroom stress-reduction.
>
> **Civics:** Based on current needs and problems, write a series of help-wanted ads designed to attract qualified people for each post in the U.S. Cabinet.
>
> **Physical Education:** Develop a two-team sport that rewards collaboration instead of competition, and teach it to the rest of the class.
>
> **History:** Find and chart a feasible new route for Columbus to take to the New World, and show how it is preferable to the route actually taken.

(Continued Next Page)

Science/Technology: Develop a system of soilless plant production suitable for the classroom.

Social: Develop a workable system for increasing positive interaction between racial, ethnic, and social groups here at school.

Directions:

Divide the class into teams of five to eight. Give each team a printed problem to solve. Urge the teams to use all relevant information that they have learned about effective teams, and instruct them to observe their own behavior and that of their group throughout the activity. Tell them that it is up to them to decide *how* to accomplish these things.

Suggest that the teams review the following concepts (covered in previous activities):
1. definition of a team
2. competition vs. cooperation
3. stages of group development
4. roles people play in groups
5. the effects of hidden agendas
6. styles of leadership
7. types of group decisions

In addition, suggest that they review **communication skills**, as well as the **steps in decision making** and **problem solving**.

As the teams complete the assignment, allow time for them to present and/or demonstrate their solutions to the class. After each presentation, debrief the team using the discussion questions below.

Discussion Questions:

— *How well did your team work together?*
— *What stage of development did your team reach?*
— *How were conflicts resolved?*
— *What were some of the roles that team members played?*
— *How were decisions made?*
— *Who provided leadership?*
— *When leadership was lacking, what did you do?*
— *What will you do differently the next time you work with a team?*

The Team and Me ———————

Experience Sheet and Dyads

Description: Using the experience sheet (provided), the students evaluate their individual performance in a group/team situation. After sharing their evaluation with a partner, they set a goal for improving their behavior.

Objectives: The students will:
—evaluate their personal behavior in a team situation.
—write a goal for improving their team behavior.

Note: This experience sheet is designed to help students evaluate their individual behavior during the "Team Problem Solving" activity; however, it may be used in conjunction with any team or group situation in which they have participated.

Time needed: approximately 30 minutes

Materials needed: one copy of the experience sheet, "The Team and Me" for each student

Directions: **Distribute the experience sheet and go over it with the students.** Say to them: *Think about a recent situation in which you were a member of a team or group. Read through the list of behaviors and decide which ones you are doing about the right amount of, which ones you would like to do more of, and which ones you would like to do less of. Make a check in the appropriate column after each item.*

Circulate and offer assistance as needed while the students complete the experience sheet.

When they are finished, have the students discuss their self-evaluations with a partner. Suggest that they skip any items that they are not comfortable sharing.

Still working with a partner, have the students write down one goal for improving their team behavior. Urge them to commit to working toward that goal over the next few weeks.

The Team and Me ———————————

Directions: Think about your behavior in a recent group or team situation. Read through the list and put a check in the appropriate column after each behavior. Then decide how you would most like to improve. Set a goal in that area and go for it!

	OK	Need to do more of	Need to do less of
Communication Skills			
1. talking in the group	_____	_____	_____
2. listening actively	_____	_____	_____
3. inviting others to speak	_____	_____	_____
4. staying on the topic	_____	_____	_____
Leadership Skills			
5. giving directions and information	_____	_____	_____
6. inspiring/encouraging others	_____	_____	_____
7. pitching in and helping others	_____	_____	_____
Problem-Solving Skills			
8. stating problems and goals	_____	_____	_____
9. asking for ideas and opinions	_____	_____	_____
10. giving ideas	_____	_____	_____
11. evaluating ideas	_____	_____	_____
Team Building Skills			
12. showing interest	_____	_____	_____
13. expressing appreciation	_____	_____	_____
14. helping achieve agreement	_____	_____	_____
15. reducing tension	_____	_____	_____
Expressing Feelings			
16. telling others what I feel	_____	_____	_____
17. disagreeing openly	_____	_____	_____
18. being sarcastic	_____	_____	_____
19. expressing humor	_____	_____	_____
Getting Along with Others			
20. competing to outdo others	_____	_____	_____
21. dominating the group	_____	_____	_____
22. criticizing others	_____	_____	_____
23. helping others	_____	_____	_____
24. being patient	_____	_____	_____

We Used Teamwork to Get It Done ——

A Circle Session

Objectives: The students will describe real situations in which a goal was attained through teamwork.

Introduce the topic: Say to the students: *Today we're going to talk about teamwork and what it can accomplish. Our topic is, "We Used Teamwork to Get It Done."*

Think of a situation in which you worked with a team of people to accomplish a goal. You can share something about a team activity in which you've participated here in class, or some other team experience you've had recently. Perhaps you belong to an athletic or debate team that won a competition. Maybe your family worked as a team to clean up the house or hold a yard sale. You and some friends may have done something together, like cook a meal, plan a party, or hold a car wash. Tell us what the team was trying to accomplish and how you felt being part of it. Take a few moments to think about it. The topic is, "We Used Teamwork to Get It Done."

Discussion Questions:
— *How did most of us feel about being part of a team?*
— *What makes a team work well together?*
— *How does the saying, 'The whole is more than the sum of its parts,' apply to teams?*
— *How does working with a team on a school assignment affect the <u>quality</u> of your work?*
— *How does it affect you motivation?*

Resources

Armstrong, Thomas, Ph.D. *In Their Own Way,* Los Angeles: J.P. Tarcher, Inc., 1987.

Ball, Geraldine, Ph.D. *The Magic Circle - Human Development Program, Level VI*, San Clemente, California: Magic Circle Publishing, 1974.

Canfield, Jack and Wells, Harold C. *100 Ways to Enhance Self-Concept in the Classroom*, Englewood Cliffs, New Jersey: Prentice-Hall, 1976.

Clark, Barbara, Ph.D. *Optimizing Learning*, Columbus, Ohio: Merrill Publishing Co., 1986.

Fanning, Patrick. *Visualization for Change*, Oakland, California: New Harbinger Publications, Inc., 1988.

Fox, Lynn C., Ph.D. and Weaver, Francine Lavin, M.A. *Unlocking Doors to Self-Esteem*, Rolling Hills Estates, California: Jalmar Press, 1990.

Frey, Diane, Ph.D. and Carlock, Jesse C., Ph.D. *Enhancing Self Esteem*, Muncie, Indiana: Accelerated Development, Inc., 1989.

Gardner, Howard. *Frames of Mind, The Theory of Multiple Intelligences*, New York: Basic Books, Inc., 1983.

Ginott, Haim. *Between Teacher and Child*, New York: MacMillan, 1972.

Glasser, William. *Schools Without Failure*, New York: Harper, 1966.

Gordon, Thomas. *Teacher Effectiveness Training*, New York: Peter H. Hyden, 1974.

Helmstetter, Shad, Ph.D. *What to Say When You Talk to Your Self*, New York: Pocket Books, 1986.

Herrmann, Ned. *The Creative Brain*, Lake Lure, North Carolina: Brain Books, 1988.

Houston, Jean. *The Possible Human*, Los Angeles: J. P. Tarcher, Inc., 1982.

Jensen, Eric P. *Super Teaching*, Del Mar, California: Turning Point for Teachers, 1988.

Kehayan, V. Alex, Ed.D. *Self Awarenss Growth Experiences*, Rolling Hills Estates, California: Jalmar Press, 1990.

Kluth, Margo and McCarthy, Dorothy. *Smile, You're Worth It!*, La Canada, California: Me and My Inner Self, Inc., 1983.

Leonard, George. *Education and Ecstacy*, New York: Dell, 1968.

Le Page, Andy, Ph.D. *Transforming Education*, Tampa, Florida: Oakmore House Press, 1987.

Maslow, Abraham. *Toward a Psychology of Being*, Princeton: Van Nostrand, 1968.

Miller, Sue. *The Wholemind Works*, Del Mar, California: The Wholemind Works Co., 1981.

Palomares, Uvaldo, Ed.D. and Ball, Gerry, Ph.D. *Grounds for Growth*, San Clemente, California: Magic Circle Publishing, 1980.

Restak, Richard M., M.D. *The Mind*, New York: Bantam Books, 1988.

Rogers, Carl. *On Becoming a Person: A Therapist's View of Psychology*, Boston: Houghton Mifflin Co., 1961.

Rose, Colin. *Accelerated Learning*, New York: Dell Publishing Co., 1985.

Toward a State of Esteem, The Final Report of the California Task-Force to Promote Self-Esteem, and Personal and Social Responsibility, Sacramento, California: California State Department of Education, 1990.

Tracy, Brian and Youngs, Bettie B. *Achievement, Happiness, Popularity and Success*, Solana Beach, California: The Phoenix Educational Foundation, 1988.

Youngs, Bettie, Ph.D. *A Stress-Management Guide for Young People*, Del Mar, California: Bilicki Publications, 1986.

Youngs, Bettie, Ph.D. *Helping Your Teenager Deal with Stress*, Los Angeles: J. P. Tarcher, Inc., 1986.

More Materials for SecondaryStudents from Innerchoice Publishing and Jalmar Press

The Tough Stuff Series
Immediate Guidance for Troubled Students

The Tough Stuff Series is a unique collection of hands-on student guided journal-workbooks designed to help students deal with the real life problems and issues they are currently facing. Each 10-16 page, fully reproducible journal workbook provides *immediate guidance* to troubled students. Topics of focus include:
- Death of a Family Member
- Death of a Friend
- Coping With Anxiety
- Overcoming Phobias
- Controlling Your Weight
- Dealing with Depression
- Understanding Anorexia
- Learning About Bulimia
- Surviving Separation and Divorce
- Living with an Alcoholic Parent
- Managing Stress
- Controlling Panic
- Educator Guide

Lessons in Tolerance and Diversity

A highly effective instructional tool that provides teachers and counselors with tools to help reduce racial, religious, ethnic and social prejudice in their schools and to promote tolerance and the celebration of diversity.

Conflict Resolution Skills for Teens

A timely book providing activities, guided discussions and reproducible handouts through which young people develop the skills and techniques necessary for effective conflict resolution. This is the best book available for teaching conflict resolution to youth.

Preparing Teens For The World Of Work
A School-to-Career Transition Guide for Counselors, Teachers and Career Specialists

This fully reproducible activity book is a timely guide designed to impact vital employability skills, and to give students an awareness of the relationship between education and the skills required for success in the work place.

50 Activities For Teaching Emotional Intelligence
Level III: High School

Emotional Intelligence impacts every area of life — health, learning, behavior and relationships. Teaching young people to understand, manage, and productively express their emotional intelligence pays big dividends in all areas of their lives and yours. This books contains a comprehensive overview of emotional intelligence theory, and each unit includes a thematic overview, stimulating activities and lively discussion topics.

The Sharing Circle Handbook
Topics for Teaching Self-Awareness, Communication, and Social Skills

The circle's unique small-group discussion process is one of the most effective strategies you can use to encourage the development of life skills. When you add this handbook to your *IMPACT!* kit, you'll gain over 100 additional circle topics!

Understanding Me
Activity Sheets for Building Life Skills and Self-Esteem in Secondary Students

These activity sheets are a perfect supplement to the experience sheets in *IMPACT!* Each one addresses a related life-skills topic, such as "Decision Making," "Being a Teenager," "Feelings," "Handicaps and Limitations," and "Friendship." All are illustrated and reproducible, with thought-provoking questions, stories, self-assessments, experiments, and games.

Contact us for more information and a *free* catalog

(800) 662-9662 *(voice)* • **(310) 816-3092** *(fax)*
Email: **jalmarpress@att.net**
On the Web: **www.jalmarpress.com**

Training Workshops

Learn how to lead circles and other IMPACT! activities in the most enjoyable way possible — through experiential training. Innerchoice Publishing conducts extremely valuable and exciting one- to three-day workshops on a wide range of topics, including self-esteem, conflict resolution, stress management, drug prevention, emotional intelligence, character education, and cooperative learning. Call for more information!

Contact us for more information
and a *free* catalog

(800) 662-9662 *(voice)* • (310) 816-3092 *(fax)*
***Email:* jalmarpress@att.net**
***On the Web:* www.jalmarpress.com**